The Politics of
Religious Apostasy

The Politics of Religious Apostasy

The Role of Apostates in the Transformation of Religious Movements

Edited by

David G. Bromley

Religion in the Age of Transformation

Anson Shupe, Series Adviser

Westport, Connecticut
London

Library of Congress Cataloging-in-Publication Data

The politics of religious apostasy : the role of apostates in the
   transformation of religious movements / edited by David G. Bromley.
          p.   cm.—(Religion in the age of transformation, ISSN
   1087–2388)
      Includes bibliographical references and index.
      ISBN 0–275–95508–7 (alk. paper)
      1. Apostasy. I. Bromley, David G.   II. Series.
   BL639.5.P64   1998
   306.6'9142—dc21   97–34747

British Library Cataloguing in Publication Data is available.

Library of Congress Catalog Card Number: 97–34747
ISBN: 0–275–95508–7
ISSN: 1087–2388

First published in 1998

Praeger Publishers, 88 Post Road West, Westport, CT 06881
An imprint of Greenwood Publishing Group, Inc.

Printed in the United States of America

The paper used in this book complies with the
Permanent Paper Standard issued by the National
Information Standards Organization (Z39.48–1984).

10 9 8 7 6 5 4 3 2 1

Contents

Preface

This book is the product of two long-standing interests I have pursued in affil-
iation/disaffiliation processes in new religious movements and movement/coun-
termovement conflict. Affiliation with these movements (usually termed
''conversion'') was the first process to be studied extensively and continues to
be the single most researched issue. Because these movements exhibited not
only high growth rates but also high membership turnover rates, it was not long
before a somewhat separate body of research developed on leavetaking. The
task of integrating the process of theoretically linking affiliation and disaffiliation
remains unfinished. At the same time, both the affiliation and disaffiliation processes occurred in the context of great controversy over the nature of the movements themselves. In the process of studying and writing about the conflict in
which these movements became embroiled, I also analyzed the intellectual and
political debates over allegations of coercively orchestrated affiliation (brainwashing) and coercively orchestrated exit (deprogramming). It was in this context that my interest in apostasy as a contested and highly politicized form of
exit developed. Subsequently, I became interested in the controversy surrounding new religious movements as a specific instance of a more general social
phenomenon that I now refer to as subversion episodes. I have begun examining
the nineteenth-century Catholic and Mormon conflicts and the contemporary
allegations of satanic cults through this framework. In these various episodes as
well as others, it became clear to me that the role of individuals who claimed
to have participated in ''subversive'' groups, who fashioned narratives about
their personal encounter with putative evil, and who became participants in
countersubversion campaigns was pivotal to the social construction of evil. As
I attempted to delineate the characteristics of the apostate role, I found it helpful
to think comparatively. It was that process which led to the typology of organ-

izations and contested exit role types. This book is an effort to examine in depth the complexity and significance of the apostate role and, in a larger context, to illuminate the processes through which subversive evil is socially constructed.

The opportunity to pursue this project emerged out of conversations with J. Gordon Melton, under the auspices of the Institute for the Study of American Religion. We discussed our mutual interest in religious conflict, an ongoing conversation that ultimately took the form of two distinct projects focusing on the conflict between religious movements and the societies in which they emerge. The present project examines the role of the apostate as a pivotal element in the social construction of subversion. The other project explores the relationship between religious movements and violence. That project is currently being developed. Initially, we anticipated a conference in Santa Barbara under Institute sponsorship at which papers on both topics would be presented and discussed. We subsequently revised those plans and decided to organize special sessions at the 1996 annual meetings of the Society for the Scientific Study of Religion, in order to move the projects along in a more timely fashion. Most of the chapters in this volume were presented in draft form at those meetings, and authors revised their manuscripts in response to the feedback they received from the editor and other contributors. Each contributor therefore had the opportunity to read most of the chapters in the process of preparing his or her own, and a number of authors made a point of referring to the work of other contributors in their chapters. I hope that this sharing of perspective among the contributors enhances the integration of the separate chapters.

I am grateful to J. Gordon Melton for his collegiality and support through the Institute for the Study of American Religion in developing this project. Thanks also to Anson Shupe, series editor for Praeger, for his suggestions and guidance throughout the development and completion of this project. Finally, both Gordon and I are grateful to the Society for the Scientific Study of Religion for helping to publicize the sessions at which the original papers for these projects were presented.

Part I

Introduction

Chapter 1

Sociological Perspectives on Apostasy: An Overview

David G. Bromley

This book has as its subject one of the most dramatic roles that has emerged around the conflict between some new religious movements and the social orders in which they have emerged, the *apostate*. Beginning around 1970, when the current cohort of "new religious movements" began to attract both members and visibility, they quickly became the center of an intense controversy that continues through the present and about which social scientists have now written extensively. The initial social science research on these groups was motivated by challenges to both established social science paradigms and by the controversy that swirled around these movements. What was particularly perplexing to scholars was what appeared to be passionate religious commitment precisely among the young, highly educated individuals who were expected to be committed residents of the "secular city."

Over the last several decades the study of contemporary religious movements has become an important area of scholarly inquiry. Of central importance have been explorations of the sociocultural conditions in which new religious movements emerged, and of affiliation/disaffiliation processes and organizational development. Research has also been spurred by the radical form of these movements and the conflict in which a number of them became embroiled. Taken together, these two sets of interests have yielded research on a number of different issues—the sharp break with conventional society; exotic experiments with alternative forms of organization; dramatic conversion experiences reported by some adherents, and casual experimentation by others; charismatic authority claimed by and accorded to some movement leaders; public expressions of anger and betrayal by many families of converts; and allegations of subversive intent and practices by the oppositional movement. Theory and research thus have focused both on the movements themselves and the societal reaction to them.

One of the most important contributions to the sociology of religion deriving from studying new religions is that it substantially broadens the field. The vast majority of scholarly work is on established, mainline religion, what I have elsewhere called "priestly religion," which sacralizes the dominant structure of social relations. The study of "prophetic religion," outsiders who contest the established order and sacralize resistance, creates a clearer perspective on the actual range of religious authorization of social relations. When the full range of religious organizations is examined, the importance of the exercise of power in constructing what is deemed legitimate and illegitimate religion becomes more apparent. It is in terms of this perspective that this volume was conceived.

Analyzing both the established and the challenging religious groups as contesting for control over powerful symbols and individual loyalties yields a different perspective on legitimate and illegitimate religion. The focus on groups that are deemed illegitimate as a product of conflict shifts to contests between competing coalitions. These political processes have been examined in some detail for new religions, although they have not been systematically integrated into a conflict-oriented paradigm. To put the matter most simply, the balance of allies to opponents is highly favorable for established, mainstream churches and equally disfavorable for challenging religious movements. The key coalitional partners on the two sides, beyond the new religions and countermovement organizations, have involved governmental agencies, churches and denominational bodies, media, families, courts and legislative bodies, and civil libertarian groups. It is out of the actions of these organizational actors that location of specific groups along a legitimate–illegitimate continuum is determined at any given historical moment.

There also are a number of key roles inside and outside of these movements that social scientists have studied. These would include movement founders/leaders, converts, moral entrepreneurs (e.g., investigative journalists), and deprogrammers/therapists. The apostate role is certainly an important one in this cluster. We focus on this role because it is integrally related to a number of the others and because it has been significant organizationally both for religious movements and the countermovements that oppose them. It is a role that integrates the organizational and coalitional levels of analysis. Indeed, the structure of this volume is organized around the role of apostates within the religious movements from which they take leave and the function of the apostate role in the oppositional coalitions, with a final chapter devoted to methodological issues raised by the variety of accounts constructed about religious movements by a range of interested parties. Following the general introduction and the theoretical essay around which the volume is organized, the third part of the book is titled "The Apostate Role and Career," the fourth "The Organizational Context of Apostasy," and the final section "Methodological Issues in the Study of Apostasy.'' While the analysis clearly focuses on contemporary new religions, several contributors call attention to comparable groups, individuals, and processes in prior cohorts of religious movements.

In Chapter 2, Bromley places apostasy in comparative perspective by identifying it as a particular kind of exit and juxtaposing apostates to two other types of exit role, ''defector'' and ''whistleblower.'' The way that disputed exits are organized and the narratives that are constructed about the process, Bromley argues, is a function of the social location of the organization. Allegiant organizations have high legitimacy, a favorable balance of allies to opponents; as a result, these organizations are extended great latitude in resolving disputes internally. Conflicts are suppressed and defectors typically exit in a fashion that does not seriously challenge organizational legitimacy. Contestant organizations operate in an environment containing both allies and opponents; their agendas are deemed legitimate but they are also subject to challenge and constraint. External regulatory units of some type form to mediate the claimsmaking that arises between the organization and groups representing competing interests. The existence of regulatory agencies reduces the capacity of organizations to maintain internal control over disputes. The whistleblowing role is one in which the exiting individual allies with the regulatory unit and an adjudicated conflict ensues over the whistleblower's character and evidence. Organizations are labeled subversive when their organizational practices and objectives are deemed illegitimate; that is, the organization is confronted by a heavy preponderance of determined opponents. Under these circumstances the organization has limited capacity to defend itself when disputes arise. Individuals are actively recruited in various ways to ally with the oppositional coalition and reconnect with conventional networks by playing a variety of pivotal support roles within the oppositional coalition. Apostates construct their prior affiliations as involuntary, recounting their organizational careers as captivity narratives.

The focus of analysis in this volume is the role of apostates in the controversy surrounding those contemporary new religious movements that are deemed ''subversive.'' Both ''apostate'' and ''subversive'' have very specific meanings here. The analytic category ''subversive'' is used in this volume to refer to organizations that are perceived and labeled ''subversive'' by oppositional groups as a tactic for status degradation that legitimates implementation of extraordinary social control measures. The typology of organization and corresponding exit role types identifies apostasy as a unique social form that emerges under very specific social conditions. Apostate refers not to ordinary religious leavetakers (the general referent) but to that subset of leavetakers who are involved in contested exit and affiliate with an oppositional coalition. The number of individuals playing this role in any given conflict may not be large; indeed, in a number of movements one or a small handful of individuals have dominated this countermovement niche. The role is distinguished not by the number of individuals occupying it but rather by its recurrence in situations of intense conflict and its centrality to countersubversion campaigns.

THE APOSTATE ROLE AND CAREER

This section contains chapters by Armand L. Mauss, Eileen Barker, Stuart A. Wright, and Daniel Carson Johnson. The common theme of these chapters is the variety of factors influencing the social construction of the apostate role. The focus is on individual motivations, role and narrative construction, role alternatives, and social factors influencing the form that the apostate role and narrative assume.

While Bromley's analysis is structural in nature, Armand L. Mauss, in Chapter 3, focuses on the quandary individuals face in preserving their identities in the leavetaking process. This is an important matter, for individuals as well as organizations have problems to solve in the leavetaking process. In an insightful analysis, Mauss offers a social psychological–level interpretation of apostasy, employing ''self-concept'' as an analytic tool to connect individual and organizational levels of analysis. Self-concept is defined as a set of identities tied to social roles. The structural situation in which exiting members of all three types of organizations find themselves requires a reconstruction of self-concept, and individuals adjust their behavior to preserve their self-concepts. He identifies the self-verification process as particularly significant in interpreting defection, whistleblowing, and apostasy. Failure to achieve self-verification yields self-discrepancy, which may take the form of a discrepancy between the actual and ideal self or actual and ought self. The former he associates with defection and whistleblowing and the latter with apostasy.

In developing his argument, Mauss draws on nineteenth- and twentieth-century Mormonism for illustrative case material. The Mormon case is an unusually instructive one since Mormonism was deemed subversive in the last century and has moved toward an allegiant position in recent decades, but continues to occupy a contestant position in some social locations. Mormonism thus demonstrates an important point—a variety of exit roles may be associated with the same organization at different times and at the same time in different locations. Mauss features the cases of William McLellin in the nineteenth century and Jerald and Sandra Tanner to exemplify apostasy, and Fawn Brodie and Sonia Johnson to illustrate twentieth-century whistleblowing.

While much of this volume emphasizes the process of exiting and the difference between members and ex-members, Eileen Barker, in Chapter 4, examines the gradation of membership and the continuum between membership and ex-membership. Exiting poses a variety of dilemmas and costs, and so some movement members are motivated to entertain other alternatives. Barker argues that movement participants may assume a variety of positions between core member and ex-member. She focuses primarily on the marginal member, juxtaposing marginals with peripheral members. The peripheral member most often is an individual who at one point was a core member, and, while still positively disposed to the movement, is unwilling to make the kind of personal commitment that the movement demands. Movement and member reach an agreement through which the individual moves, with movement recognition and acceptance, to a peripheral position within the movement. For the groups under consideration here, this typically means separate living arrangements and part-time participation. The existence of peripherals is not without benefit to the movement, as peripherals may reduce tensions between the movement and the larger social order.

By contrast, a major distinguishing characteristic of marginal members is that they hold an ambiguous, unrecognized status within the movement. While disputing some movement belief and/or practice, marginals are individuals whose identities continue to be tied to the movement and who continue to be treated by the movement as core members. This position, of course, creates tension both for movement and member alike. Barker argues that marginals position as they do because they reject peripheral membership, which offers the advantages of neither core member networks nor external, non-member networks. Turning Bromley's argument on its head, Barker proposes that for movements in high tension with their environments, some individuals elect marginal status precisely to avoid centripetal pressure from the movement and centrifugal pressure from external networks. They thus avoid the kind of narrative account and return to the pre-movement self that may be required of apostates. These relationships become even more complicated over time as a second generation emerges within the movement. Members of a generation raised within the movement but lacking first generation commitment to the movement may drift into a marginal status and even form networks at the margin, a development which creates additional challenges to movement solidarity.

Since apostasy is a special form of exit, identifying factors associated with the adoption of an oppositional stance is a pivotal issue. In Chapter 5, Stuart A. Wright observes that most individuals exiting religious movements labeled subversive are not hostile to the groups with which they were formerly affiliated. Therefore, in his chapter, Wright first conceptualizes apostasy and then identifies a series of social factors linked to the form. In seeking to explain the occurrence of apostasy, he draws on the concepts of narrative and role. The characteristic apostate account is fashioned as a captivity narrative with "warfare" and "hostage-rescue" as central motifs, leading to the use of derivative concepts such as "enemy" and "casualties." The corresponding role paralleling the captivity script is that of "victim" or "survivor," which is proffered and confirmed by countermovement affiliated counseling practitioners.

Based on this conceptualization and building on his considerable previous work on exiting religious movements, Wright identifies a series of structural and processual factors that influence the nature of leavetaker orientations to their former groups. Among the most important structural factors are the primacy of the role (which increases the importance of a socially acceptable account for one's actions) and the social value of the former affiliation (with more culturally disvalued groups yielding more negative assessments). Processual factors include mode of exit (where lower degrees of voluntariness correlate with a more negative orientation) and location of new social networks (with connection to oppositional coalitions yielding a more hostile stance). Wright goes on to examine the way in which former members may become "professional ex-s" and develop credentialed careers in which they affirm and reproduce their own orientations in clients.

In Chapter 6, Daniel Carson Johnson offers a provocative analysis of the limiting form of apostasy, "apostates who never were." The significance of the apostate role is clearly evident in these cases. If actual individuals with the requisite characteristics are lacking, those attributes, and sometimes entire identities, are fabricated. These apostates may exert immense influence in a religious conflict but, at least in the cases at hand, ultimately are exposed as having fictive movement identities. Johnson selects a variety of notable cases from nineteenth- and twentieth-century subversion episodes through which to document this construction process—from the last century imposter nuns Rebecca Reed and Maria Monk—and from the present era counterfeit satanic priest Michael Warnke, Catholic priest Alberto Rivera, and satanic ritual abuse victim Lauren Stratford.

Johnson focuses on the narratives of these apostates as a distinctive literary genre. He argues that these narratives stretch the "membrane" between fiction and non-fiction to the limit. Apostate narratives involve what Johnson terms "autobiographical laxity" and "artificial contextualization." With respect to the former, the timing and length of membership as well as the source of initiative and motivation in affiliating are likely to be reconstructed. Some of these narratives even "go all the way," as the very fact of membership itself is a fiction. It is such constructed membership histories that sustain these apostates in their roles. With respect to the latter, the context of the group is fictionalized to varying degrees. One of the most important ways that this occurs is through contextual introductions. Apostate narratives often are preceded by statements from allies that contain more general denunciations of the subversive organization, or are endorsed in congratulatory reviews. In either case a subversive historical context for the group is created outside the boundaries of the apostate account. Some of these narratives too "go all the way," as the very existence of the organization is a fiction. The fact that this form of narrative is produced cannot be traced to individual flights of fancy but rather must have a structural source.

The narratives produced by apostates exhibit stylistic commonalities that contribute to their audience impact. These include defensive posture designed to pre-empt scrutinizing and questioning of the narrative (through pleas, corroboration, attestation, and challenges); a dwelling on irrelevant details, which injects an entertainment quality into the narrative; selective revelations that lend the account an air of mystery and fascination by leaving implications to the reader's imagination; and recognition of risk and duty, which raises the credibility and lowers the responsibility of the apostate by assertion of the perilous circumstances to which he or she has been subjected.

Johnson argues that it is the political structure in which apostasy occurs that yields these stylistic continuities. The key elements in the political structure he identifies are the sponsoring audience, narrative distancing, and truth-telling. The sponsoring audience actually promotes and shepherds the apostate narrative once it has been fashioned. The support and certification of the sponsoring audience builds the credibility of the account and the certitude and confidence of the apostate–narrator. The distancing of the narrative paradoxically enhances it be-lievability, even if through the suspension of disbelief, and broadens its appeal. Separating the narrative spatially, temporally, and informationally from the re-ceiving audience renders the narrative mysterious and unverifiable even while its veracity and accuracy are being proclaimed. The category of participants Johnson calls truth-tellers functions to critique the extreme claims of apostates. Drawn from the ranks of "moderates," the truth-tellers find the apostate nar-ratives destabilizing, polarizing, and provocative. The protestations of truth-tellers, however, offer yet another opportunity for repetition of the charges, the raising of fears of collusion with the enemy, and evidence of the insidiousness of evil.

THE ORGANIZATIONAL CONTEXT OF APOSTASY

Part IV of this volume includes contributions from John R. Hall and Philip Schuyler, James T. Richardson, Susan J. Palmer, and Anson Shupe. These chap-ters examine both the role of apostates within the countermovement and the impact of apostates in the movement–society conflict. As these chapters make clear, a relatively small number of apostates have had considerable impact in some movement–society conflicts and they are integral to countermovement or-ganization and influence.

Chapter 7 develops a general model of religious violence in which the role of the apostate is a key element. Eschewing an essentialist position, Hall and Schuyler argue that religious violence is rooted in social conflicts between uto-pian religious movements and ideological proponents of an established order. Religious movements that locate outside the dominant structure of social rela-tions and are organized totalistically create a gulf between themselves and the larger social order and can assume a militant stance. The culmination of con-frontation between movement and established order in violence or collective suicide offers a means through which the movement can preserve its sense of legitimacy by refusing to capitulate to state authority or external definitions of its identity.

Hall and Schuyler develop a model of movement–societal confrontation that contextualizes the role of apostates. They first identify a set of necessary pre-conditions and then a second set of additional conditions that, taken together, increase the likelihood of violent confrontations. The former include organiza-tion as a charismatic religious social movement, an apocalyptic ideology; inter-nal organization capable of maintaining solidarity, legitimacy sufficient to exercise collective social control, political and economic viability, and strong social boundaries and cognitive isolation. The latter factors, which are at the heart of the analysis, include mobilization of a solidary group of cultural opponents, shaping of news media coverage through the oppositional frame of reference, and the invocation of state authority. The combination of these conditions undermines the capacity of a movement to persist as an authentically apocalyptic movement. Violence becomes a means of aggression against detractors and an affirmation of self-determination. Three contemporary cases of religious violence are used to interpret through the model: the Peoples Temple, Branch Davidians, and Solar Temple.

In the case of the Peoples Temple, there was ongoing conflict between the movement and an oppositional coalition, Concerned Relatives, that included both relatives and former members. The oppositional group was not very successful in its efforts to mobilize the various governmental agencies it contacted, but it did increase the "siege mentality" within the Peoples Temple and it served as a catalyst in the conflict between the movement and its opponents. Apostates played a major role in organizing the opposition. For example, apostates approached the Internal Revenue Service with information about financial practices within the movement, which was a factor in the migration of the Peoples Temple to Guyana. And it was the opposition that initiated state involvement in the form of the visit of Congressman Leo Ryan and a delegation (including opponents and media) on a "fact-finding mission" to Jonestown. Disaffected members leaving Jonestown with Ryan promised further opposition and negative media coverage. It was at that juncture that several members of the Ryan delegation were murdered, sealing the fate of the movement and triggering the mass suicide that quickly followed.

The Branch Davidians, a splinter group once affiliated with the Seventh-Day Adventist Church, had occupied various sites around Waco for half a century prior to the two violent encounters with federal authorities. The Davidians experienced a number of defections from the group following the assumption of leadership by David Koresh. The disaffected members sought to enlist the support of various state agencies but faced the same lack of enthusiasm as had opponents of the Peoples Temple. However, the network was able to generate negative media coverage, and in the process raised the specter of mass suicide. In this episode, a single apostate, Marc Breault, played a central role in drawing a network of apostates together. The state child welfare agency and federal Bureau of Alcohol, Tobacco, and Firearms (ATF) both were influenced by this network as each had unsuccessfully sought to intervene against the Davidians on child abuse and weapons possession charges, respectively. The ATF relied heavily on apostates to generate the evidence used to secure the warrant that triggered the first violent confrontation with the Davidians. The ATF's concern about a potential mass suicide significantly influenced its strategy in confronting the Davidians. The deadly encounters between movement members and law enforcement officers left the movement members with no realistic option for continuing as an autonomous collective entity.

Like the Peoples Temple and Branch Davidians, the Solar Temple experienced a series of defections and the potential for embarrassing disclosures about the movement from those individuals. Again, one major leavetaker, Rose-Marie Klaus, played a major role as an apostate. As an outgrowth of a marital dispute with her husband and conflict with the movement, Klaus made contact with a countermovment organization and offered damaging information about the movement. As a result of a convoluted series of events, several movement leaders were prosecuted on a weapons possession charge. That incident, in turn, triggered a series of investigations by other governmental agencies. The movement increasingly began to perceive itself to be the target of a government conspiracy. As Hall and Schuyler conclude, although the shift from "earthly apocalyptic survivalism to passage beyond the earthly apocalypse" occurred several years prior to the initial Transit, the emphasis on "departure" emerged in the context of increasing organized opposition.

In Chapter 8, James T. Richardson examines the important issue of the impact of apostates on the movements that they oppose. Only a small number of individuals ultimately play apostate or whistleblower roles, but the effects of their actions often far exceed their numbers. Richardson focuses on some of the most high-profile instances of the special case in which apostates turn whistleblowers and become particularly influential in shaping social control and public opinion alike. In working through his argument, Richardson draws on cases involving three contemporary religious movements that triggered the cult controversy (the Unification Church, Hare Krishna, and The Family), one movement that has become embroiled in controversy more recently (the Church Universal and Triumphant), and a church with a much longer history (Christian Science) that had achieved considerable acceptance but now faces renewed opposition to its spiritual healing practices. In each of these episodes Richardson analyzes the impact of former members who played some combination of the apostate and whistleblower roles, beginning with the former and moving to the latter.

In the episode involving the Church Universal and Triumphant, a former member brought suit against the church on a variety of grounds, some of which were based on alleged brainwashing activity by the church. He received a large financial settlement, including a personal award against the church's spiritual leader, and his campaign against the church was a significant factor in its decision to relocate geographically.

In the Unification Church case, two former members brought suit against the church on brainwashing-related charges. The case went through trial and appeal all the way to the United States Supreme Court before finally being settled out of court for an undisclosed sum. Richardson reports that in addition to the protracted negative publicity and the financial settlement it was forced to incur, the church restructured its recruiting procedures and reallocated financial resources. The case also kept alive the legal viability of brainwashing-related legal claims.

The family of a former member of Hare Krishna sued the California branch of that movement on wrongful death and brainwashing-related charges. The case was a complex one in which the daughter, who was legally a minor when she joined the group, was deliberately hidden from her parents by the group. She was subsequently expelled from the group in the face of threatened legal action. The family ultimately did sue the Krishnas following the father's death, which the family attributed in part to the stress associated with the family–movement conflict. The result again was a case that went all the way to the United States Supreme Court before being settled out of court. The Hare Krishnas suffered a large financial penalty (including punitive damages), were forced to accept a lien on all of their property in order to finance the appeal process, and subsequently revised their recruitment procedures as a result of the case.

In a series of incidents involving The Family, a small group of apostates orchestrated a campaign around the world to bring child abuse charges against the group. The result was a number of official interventions in which children were physically removed from movement "homes," sometimes for extended periods. In none of these cases did official investigations substantiate the allegations, but the group nonetheless bore major financial costs; experienced extremely negative media coverage; and was compelled to agree as part of legal settlements to restructure its relationships with former members, increase contact with family members of current members, and revise its child education programs.

Finally, the Christian Science case is instructive because it demonstrates how the legitimacy accorded religious organizations may change in either direction as a function of changes in the environment as well as in the organization itself. After achieving legal protection for its spiritual healing methods in many states, Christian Science has come under increasing fire again in recent years. One former member in particular has been influential in mobilizing a network of other former members, medical professionals, and child welfare advocates. The church has experienced negative publicity and unfavorable legal decisions; as a result, the church has modified its official stance on employing spiritual healing in the case of children. Richardson thus concludes that apostates and whistle-blowers, although often few in number, have had a substantial impact on the image, resources, organization, and practices of a range of religious groups.

In Chapter 9, Susan J. Palmer offers a detailed analysis of both the changing role and organizational impact of apostates in a single case, the Northeast Kingdom Community Church. The saga is an interesting one since on a number of counts the group has a rather unexceptional history yet was involved in a very dramatic confrontation with the state. The group became a focus of national attention in 1984 when Vermont state authorities conducted a pre-dawn raid on its community at Island Pond and took over 100 children into protective custody. The Messianic Communities, as they are now called, are most distinctive by virtue of having a controversial prophetic leader, communal organization, and a millenarian ideology. As do a number of conservative Christian groups, the Messianic Communities advocate strict discipline and corporal punishment of willfully disobedient children. The millenarian expectations of the group and child discipline practices converge as members seek to protect children from corruption by the secular world and to insure that their children will be instantly responsive to signs of impending world transformation. As Richardson points out in Chapter 8, controversial child socialization and discipline practices easily are designated as abusive in the present environment, and child abuse is an incendiary legal charge.

Palmer traces the history of movement–societal conflict and the role of apostates in that conflict through three phases. The Messianic Communities became embroiled in controversy early in their history when a number of members were coercively deprogrammed and the decisions in several child custody cases uniformly awarded custody to the non-affiliated parent. It was in this turbulent climate that the primary movement apostate, Juan Mattatall, emerged. Despite the controversy that swirled around Mattatall, he became a major influence on the movement's history, even after his own death. Mattatall was accused of child sex abuse by the movement and ultimately rejected by both his wife and the community. He became a public opponent of the movement in the context of seeking custody of his children. Despite the fact that sex abuse charges were repeatedly leveled at Mattatall and he was ultimately killed by his mother in an apparent reaction to these incidents, his allegations against the Messianic Communities have continued to resurface. A coalition formed around Mattatall that continued to oppose the movement and ultimately lobbied for the dramatic 1984 raid.

During the second phase, the conflict between the movement and the larger society escalated as church elders began to perceive a concerted campaign against the movement and authorities began to conclude that movement secrecy, evasiveness, and non-cooperation impeded legitimate public oversight. A variety of minor conflicts and ambiguous events thus were converted into major public conflicts during this period. A number of individuals found themselves being cast in the apostate role, despite their own ambivalence, as the oppositional coalition sought to fashion a case for public intervention.

In recent years both sides have stepped back from the brink. The Messianic Communities have restructured their lifestyle, sought more congenial relationships with the surrounding community, and openly courted allies with mainline institutions; and authorities have refrained from intervention and conflict escalation. Still, tension remains around children as a number of custody decisions have been unfavorable to the group and parents within the movement, with or without group sanction, have concealed children from authorities in custody cases.

While most of the chapters emphasize the impact of apostates on the movements they oppose, in Chapter 10 Anson Shupe examines the reciprocal role that apostates play in the anti-cult movement. Shupe begins his analysis by identifying the key resource that apostates bring to countermovements—direct, personal experience with putative evil. The narratives that apostates construct function to legitimate countermovement ideology. In designating and analyzing these narratives, Shupe asserts, there is no presumption concerning the truth or factuality of the atrocity stories that apostates recount. As he notes, the apostate role is not unique to contemporary countermovements; in fact, it has been a prominent feature of countermovements through American history. However, the role that apostates play is not an invariant one; it changes with the development of the countermovement.

Shupe documents how the role of apostates in contemporary anti-cultism has shifted during three time periods. His analysis is quite parallel to Palmer's except that the focus is on the organizational needs of the countermovement. The earliest apostate testimonies were central to a highly decentralized, emergent anti-cult movement. These accounts, in classic atrocity story format, were largely reported by journalists in local and regional newspapers and magazines. The narratives served to create awareness of the cult problem and mobilize support among the general public, media representatives, and public officials. Later, autobiographical accounts in book form recounted similar stories. However, Shupe argues that the value of apostates began declining at this time, except as an internal solidarity-building mechanism, as professionals replaced family members in anti-cult leadership positions. During the most recent period, apostate accounts have declined both in their utility to the anti-cult movement and in media interest. Shupe attributes this decline to migration of media to new sources of sensational stories, the clichéd quality of the narratives, shifting public concerns, and professionalization within the anti-cult movement. As the countermovement institutionalized and professionalized, the apostates shifted from frontstage to backstage, supplanted in a public leadership role by professionals with the credentials to generate greater institutional legitimacy.

METHODOLOGICAL ISSUES IN THE STUDY OF APOSTASY

It is consistent with the argument that orients this volume that a variety of interpreters construct narratives about religious movements and their relationship to the surrounding social order. The groups' self-accounts often have been granted little legitimacy. Oppositional groups have also faced legitimacy problems, although public opinion probably is more sympathetic to the latter than the former accounts. Scholars have fashioned interpretations that address various disciplinary theories/issues and, secondarily, matters of public debate. In constructing their narratives, scholars face the question of how to interpret and incorporate information from other sources. This is a critical issue to the extent that research data are gathered from or influenced by movement allies and opponents. It is therefore appropriate that the concluding chapter of this book by Lewis F. Carter explores this issue.

Carter begins by defending the importance of triangulation, "using a number of data sources with differing perspectives," in constructing scholarly narratives. He illustrates the way that triangulation methods may be employed to sort out complex events and variant accounts in a case study of a contested incident involving Rajneeshpuram. As a prelude to his analysis, he identifies and examines four important sources of information about religious groups: believers, ethnographers, apostates, and opponents. Each source, he asserts, has different strengths and weaknesses, and it is important to assess the knowledge, motivation, and context of the information of various parties rather than presumptively equating categories of person and information.

Believer is a label that is applied to a broad range of organizational participants who typically share in common being positively disposed to the organization. However, believers may have very different types and levels of information, particularly in hierarchical movements, Carter argues. Barker's (Chapter 4) distinction between peripheral and marginal is instructive here and confirms the general line of argument. It is therefore important to determine what knowledge believers might reasonably be expected to have in a given group and location, and even their personal qualities of inquisitiveness and perceived trustworthiness may influence this.

Apostates also may be an important source of information. Carter here distinguishes between ordinary leavetakers (the generic use of apostate) and "career apostates," which more closely parallels Bromley's usage in the introductory chapter. Some former members have extensive knowledge of the organization, and "moderate" former members may possess the virtue of insider knowledge and outsider detachment. "Extreme" former members are likely to be more available to scholars or others as they possess heightened motivation as well as a negative orientation toward the organization.

Ethnographers also are influenced by their location with respect to the group. As Carter observes, it is difficult to engage in participant observation without spending extended time inside of the organization and learning the internal language and perspective. Social scientists historically have sought to maintain a certain detachment and "objectivity," which may be more elusive than they suppose. Ethnographers are insiders at one time and outsiders at another, and they may experience a certain amount of resocialization as they move from inside to outside the organization. As a result, their perspective too shifts with their social location. The cautionary tales that anthropologists tell about "going native" are instructive on this point.

Finally, opponents sometimes develop extensive information about their former groups. The case of Jerald and Sandra Tanner, about which Mauss writes in Chapter 3, is an excellent case in point in this volume. The information that opponents have may have direct and indirect effects on the research process. On the one hand, groups share information and respond to problems and opposition that other groups encounter, which creates an indirect effect. On the other hand, opponents (as well as groups themselves) supply information to scholars; they may gain legitimacy and corroboration for their version of events to the extent that the information they gather is incorporated into scholarly narratives.

In sum, then, the contributors offer a variety of theory, data, and substantive insights that extend and modify the model proposed in Bromley's introductory chapter. While there is general agreement that the typological distinctions Bromley has constructed are useful ones, the contributors collectively create a richer, more complex mosaic. Collectively, the volume contributors suggest the fruitfulness of research on individual apostate careers and of their organizational careers; the movement of individuals between the three types of contested exit roles and of groups between the three organizational types; the occurrence of circumstances leading to the various "mixed" exit role and organizational types; and the political processes that preserve the network alliances that create and sustain the organizational locations and the intra-organizational social control mechanisms. The lengths to which countermovements will go in constructing (and even fabricating) apostates and which movements will go in attacking and discrediting these individuals; the intensity with which some individuals will embrace the apostate role and others abjure it; and the veracity attributed to apostate narratives during periods of intense conflict and their folkloric treatment at other times all suggest powerful motives and forces at work. The ultimate value of this volume is not found in final answers to all of these issues but in its argument for their inclusion in the social science agenda and their theoretical salience in understanding social movements and countermovements.

Part II

A Comparative Approach to Organizational Exit

The Social Construction of Contested Exit Roles: Defectors, Whistleblowers, and Apostates

David G. Bromley

In all human organizations individual participants enter and/or exit, but entry and exit processes may or may not assume external social significance. To the extent that individual exiting involves larger social significance, a variety of parties may become involved in structuring the exit process and interpreting its meaning. In some cases the exit process is socially contested, and under this condition organizations possess a differential capacity to determine the outcome of disputes. The focus here is on a unique type of contested exit, which I shall refer to as *apostasy*. (This use of apostasy must be distinguished from the more general use of the term that refers to simple leavetaking.) Apostasy may be defined in preliminary fashion as a role that is constructed when an organization is in a state of high tension with its surrounding environment and that involves an individual exiting the organization to form an alliance with an oppositional coalition. While I am primarily concerned with apostasy from new religious movements (NRMs), a comparable analysis could be undertaken of apostasy in a variety of other social movement or institutional contexts. The distinctive qualities of the apostate role are demonstrated by comparing apostates with two other contested exit roles.

I shall argue that although, or precisely because, apostates typically constitute only a small proportion of leavetakers, apostasy is a significant phenomenon both socially and sociologically. From a social/political perspective, apostates have been a significant component of the campaign to invoke social control measures of various kinds against NRMs over the last several decades. There have been numerous instances of NRMs becoming embroiled in extended altercations with apostates; apostate testimony of various kinds has been pivotal in enforcement actions by social control agencies and in civil litigation initiated against NRMs; apostate accounts have been prominently featured in media coverage of NRMs; and public opinion has been heavily influenced by apostate accounts of both their personal experiences and the nature of NRM organization.

Apostasy is important from a sociological standpoint both theoretically and methodologically. It is a unique social form that has been recreated in numerous cases historically when tensions between social movements and larger society have reached high levels. Apostates have been an integral element of countermovement organization and strategy in such circumstances; countermovements arguably could not have successfully mobilized opposition and imposition of sanctions without this role-resource. Apostates thus have in some cases significantly shaped the subsequent course of the target social movements. From a methodological standpoint, apostates are particularly relevant to sociological interpretation of NRMs. The high visibility of the apostate role has tended to obscure ordinary leavetaking as well as other forms of contesting organizational policies and exiting. Likewise, apostate accounts of group practices and individual experiences have been most accessible to social scientists and others. It is clear that research on NRMs, and other groups in high tension with the larger society, particularly requires a variety of sources of organizational and account data in constructing sociological interpretations of such organizations (Zablocki 1996).

Coser (1954, p. 250), following Max Scheler, defines apostasy in terms compatible with the argument to be developed here. He writes, the apostate is not simply one who has experienced a dramatic change in conviction; rather the designation refers to "a man who, even in his new state of belief, is spiritually living not primarily in the content of that faith, in the pursuit of goals appropriate to it, but only in the struggle against the old faith and for the sake of its negation." Coser and Scheler adopt a social psychological orientation to apostasy, but their emphasis on the negation of former beliefs and commitments and the continuing implications of the past relationship for subsequent behavior goes to the heart of the matter. I shall take a broader, more structural perspective, analyzing apostasy as a specific social form that is constructed and supported only under very distinctive social conditions.

I develop the distinctive qualities of apostasy by first specifying three types of organizations in contemporary American society based on level of tension with the surrounding environment—Type I (Allegiant), Type II (Contestant), and Type III (Subversive)—and three corresponding types of exit characteristic of these organizational forms—Defector, Whistleblower, and Apostate. Apostasy in its strongest manifestation is then distinguished as a social form that is created in a situation of intense conflict and power imbalance where claims of subversion are advanced against a group (in this case a NRM). This form of claimsmaking is employed to authorize an expansion in the scope and severity of social control measures. Dramatic, compelling evidence of the alleged evil is imperative to mobilize and sustain an opposition coalition and neutralize potential resistance. Apostates play a pivotal role in creating such evidence, offering personal testimony in which they attest to witnessing and being compelled to participate in the target movement's nefarious activities. The role is constructed in interaction between the individuals exiting putatively subversive movements and one or more parties in the oppositional coalition.

THREE TYPES OF ORGANIZATION

Social organizations may be distinguished on the basis of the degree to which their interests coincide with other organizational units in their respective environmental fields. The three kinds of organization developed here are presented in ideal-type form, based on the degree of autonomy and legitimacy accorded to them, which actual organizations approximate to varying degrees. To put the matter most directly, organizations whose interests coincide to a high degree with dominant organizations in their environmental field are accorded a high degree of legitimacy and considerable latitude in structuring their own operations while low coincidence of interests yields a label of illegitimacy and corresponding elevated surveillance and control. The three types can therefore be conceived as being arrayed on a continuum, from lowest to highest tension with their external environments. The tripartite typology is constructed as a heuristic device through which to emphasize the differences among organizations. This analytic method should not be interpreted as denying or diminishing the importance of mixed types and movement between types. To the contrary; variations around typological characteristics would be expected to constitute the rule rather than the exception and reveal the politically contested nature of actual organizational histories.

Allegiant Organizations

Type I (Allegiant) organizations are those whose interests coincide to a high degree with other organizations in their environments; therefore, most external organizations are positioned either as neutrals or coalitional allies. Organizations which exemplify this category include therapeutic/medical organizations, mainline churches, colleges, professional organizations, and various voluntary associations. Allegiant organizations are able to exercise considerable autonomy in conducting their organizational missions. Possessing this status carries with it weighty social expectations—that external groups and internal members will find little need or basis for serious or frequent claimsmaking against the organization. Allegiant organizations typically legitimate the exercise of their authority in terms such as "trusteeship" and "service," and they engage in a variety of organizational practices intended to foster and sustain that definition.

Under Type I conditions, both internal and external claims against the organization are difficult to muster for several reasons. First, the dispute settlement process is structured and managed by the organization itself, which enhances the capacity for organizational self-protection. The result is *dispute containment* as the organization is in a position to control the definition of and records pertaining to any dispute. In the best sense, internal organizational control means responsively redressing legitimate grievances; alternatively, the organization may use internal control mechanisms to intimidate claimants, conceal violations, and prevent internal opposition from coalescing. In either event, disputes are contained, and relatively few cases become matters of public record. Second, the organization is deemed by both participants and outsiders to be exercising legitimate authority, resulting in more stringent testing of claimsmaking against the organization. The burden of proof is squarely on the claimsmaker. Indeed, in the limiting case there may be no category of violation to be adjudicated. Where claimsmaking is successful, the language in which it is constructed tends to be "violation of trust" with claimants depicted as "victims of betrayal or abuse." Only when there is a succession of claimants whose claims can be linked into a broader pattern (i.e., a scandal) is there any substantial opportunity for oppositional coalitions and pressure for diminution of organizational autonomy.

Allegiant organizations seek to sustain autonomy by aligning organizational structure with external organizations, engaging in service activities commensurate with trustee status, and assuming responsibility for appropriately resolving disputes. Therefore, there are unlikely to be established oppositional groups possessing a mandate to advance or adjudicate claims against these organizations. The absence of external allies means that any claimants that do exist have few resources available to pursue claims, whatever their motivation.

Contestant Organizations

Type II (Contestant) organizations have a moderate level of coincidence and, correspondingly, a moderate level of tension with other organizations in their environments. The clearest examples of organizations in this category are the plethora of profit-making economic organizations. Contestant organizations are dedicated to the pursuit of organizational self-interest, which yields an environment populated with both allies and opponents. They are able to exercise limited autonomy in conducting their organizational missions as the legitimacy of pursuing private interests is deeply embedded in property rights and in cultural themes such as "freedom" and "success." While these organizations can successfully advance claims to pursue their particular organizational interests, countervailing internal and external claims challenging those interests also are accorded legitimacy. Contestant organizations are therefore involved rather routinely in disputes with other organizations, and the social expectation is that normal competition and conflict will involve these organizations in an ongoing pattern of claimsmaking. The normative boundaries that constrain unfettered pursuit of organizational interests are those such as "good citizenship" and commitment to "public interest."

In Type II situations, internal and external claims against an organization are considerably easier to mobilize than in Allegiant organizations, but Contestant organizations still face some major constraints. They have specific, enforceable obligations that are codified in regulations, laws, or contracts. Dispute settlement most often involves the creation of external third parties that stand between the organization and various internal and/or external claimants. The result is dispute adjudication in which the organization has stipulated rights but not unilateral control. The positioning of the regulatory unit between competing interests varies, but organizations inevitably lose some degree of control over dispute resolution because regulatory agencies possess their own priorities and forms of empowerment, seek to preserve their own position and legitimacy, and translate disputes into categories consistent with their regulatory mandates. Because the organizations possess legitimacy (i.e., rights, presumption of innocence), the various types of rules governing them address specific practices, and regulatory agencies have specific interests and forms of empowerment, there is a strong tendency toward *dispute narrowing* and negotiated settlements that limit organizational liability. Successful claimsmaking is constructed in terms of "malfeasance" or "violation of interest or equity." In the event there is a progression of claimants whose testimony suggests more pervasive wrongdoing, then pressure increases for greater enforcement powers lodged in external units and criminal rather than civil enforcement.

Contestant organizations attempt to maintain their positions by utilizing organizational resources to influence the regulatory process, conducting public relations programs that depict their organizational interests as coinciding with community interests engaging in service activity that is reflective of public spiritedness, and resolving disputes in a fashion that will be deemed fair and equitable (Braithwaite 1985; Reichman 1992). When conflicts do occur, opponents have some capacity for claimsmaking through appeal to regulatory units.

Subversive Organizations

Type III (Subversive) organizations have extremely low coincidence of interests with other organizations in their environment. Indeed, "subversive" is a label employed by opponents specifically to discredit these organizations. Organizations labeled Subversive are confronted by a broad coalition of opponents and few allies. The result is a very high level of tension between organization and external environment and concerted effort by opponents to label the organization as dangerous and pathological. Organizations that illustrate this type include some of the more controversial alternative religious movements, radical rightist and leftist political movements, and various forms of underground economies. Organizations regarded as Subversive are accorded virtually no organizational legitimacy and therefore face continuous opposition and constraint in pursuing organizational goals. In fact, their existence and functioning are regarded as inherently subversive to the goals and functioning of other "legitimate" organizations.

Under Type III conditions, claims against the organization are easily marshalled and tend to proliferate rapidly; indeed, organizations labeled Subversive are likely to be the targets of social control initiatives designed to contain, suppress, or destroy them. Dispute settlement processes are substantially controlled by oppositional coalitions. Because organizations labeled Subversive are regarded as particularly dangerous, special control agencies with extraordinary authority are formed or existing agencies are granted expanded powers. The expectation is that violations will be frequent and serious, and the organization is afforded little deference when violations are suspected. Instead, the organization is likely to be confronted with unilateral, pre-emptive, coercive control measures such as covert surveillance, planting of undercover agents, or even instigation of provocative incidents by agent provocateurs (Marx 1974). Command over the dispute settlement apparatus means that the oppositional coalition controls the definition of alleged violations and can widely disseminate information collected during investigation and prosecution processes. The result is a *dispute broadening* process that incorporates a range of organizational attributes and practices as external control organizations define their missions in terms of repressing such groups, operate with numerous allies, and face few restraints.

From the perspective of their opponents, Subversive organizations embody quintessential evil and are considered to pose a maximum degree of threat to the established social order. They are portrayed as qualitatively different from other organizations in that evil is rooted in their essential qualities rather than in specific patterns of behavior (Katz 1975). The countersubversion ideology that is constructed to legitimate expanded control over putatively Subversive groups alleges several elements are integral to their organization and operation (Bromley 1994a, 1994b). First, Subversive organizations are organized, secretive, conspiratorial groups that are large and rapidly growing. Second, these organizations are based on principles and pursue goals that are the inverse of and subversive to the central principles and goals of the legitimate social order. Third, they have gained control over some segment of the conventional social order, which now constitutes their base of operations. The very real possibility exists, therefore, that some major institution or even the entire social order may fall under subversive control. Finally, they possess a unique capacity or power that is fundamentally destructive to the essential integrity of normal individuals and social groups. This power is capable of destroying the primary basis of individual autonomy and collective loyalty, and it is believed to progressively undermine the capacity for resistance. Claimsmaking is thus cast in terms of manipulation, coercion, or even captivity at the hands of subversive agents. This countersubversion ideology becomes the working basis for the exercise of social control. Because Type III organizations are presumed to be so nefarious, the burden of proof in dispute resolution proceedings shifts to the organization, whatever the legal formalities.

Organizations labeled Subversive face great difficulty in defending themselves against implementation of coercive control measures. They may develop a public spokesperson role through which to defend themselves, but their claims often are not given a public forum or are publicly denounced. They are likely to try to compel opponents to file specific, formal charges that will be adjudicated through normal due process, thereby circumventing subversion control measures. They also enlist the assistance of organizations that defend universally granted protections, such as "civil rights" and "human rights," both to shield themselves and to enhance their credibility. Another common strategy is identifying as situational allies organizations that may be adversely impacted by expanded social control mechanisms. Finally, these organizations may make major organizational concessions, particularly where the opposition has targeted some specific policy or practice. In highly polarized situations, these various tactics are likely to do no more than slow down countersubversion initiatives.

TYPES OF ORGANIZATION AND TYPES OF CONTESTED ROLE EXIT

The three forms of organization delineated in the preceding section—Allegiant, Contestant, and Subversive—are distinguished in terms of the extent to which the organization is in tension with the surrounding environment and the extent to which the organization is able to control the process by which disputes to which it is party are settled. I have argued that type of organization is strongly related to both external incentive to exercise control over an organization and its capacity to avoid such control.

To focus the analysis now on the exiting process, all types of organizations experience some rate of participant exodus (Ebaugh 1988a; Murnighan 1981), and exiting participants are a potentially important source of information that could be used to discredit the organization. However, it is important to emphasize that most exiting does not involve formal or public airing of disputes between organization and exiting member. Both departing individual and organization leaders may have pragmatic reasons for avoiding contested exit. Individuals may be genuinely ambivalent about their organizational experience, continue to accept the organization's worldview even while rejecting current policies and practices, attempt to preserve friendships or other ties to the movement, or even hope to reform the organization from outside in an informal and non-confrontive fashion. For its part, the organization may well refrain from contesting exits in order to conceal the existence of internal dissent, avoid energizing internal opposition to repressive control practices, accept exits it cannot prevent rather than heightening hostility over the exit process itself, or hope to garner continued support from individuals who may remain nominally connected to the organization. Whatever the nature of individual or situational motivations, I argue that organizations in the low-tension positions are most likely to be able to control the exit process so as to prevent public dispute, while organizations in a high-tension position are much less likely to be able to do so (Richardson et al. 1986). I therefore identify three distinctive contested exit roles—Defector,

Whistleblower, and Apostate—that are characteristic of Allegiant, Contestant, and Subversive organizations, respectively. Integral to developing this argument is the assertion that several conditions that might explain differences in contested exit behavior are in fact common to all three types of organizations.

First, as Becker (1963) has observed, from an external perspective things are often not as they seem or should be within organizations. Across a range of organizations, there are accepted, well-established internal practices that could be the basis for claimsmaking against the organization if they became known externally (i.e., "normal deviance"). For example, there are long-standing patterns of physical and sexual abuse within families (e.g., Strauss, Geles, and Steinmetz 1980); collusive relationships by regulatory agencies and bribery of public officials (e.g., Gardiner and Olson 1974); brutality and complicity in illicit activity by police agencies (e.g., Kray 1972); and restraint of trade, deceptive advertising, and sale of harmful products by corporations (e.g., Simon and Eitzen 1990). These practices have gone on for extended periods of time and are rather widely known within, and sometimes outside, the organizations involved. Indeed, quite commonly the participation of a substantial number of internal and/or external parties is indispensable to the persistence of such practices. There are a number of reasons that normal deviance often remains unexposed. Members of organizations are socialized into and accept both conventional and deviant practices when they enter the organization. Members also develop personal and organizational loyalties that lead them to protect colleagues and the organization even if they harbor personal reservations. Finally, individuals have strong personal interests in avoiding placing their career positions within organizations at risk. Whatever the causes of concealment, it is clear that within most organizations there exists a shared pool of information about contestable practices that can be revealed under certain conditions.

Second, disputes are endemic to all types of organizations. The pervasiveness of marital conflict and divorce (Miller 1990), disagreement-based termination and resignation of employment (e.g., Weisband and Thomas 1975), denominational conflict and schism within churches (e.g., Ammerman 1990), the necessity of force to gain compliance across a range of relationships and ongoing resistance to such measures (Scott 1985), the numerous types of third parties built into social structure whose primary function is conflict resolution (Black 1993), and the formation of protest movements of various kinds within formal organizations (e.g., Zald and Berger 1978) all bespeak the pervasiveness of disputing. There is no shortage, it would seem, of divisiveness within most types of groups, and these disputes constitute potential motivation to reveal discrediting information about the organization.

Third, organizations tend to respond to internal disputes in predictable fashion. In most cases in which trouble emerges in the context of organizational relationships, the problematic condition is resolved prior to any formal, public visibility (Emerson and Messinger 1977). One common response, for example, is individual-initiated relocation or organizationally sponsored reassignment. However, in all organizations when trouble does not recede it is identified categorically, responsibility is attributed to some source, and claimsmaking activity commences (Felstiner, Abel, and Sarat 1980–1981). Organizations may respond to internal dissidents by "reforming" organizational norms or practices so as to eliminate a dispute; they may also choose not to confront dissidents and simply tacitly accept contested practices. However, a common response appears to be to react punitively (Harshbarger 1973). Individuals may alternatively be punished through surveillance, intimidation, isolation, reduction in rights/privileges, lowered status, or expulsion. While sanctions may suppress resistance, they also may sustain hostility that can be released later as conditions permit. Alternatively, individual participants may perpetuate disputes by resisting control measures. They may choose "voice" over accommodation or exit (Hirshman 1970). Having a sense that the organization has gone wrong and requires reform, individuals may choose to stand and fight, concluding that the chances for influencing the organization are greater internally than externally. The internal heretic role is, of course, unstable and fraught with problems, and heretics ultimately may elect to gain additional leverage in the conflict by involving external parties. Conventional, widely employed control strategies thus are likely to create pools of potential allies for oppositional groups.

Fourth, while contested exits may provide the most obvious source of later opposition, under certain conditions former members may be recruited into oppositional roles. Since prior disputes are not necessary for later opposition, the pool of former members who are potential recruits for oppositional roles is substantially larger than the number of highly visible dissidents. Further, even if rates of exit do differ among organizational types, large numbers of former members are not necessarily required to support an oppositional campaign.

Finally, leavetaking is a source of considerable ambivalence (i.e., "mixed emotions") that must be resolved (Weigert 1991). Leavetakers are likely to harbor conflicting feelings about their former relationships, as participants in all types of organizations normally develop some degree of commitment to the organization and to their position within it. Therefore, they may well remain attracted to the organization even while they feel compelled to separate from it. At the same time, each of the three forms of exit considered here involves some degree of formal rejection by the organization even though personal connections and relationships may remain. Further, external audiences express ambivalence toward leavetakers as their character and loyalties are called into question during the exiting process. The way that ambivalence is resolved varies by type of organization, but it is an important motivator for reconstructing role relationships and biographical narratives to account for such changes. Ambivalence thus may provide a significant motivation for exiting organization members to assume oppositional roles as a means of tension reduction.

Defectors

The term "defector" (or even "deserter") traditionally has been applied to leavetaking in a variety of institutional contexts—familial, military, religious—

in which role occupants are defined as having a strong commitment and responsibility to the organization and their status within it. As employed here, the defector role may be defined as one in which an organizational participant negotiates exit primarily with organizational authorities, who grant permission for role relinquishment, control the exit process, and facilitate role transition. The jointly constructed narrative assigns primary moral responsibility for role performance problems to the departing member and interprets organizational permission as commitment to extraordinary moral standards and preservation of public trust.

Disputes and Defectors. The high moral standing of allegiant organizations allows them both to socialize members so that individual intentionality and organizational logic coincide and to make substantial personal claims on members (Becker 1958). Individuals may either resist organizational claims, leading to internal disputes, or be unable to comply with them, creating a sense of personal failure. Whatever the source of initial disputes or doubts and subsequent informal discussions about them with leaders, formal action is almost certain to be triggered if behavior threatens organizational functioning or solidarity. Members have considerable reason for reluctance to sever relationships for which they often have made considerable personal sacrifice and to which they have serious commitment, and so the response to initial problems is likely to be renewed commitment and effort. One important result of a high congruence of individual intentionality and organizational logic is that members are likely to encounter considerable difficulty in formulating an alternative to the organizational interpretation for the problems they face. Their inability to say what is wrong in other words tends to cut off any possible dispute at the most preliminary stage.

If remedial efforts are unsuccessful, the process of exiting involves negotiations between the member and organizational leadership rather than with external parties (although the reaction of outsiders may also be assessed), and it may be constructed as an organizationally sponsored and controlled separation ritual. In cases where organizational authorization is greatest, external parties support organizational processes with the result that the member has no recourse to external allies. In essence, the individual must request permission from organizational authorities to disaffiliate if the separation is to occur on favorable terms. Since the organization possesses a high degree of legitimacy and controls the dispute resolution process, it can suppress contested exit by administering the exiting process and the narratives that interpret this process. The organization therefore is able to maintain control over cases that would be potentially discrepant with its privileged position. Given this high degree of control, it is difficult for members to locate others who might collectively reinterpret private troubles as organizational problems and mount organized protest. In the unlikely event that an exiting member opts to attribute problems to the organization, the burden of proof is squarely on the claimant, who lacks both internal and external allies. In essence, no matter what the validity of the defector's claims might be in theory, the inability of the individual to articulate grievances and to validate and support claims leaves defectors without meaningful recourse.

Defector Narratives. The high level of legitimacy and moral rectitude attributed to allegiant organizations allows them to translate problems into organizational terms and categories that place primary responsibility for failure on the member. The account that is negotiated typically is one in which the exiting member professes sincere intention and acknowledges failure despite genuine, persistent effort. Departing members are likely to reaffirm the organization's values and goals; the organization professes regret but understanding. This resolution leaves the organization positioned such that it has exercised appropriate responsibility to both exiting member and the larger society. No great stigma attaches to either side, although the exiting member shoulders ultimate responsibility. Control over records of the exit account maintains confidentiality and preserves organizational power.

Defector Careers. Once outside the organization, defectors are most likely to seek a transition into a new social network. The post-membership career therefore is of limited duration and directed at stabilizing personal life and reconstructing personal identity. To the extent that the former organization was the source of a distinctive lifestyle and identity, there is inevitably a period of instability as individuals find themselves between identities, and the former identity colors current identity-building efforts. The defector is faced with a negotiated exit agreement that renders personal opposition problematic, and in any event the absence of pre-existing oppositional groups significantly restricts the political and economic opportunity for a former member career. In some cases former members form ex-member support groups that operate to facilitate the period of role transition for others, and limited ex-member careers may be fashioned through administering such groups.

Defectors from Allegiant Religious Organizations. The extent to which religious organizations can maintain internal social control over disputing and the exit process is nicely illustrated by the history of exit among priests and nuns within the Catholic Church, although a similar case could be advanced for other churches as well. Prior to the Second Vatican Council, by all accounts the rate of exit by priests and nuns was extremely low (Ebaugh 1988b; Hoge 1991). The opportunity for disputes to surface publicly within or outside the church has been limited by the spiritual authority of the church internally, its legitimacy externally, and, in the case of religious orders, by totalistic organization. Nonetheless, it is clear that during various historical periods there has been a pattern of violation of sexual norms, for example—in the form of homosexuality, heterosexual relationships, and, most recently, pedophilia—that could have been very damaging to the church at any time if revealed publicly (Boswell 1981; Curb and Manahan 1985; Shupe 1995; Sipe 1991; Wong 1983). There have also been persistent disputes in the form of resistance to the totalistic lifestyle within religious communities, centering on issues such as authority structure, lack of spiritual commitment by other priests or nuns, and constant demands for self-sacrifice (Daichman 1990; DellaCava 1975). However, institutional defenses against the internal and external leakage of potentially discrediting information have been very effective. Goldner, Ritti, and Ference (1977, p. 540) found that priests traditionally have not had access to what they term "cynical knowledge" (information that "presumably altruistic actions or procedures of the organization actually served the purpose of maintaining the legitimacy of existing authority or preserving the institutional structure") until they were well socialized and integrated into the priesthood (1977, p. 546). As a result, organized internal opposition is unlikely. Even more compelling is the evidence that pedophilia involving a substantial number of priests has been occurring clandestinely over a period of decades (Shupe 1995).

Priests and nuns who ultimately have left their religious roles often agonize over that decision, sometimes for many years (Armstrong 1981; Wong 1983). When it becomes clear that priests or nuns are moving toward exit (i.e., laicization or vow dispensation), church officials have maintained close control over the process. Nuns would be escorted from the convent at night to prevent interaction with other nuns, and any future contact with the former nun was strictly prohibited (Ebaugh 1988a, p. 170). In addition, it has not been uncommon for family members, who would be expected to be nuns' strongest allies, to resist exit as well. In her study of former nuns, Ebaugh (1988b, p. 110) reports opposition from family members and other Catholics to be a significant impediment to nuns' exiting their roles. Eight of the nuns she interviewed "procrastinated leaving their convents because of intense disapproval from parents. Three of them were threatened with disinheritance should they leave. All eight admitted that parental disapproval caused them to reconsider earlier decisions to exit and resulted in their postponing their decisions, sometimes for many years." Similarly, priests perceived that both church and family would repudiate them (Jehenson 1969, p. 292). One former priest writes that "If I were to leave the priesthood because celibacy makes no sense and hides the very Christian love it once was meant to serve, I would be a renegade, a traitor, a man without a home" (Kavanagh 1967, p. 11).

The spiritual authority of the church and its control over the exit process are reflected compellingly in the construction of exit accounts. For example, Goldner, Ritti and Ference (1977, p. 547) report that priests seeking exit have tended to attribute their laicization to individual rather than organizational failings: "In the past, leaving the active priesthood was an individual act and an occasion for stigmatizing the individual priest. . . . leaving was interpreted as a weakness of the individual priest—an inability to cope or to maintain the strength needed as a participant in this highly demanding endeavor" (Goldner, Ritti, and Ference 1977, p. 547). The church has reinforced this perspective by pressuring exiting priests to make admissions of individual weakness part of the formal record in some cases. Indeed, during the Vatican II reform process, the committee on priestly renewal within the Senate of Priests reported that "It is a verified fact that some applicants have been told that a favorable decision is more likely if they will testify to immoral conduct or psychological disability on their part'' (Goldner, Ritti, and Ference 1977, p. 548).

Priests and nuns leaving their religious communities faced a particularly challenging transition when religious communities securely enveloped members and few members exited. Their primary goal became to establish a conventional lifestyle and identity and to put former commitments behind them. Because their religious communities terminated all contact, they had little alternative to rebuilding alternative lives. Ebaugh reports that nuns making the transition to secular lives continued to have strong feelings of ambivalence. Most remained devout Catholics; at the same time, it was not uncommon for them to harbor considerable resentment toward their former orders (1988a, pp. 26, 47). However, the hostility they experienced subjectively was rarely translated into public disputes or external attempts to reform religious orders.

Whistleblowers

The term ''whistleblower'' is adopted from its common usage in economic and political institutions. The whistleblower role is defined here as one in which an organization member forms an alliance with an external regulatory unit through offering personal testimony concerning specific, contested organizational practices that is then used to sanction the organization. The narrative constructed jointly by the whistleblower and regulatory agency is one which depicts the whistleblower as motivated by personal conscience and the organization by defense of public interest.

Disputes and Whistleblowers. Whistleblowing most often surfaces within corporate and governmental institutions in the context of internal resistance to established organizational practices (Perrucci, Anderson, Schendel, and Trachtman 1980; Weinstein 1977). A common source of widely publicized whistleblowing cases in recent years has been disputes between professionals and administrators concerning specific organizational priorities and practices within bureaucratic settings. Organizational participants have considerable personal incentive to avoid the public confrontation entailed in whistleblowing. Their loyalty to the organization is certain to be challenged by leadership; organizational colleagues may distance themselves; career potential within the organization is diminished; transfer to other organizations is jeopardized by attributions of disloyalty; and legal liability may be incurred if information disclosed is deemed proprietary. Formal organizations typically espouse the right to internal disagreement (i.e., belief, speech). However, if normal decision-making channels, organizational incentives, and informal safety-valve mechanisms do not succeed in suppressing overt dissent, leaders will invoke sanctions. Often this involves precipitating incidents of such a nature that sanctions can be imposed for rule violations rather than exercise of privileged freedoms (Harshbarger 1973; O'Day 1983). While the intent of the whistleblower usually is to employ external allies to effect change within the organization rather than personally switching sides, the end result tends to be permanent marginalization or exit.

The process of exiting as a whistleblower differs from that of a defector in that the individual at some point begins active negotiation with representatives of an external regulatory unit. These units have oversight responsibility to a coalition of individuals or groups whose interests they represent, but they face a continuing problem in identifying organizational violations, particularly when the operating assumption is organizational legitimacy. The historical record indicates that organization members, whether involved or non-involved in normal deviance, usually will not assume the risks associated with whistleblowing. It is therefore in the interest of regulatory units to offer incentives, in the form of rewards for whistleblowing and protection from retaliation. Whistleblowers play a pivotal role in organization–regulatory unit relationships as they provide otherwise unobtainable information, enhance the regulatory unit's claims to defense of public interest, and diminish any organization claims of overzealous or partisan regulatory activity. Since the regulatory unit, with the testimony of the whistleblower, may capture the moral highground and control the dispute resolution process, the organization is unable to merge dispute and non-dispute–precipitated exits to its advantage. Rather, the regulatory agency controls this process, and it may therefore be able to cast the whistleblower as hero rather than heretic. Further, ''whistleblower'' becomes a positive label that regulatory agencies are able to bestow retrospectively to lend credibility to individuals who offer testimony to them under a variety of circumstances.

Whistleblower Narratives. Exposing illegal or immoral conduct within organizations is defined as a general civic responsibility, and members of the professions and civil service are specifically pledged to place public welfare ahead of personal interests (Bok 1982, pp. 211–12; James 1980). The reality, of course, is that organizations regard public exposure of normal deviance as disloyalty and commonly respond to whistleblowers by attempting to impugn their motives, tactics, and credibility. The conflict is one in which both the regulatory unit and the organization possess considerable resources and legitimacy. The narrative that is most effective in buttressing whistleblower and regulatory unit position asserts that the whistleblower became involved in deviant practices as a result of ignorance, deception, or pressure; has pursued all internal means of recourse before going public; was not recruited; is acting out of personal conscience; has no personal interest in pending adjudication; and has assumed considerable personal risk in whistleblowing. At the heart of the narrative is evidentiary material documenting a specific pattern of rule violation. This account simultaneously elevates the moral standing of both the whistleblower, as an exemplar of public virtue, and the agency, as a defender of public interest, while camouflaging any political motivations and struggle within the organization. In effect, this account distinguishes the whistleblower from the informant, who has a personal interest in providing information and testimony. Organizationally sponsored campaigns to discredit whistleblowers may simply serve to enhance this image.

Whistleblower Careers. Beginning as they usually do with the objective of winning an internal conflict, individuals who become whistleblowers often have no intention of exiting the organization. It appears that many naively assume that once the dispute is resolved, they will pursue normal careers in a now reformed organization. However, whistleblowers lose most allies within the organization by betraying organizational trust. Exclusionary activity then pushes the whistleblower toward a closer alliance with the regulatory unit. At the same time, whistleblowers also lose considerable control over whatever initially precipitated the conflict, once external regulatory agencies become involved in the dispute. The latter pursue their own missions and translate disputes into agency-relevant categories. Most importantly, the process of dispute resolution in contestant organizations requires proffering specific charges for adjudication. This process effectively limits the lifespan of individual whistleblowers, as their formal role ends with the termination of adjudicatory proceedings, and regulatory units move on to other cases.

In one sense, the transition following whistleblowing appears to be one of modest proportions as the whistleblower often seeks to maintain organizational membership and is involved in a limited dispute between two legitimate organizational entities. However, the transition process can be extremely difficult, as whistleblowers find that their disloyalty has the consequence of sealing off alternative opportunities. The record strongly suggests that even if regulatory agencies are able to offer whistleblowers protection against overt retaliation, their organizational positions become marginal and untenable in the long run. In a few cases, whistleblowers carve out careers as "crusaders" or find positions in advocacy groups if the issues raised are the source of continuing conflict.

Whistleblowing in Religious Organizations. Whistleblowing involving religious organizations is relatively uncommon, and the form it assumes only approximates corresponding activity in economic and political organizations. Constitutional limitations on state regulation of religion precludes the kind of public sector regulation that is so prevalent in monitoring economic and political deviance. Further, because mainline churches are allegiant organizations, most have internal tribunals that regulate their own affairs. Appeals that in other institutional contexts would be directed outward are therefore turned inward.

The case of Worldwide Church of God is the exception that proves the rule, nicely illustrating the limitations of regulatory intervention into church affairs (Wiley 1979; Worthing 1979). Established in 1933 by Herbert W. Armstrong (as the Church of God), the church grew at a modest rate until the 1960s, when it began a period of extraordinary membership increase. During this period the church, which was always somewhat controversial by mainstream standards, also experienced a series of internal controversies and public scandal. After a protracted internal dispute over financial policy and practices in which their allegations were rebuffed, a small coterie of dissidents resigned in protest and almost immediately launched a civil suit against the church. What transformed this internal dispute into a regulatory action and internal dissidents into whistleblowers was the availability of an external ally in the office of the Attorney General. In an *ex parte* hearing, state officials convinced a judge to issue a receivership order that placed the church under the virtually total control of a court-appointed receiver for several months. The initial action was successful because state authorities convinced the court that churches should be treated as public charitable trusts and therefore as subject to broader government control. The receivership was later rescinded and the lawsuit dismissed when an appellate court reasserted the privileged position of churches, ruling that the suit was from its "inception constitutionally infirm and predestined to failure" (Melton 1989, p. 706). The vigorous opposition to this episode by mainline churches resulted relatively quickly in state legislation intended to preclude any future incidents of this kind.

The recent priest-abuse cases in the Catholic Church make the other side of the case, indicating the combination of circumstances that must obtain for a church with greater power and legitimacy to become vulnerable to whistleblowing. There is considerable evidence of ongoing sexual activity, homosexuality, heterosexual liaisons, and pedophilia that violated official church doctrine and public pronouncements over a long period of time (Shupe 1995; Sipe 1991). The record suggests that many cases were never reported; in those that were, families were stunned at discovering their children had been sexually abused by their priests, and dutifully reported the victimization to church leaders. The church handled cases internally, which typically meant remanding the priest to a treatment facility or reassignment. Several factors apparently combined to alter the situation in favor of external control and whistleblowing (Jenkins forthcoming). Internally, there was a decline in centralized authority as well as a major schism between liberals and conservatives accompanying the Second Vatican Council. Both liberals and conservatives began leaking information about sexual improprieties for their own purposes as each side sought to influence the direction reforms would take. Externally, the more aggressive stance of investigative reporters and the increasing availability and lucrativeness of civil suits to law firms created a powerful pair of coalitional allies for families confronted with church non-responsiveness. In this volatile context the church sought to suppress information about priest abuse. It was only after families encountered non-responsiveness and intransigence that they began taking their cases to the media and the civil courts (Bromley forthcoming). The external agencies defined whistleblowing families as courageous survivors of unconscionable institutional irresponsibility, and the church suffered financial and reputational loss. At the same time, this episode also demonstrates the capacity of organizations possessing substantial legitimacy to exercise damage control even during serious crises. In this instance, legal suits have permitted the church to negotiate of out-of-court settlements in which records usually are sealed as part of the agreement. Further, litigation of cases individually creates a focus on individual incidents rather than on institutional polices and upper-level leaders.

One result of restrictions on external political regulation is that independent groups approximating regulatory agencies have been formed within the religious institution sector, most frequently formed by elements of the conservative Christian tradition. Within the conservative Christian community the sacred text is taken as literal truth; it constitutes the ultimate basis for authorizing social relations and serves as the source of the received spiritual tradition that underpins religious legitimacy. These churches therefore are implacably opposed to legitimating alternative versions of the sacred texts. Various conservative Christian organizations—such as the Christian Research Institute, Moody Bible Institute, Christian Apologetics and Information Service, and Spiritual Counterfeits Project—have been formed to defend the theological boundaries of "legitimate Christian churches" (Shupe and Bromley 1980). The targets of these regulatory efforts traditionally have been sectarian churches such as the Jehovah's Witnesses, Mormons, and Seventh-Day Adventists. Given cultural support for religious diversity and tolerance and the increasing marginality of conservative religious forms, these religious regulatory units lack the public standing of their political counterparts. As a result, they are perceived as partisan and function without significant sanctioning power beyond the capacity to deny the mantle of legitimacy within their limited niche in the religious institution sector.

Sectarian churches have exhibited both high conversion and high defection rates (Nelson and Bromley 1988), and one major source of discontent among members has been their high authority/high demand structure. Whatever the sources of disputes with these churches, numerous members exiting these groups have been recruited to brief whistleblowing careers. Religious regulatory units rely heavily on individuals who resemble secular whistleblowers in offering public testimony, but the basis of dispute is theological beliefs and related practices. Employing a standard of "theological truth," these agencies reconstruct conflicts in terms of prior spiritual "deception" and subsequent recognition of "truth." One of the most common forms through which religious whistleblowers offer testimony is printed tracts that regulatory agencies distribute as a means of denying legitimacy to what they regard as the ongoing deceptive practices in which "pseudo-Christian" churches engage. Typical titles include "I Was a False Witness" (Cetnar 1982), *Apostles of Denial: An Examination and Expose of the History, Doctrines and Claims of the Jehovah's Witnesses* (Gruss 1970), "Set Free by the Truth" (Schmuck 1977), "One Mormon's Journey to Christ" (Curtis 1977), *From Housewife to Heretic* (Johnson 1981), and *Out of Darkness, Into the "Sonlight"* (Tanner 1960). For the most part, these whistleblowers pursue only brief careers, usually in the context of a transition between churches. However, some longer-term careers are possible in administering regulatory units or supplying the investigatory reports these units regularly issue.

Apostates

The term "apostate" historically has been applied to general religious leavetaking as well as to oppositional leavetaking, and it is the latter usage that is employed here. The apostate role is thus defined as one that occurs in a highly polarized situation in which an organization member undertakes a total change of loyalties by allying with one or more elements of an oppositional coalition without the consent or control of the organization. The narrative is one which documents the quintessentially evil essence of the apostate's former organization chronicled through the apostate's personal experience of capture and ultimate escape/rescue. It is the avowed inability of the former member of a Subversive organization to have done otherwise, a claim which is accepted by the oppositional coalition, that distinguishes apostates from traitors.

Disputes and Apostates. The high level of tension between organizations labeled Subversive and their surrounding environment means that individuals joining them almost inevitably distance from conventional social networks. Groups deemed Subversive most often constitute organized projects that posit and model an alternative version of social order that clashes sharply with the prevailing structure of social relations, and they therefore attract a range of individuals who are in resistance to the dominant order. New affiliates are important both in organization building and as validation of the organization's repudiation of the existing social order. Strong ingroup solidarity develops among the core group of members as a result of organizational commitment-building mechanisms, personal sacrifices for the cause, and unremitting societal opposition (Kanter 1972). At the same time, such organizations historically have demonstrated a tendency toward political infighting and schism as competing visions of an alternative social order are offered and as struggles for control over organizational apparatus transpire. Further, disaffiliation rates may be high as affiliates simply experiment with the alternative forms of social relations proposed by the organization. These organizations often devote considerable effort to containing dissent and disenchantment through positive incentives and negative sanctions that closely parallel those employed in Allegiant and Contestant organizations. The organizational response to defection ranges from inattention to rebuke, and contact with disaffiliates usually is abruptly terminated or becomes a kind of ritualized reconversion effort. However, a key difference between Subversive organizations and the other two types is that for the former there is a plethora of allies to whom exiting members can turn for support. Because the organization possesses little legitimacy, it may be able to control the internal dispute resolution process as long as individuals remain members, but it has a very limited capacity to control external intervention in exit and post-exit processes. One critical result of external intervention is that dispute and non-dispute–precipitated exits are converted into the former as external opponents actively recruit exiting members into the oppositional coalition, provide social networks through which exiting members can reinterpret personal troubles as organizational problems, and control role transition on favorable terms. There is likely to be a price for re-entry. Former members may have to confess to disloyal conduct or plead loss of free will as a result of subversive influence. The burden of proof is on the organization to refute claims by exiting members, and there may be little opportunity to do so.

Apostate Narratives. Given the polarized situation and power imbalance, there is considerable pressure on individuals exiting Subversive organizations to negotiate a narrative with the oppositional coalition that offers an acceptable explanation for participation in the organization and for now once again reversing loyalties. In the limiting case, exiting members without any personal grievance against the organization may find that re-entry into conventional social networks is contingent on at least nominally affirming such opposition coalition claims. The archetypal account that is negotiated is a "captivity narrative" in which apostates assert that they were innocently or naively operating in what they had every reason to believe was a normal, secure social site; were subjected to overpowering subversive techniques; endured a period of subjugation during which they experienced tribulation and humiliation; ultimately effected escape or rescue from the organization; and subsequently renounced their former loyalties and issued a public warning of the dangers of the former organization as a matter of civic responsibility (Ebersole 1988; VanDerBeets 1972). Any expressions of ambivalence or residual attraction to the former association are vigorously resisted and are taken as evidence of untrustworthiness. Emphasis on the irresistibility of subversive techniques is vital to apostates and their allies as a means of locating responsibility for participation on the organization rather than on the former member. This account avoids attribution of calculated choices that would call for invoking the label of traitor. Further, a broad allegation of subversion allows a diverse array of opponents to unite under a common banner and formulate a variety of claims in terms that will mobilize or neutralize a broad spectrum of interests. Upon the rendering of an acceptable narrative, the oppositional coalition accepts pledges and tests of loyalty and professions of regret as the basis for reintegration into social networks to which it controls access.

Apostate Careers. Apostates generally have greater career possibilities than whistleblowers. Since they are exiting highly stigmatized organizations, however, many exiting members seek to make role transitions as inconspicuously as possible. Their capacity to move back into conventional social networks unobtrusively depends in large measure on the breadth, power, and aggressiveness of the oppositional coalition. Exiting organization members may be able to circumvent the oppositional coalition, or negotiations for re-entry may be conducted out of public view. In such cases the apostate career is muted and transitory. Even here, however, explicit or implicit confession that the organization is indeed subversive in character, renunciation of prior affiliation, and new declarations of loyalty are likely to be required. To the extent that the oppositional coalition confronts exiting members, or leavetakers pursue grievances against the organization, the apostate role assumes a more public form. Whether or not the transition occurs in or out of public view, it is likely to assume a ritualistic form. The exiting member's identity and loyalty remain indeterminate, and rituals of passage are constructed to transform individual identity and validate the locus of social loyalty. In its public form apostasy primarily involves participation in various types of degradation ceremonies that feature moral denunciations of the organization, with the personal ordeal of the apostate as the testimonial centerpiece.

Protracted conflict between the organization and oppositional coalition creates opportunities for extended apostate careers. Apostates may pursue a variety of strategies to solidify their careers: consolidating their experience and acquiring credentials that support a more permanent social niche; reconstructing their position and experience within the organization, particularly status inflation, so that their testimony becomes more valuable in sanctioning the organization; modifying the narrative content so that it appeals to the specific interests of one or more elements of the oppositional coalition; and embellishing the narrative so as to maintain niche viability, particularly when the existence of a cohort of apostates creates role competition.

As in the case of the whistleblower role, the credibility of apostates rests on both their former organization relationship and rejection of that relationship. However, the apostate role is more extreme in this regard, as apostates must completely renounce the former organization even while their careers depend upon highlighting and displaying their former membership as the basis of their credibility. More than for the other exit roles, then, former status is the basis for their current status. This, of course, complicates role transition since apostates must display as their credentials the attributes that also are the source of their stigma. As Ebaugh (1988a, p. 158) notes in describing the difficulty of making the transition from deviant to conventional roles, "the people making such socially desirable changes are often caught in 'no man's land' because they lose the strong primary group's association with their fellow deviants and find it hard to be accepted in mainstream society. They are often caught in between the two worlds and find little acceptance from either world." This problem is accentuated for apostates since their participation in mainstream society is predicated on preserving their prior identity.

Apostates from Religious Organizations. The NRMs that initially were at the center of the cult controversy—the Unification Church, Hare Krishna, and The Family (originally named the Children of God)—share a prophetic orientation and communal organization (Bromley 1997). Their ideologies predict imminent, radical transformation of the social order, and they have organized as tight-knit communities that distance themselves from a world they conclude is corrupt and moribund. These movements not only reject the dominant forms of social relations, they sacralize the antithesis by supplanting family relationships and secular careers with collectivist relationships and spiritual careers. The new commitments are accorded the highest moral priority and insulated symbolically and organizationally from countervailing influence. Although the NRM controversy later broadened to include multifarious religious movements, as well as more established religious organizations allegedly displaying dangerous or destructive tendencies, it was these prophetic movements that served as the initial impetus for ideological and countermovement organization.

Particularly at the height of prophetic NRM mobilization, the core of committed members separated themselves from conventional society and poured enormous personal and collective energy into building models of an alternative social order. However, research on NRMs has consistently shown that for most individuals NRM membership has constituted a period of experimentation rather than long-term commitment (Robbins and Bromley 1992). As a result, many of the NRMs that triggered opposition experienced steep declines in membership by 1980, following a few years of extremely rapid growth, when affiliation rates tailed off while disaffiliation rates remained robust (Barker 1988). Most of the individuals who experimented briefly with NRMs exited without clearly artic-ulating reasons for disaffection and left with little discussion or planning (Beck-ford 1985). At the same time, their monolithic appearance notwithstanding, NRMs have demonstrated a persistent pattern of internal dissension and conflict that has produced member defections. Internal problems include struggles for control over movement organization and resources at upper ranks, disillusion-ment with change or lack of change within the movement among both leaders and followers, and resistance to the severe discipline and sacrifice demanded of lower-ranking members (Bromley 1988b; Wright 1988). There has therefore been an ample supply of members exiting NRMs both with and without griev-ances.

It was the families of NRM members that first mobilized to oppose NRMs in response to conversions that they interpreted as total, permanent changes in loyalty. Rather quickly a loose confederation of family-based voluntary asso-ciations formed, which gradually evolved into a national anti-cult movement (ACM), to orchestrate the countersubversion campaign against NRMs (Bromley and Shupe 1993; Shupe and Bromley 1980). The problem that the ACM faced was that constitutional protection of religious liberty precluded the creation of a governmental regulatory agency that could act for the constellation of groups with an interest in controlling NRMs. The ACM pursued a variety of strategies through which to legislate distinctions between legitimate and illegitimate relig-ious groups and between conversion and brainwashing (Shupe, Bromley, and Oliver 1984). However, these efforts were largely unsuccessful. Even the apoc-alypse at Jonestown, which exceeded in carnage even the ACM's direst predic-tions, failed to galvanize governmental action (Shupe, Bromley, and Breschel 1989).

Left with few viable avenues of appeal to public officials, the ACM attempted to ensconce itself as a social control organization, assuming the functions of an information clearinghouse, lobbying group, accrediting agency, and policing unit. In these various capacities the ACM was variably successful. It did become a major source of public information about NRMs, significantly shaping public opinion (Bromley and Breschel 1992). The countermovement also scored some successes in lobbying public officials. On a number of occasions state and fed-eral legislative hearings and investigations were held that showcased ACM claims and grievances. Indeed, at the height of the cult controversy, media cov-erage and legislative hearings functioned as public degradation ceremonies dominated by elements of the countermovement coalition. The ACM also assumed a more militant, activist role as the deputized agent of families in orchestrating the physical extraction of NRM members. During the 1970s the ACM was relatively successful in extracting members from NRMs, but over time, resistance intensified to what amounted to delegation of police power to a private group (Bromley 1988a).

The foundation on which ACM organization and its organizational initiatives rest is a cult/brainwashing ideology that labels NRMs as subversive organizations by distinguishing what are depicted as pseudo-religious groups ("cults") from their legitimate church counterparts and pseudo-conversions ("brainwashing") from legitimate spiritual transformations. According to this ideology, rapidly growing cults are unprecedented in their totalistic organization, manipulative tactics, and psychological destructiveness. The most significant distinguishing characteristic attributed to cults is a potent psychotechnology (brainwashing techniques) capable of dramatically altering individual belief and behavior and of creating long-term emotional damage to anyone subjected to it. Unscrupulous gurus are ultimately responsible for developing these techniques to exploit innocent followers for their own pleasure, power, and profit, with innocent and vulnerable young adults ("children") as the primary targets. The rapid growth in size, wealth, and power of cults poses an ever greater threat to both individuals who become enmeshed in them and to social institutions which they infiltrate. Strong countermeasures—warning families of the dangers, rescuing individuals incapable of extricating themselves, and revision of laws and constitutional privileges behind which they hide—are advocated. The cult/brainwashing ideology serves as the symbolic umbrella under which the disparate groups arrayed against NRMs unite.

Apostate testimony is central to the entire range of ACM-sponsored social control initiatives. However, because the ACM lacks official authority to control NRMs and to reintegrate former NRM members into conventional social networks, it actually has incorporated only a small percentage of former members into the countermovement. By far the largest proportion of members exit voluntarily after some period of experimentation and typically seek a low-profile re-entry into conventional networks by resuming familial, occupational, and educational endeavors. Limiting visibility reduces the likelihood of their having to make a public accounting for involvement in a stigmatized group. Research on former NRM members suggests that their assessments of NRM experience span the entire range from positive to ambivalent to disillusioned (Wright 1984; Rothbaum 1988; Jacobs 1989). However, most leavetakers do not adopt an openly adversarial relationship with their former movements, and therefore it is the small segment of countermovement-affiliated former members that dominates the public arena.

The ACM therefore has recruited apostates through two other forms of exit, deprogramming and exit-counseling, that are more directly under ACM control (Lewis and Bromley 1987). For both of these exit types, ACM-allied deprogrammers and therapists act as deputized agents of families to enforce demands for disaffiliation and to coordinate the role transition process. The key difference between the two is that deprogramming initially was a unilateral, pre-emptive action based on coercive control of the deprogrammee; it also came to be used as a confirmatory post-exit ritual, even when NRM members disaffiliated on their own initiative. Based on ACM ideology that NRM members had been psychologically subjugated through cult mind-control processes, the first deprogrammings were organized as elaborate rituals resembling exorcisms. Early entrepreneur-deprogrammers, who offered their "rescue" services to families, treated deprogrammees as quite literally possessed, dangerous to themselves and to others (see, for example, Bromley 1988a, pp. 262–65; Shupe and Bromley 1978). The deprogramming ritual was conceived of as an ordeal in which a struggle took place between the cult-imposed personality and the deprogrammee's natural, pre-cult personality. Successful deprogramming, which resulted in the deprogrammee confessing to having been brainwashed and disavowing NRM affiliation, was interpreted as a victory of the latter over the former. While failures did occur, deprogrammers succeeded in an overwhelming majority of cases (Bromley 1988a) because members were overwhelmingly noviates, experimenting with membership, ambivalent about the progressively greater commitments and sacrifices they faced, and confronted by dramatic, resolute intervention by their families. As resistance to coercive deprogrammings mounted, countermovement activists discovered that non-coercive counseling processes also yielded high rates of disaffiliation. Exit-counseling involving varying degrees of voluntarism then began to replace coercive deprogramming in most instances. The ACM's objectives were realized, whichever method was employed, as former members re-integrated into conventional social networks and re-formatted their doubts and disputes into an account consistent with the ACM's cult/brainwashing ideology. In essence, affirmation of ACM ideology becomes the basis for role transition.

Apostates whose role transitions are coordinated through ACM-sponsored identity transformation rituals typically fashion their personal sagas as captivity narratives. Although the specific details of these personal narratives vary, the following summary/synthesis of these narratives is one of journey into and out of captivity: While operating in what they believed to be safe space, such as a college campus or center of tourism, individuals who were innocently engaged in conventional activity encountered cult recruiters. Camouflaging their true identities and affiliations, the recruiters employ some combination of deception and manipulation to induce the individual to attend a cult-sponsored and -controlled function, often under the guise of an educational, recreational, or therapeutic experience. Individuals are then induced to move to an isolated, cult-controlled location (such as a camp, retreat, or commune) where contact with or exit to the outside world is extraordinarily difficult. Once under the physical control of the cult, individuals are subjected to potent mind-control techniques (disguised as spiritual, community-building, psychotherapeutic training) that rapidly undermine their capacity for rational, autonomous decision making. After the initial programming process is completed, individuals, now in a state of psychological captivity, are deployed on various cult-sponsored missions to gain new recruits, raise money, or work in cult-run organizations and projects designed to increase the leaders' wealth and power. These often involve participating in a variety of activities that are illegal and/or subversive. During this period cult members are subjected to ongoing re-programming as well as extreme personal exploitation, humiliation, and degradation. Some individuals possess a sufficient residue of free will to escape cult control or become separated from the group while on missions for a sufficient time to weaken the effects of cult programming. Others fall so fully under cult control that physical extrication from the organization is necessary. Subsequent deprogramming and/or extended therapy with experts in cult mind control is then necessary to eliminate completely the effects of cult programming. The deprogramming/exit-counseling ritual, with its corresponding captivity tale, effectively restores social order. The individual is able to account for a radical departure (Levine 1984) and participation in a Subversive group without having to assume responsibility for personal actions or to accept conferral of a mental illness label. Parents need not accuse wayward offspring of family betrayal or mitigate any public embarrassment attending the family crisis, and are free to move toward restoring familial relations. The ACM gains confirmation of its cult/brainwashing ideology and support from client families.

Apostate recounting of captivity tales is pivotal to the ACM's achieving its social control objectives. The allegations of deliberate use of potent psycho-technology to undermine individual free will and the systematic organizational practices that would sabotage an array of central social institutions are used to document subversive capacity and intent. Apostates occasionally offer evidence of NRM wrongdoing that can serve as the basis for legal action. Even though success in civil and criminal proceedings can be counted as a victory and may bolster countermovement morale, legal forums also allow defendant groups to rebut allegations and they narrow accusations to specific offense categories. In general, therefore, apostates do not function as witnesses or whistleblowers; their primary function is moral condemnation of NRMs (Bromley and Shupe 1979).

The apostates' recounting of their personal captivity and of the organizational atrocities they witnessed highlight countermovement lobbying campaigns, media reports, investigatory hearings, trial testimony, and deprogramming sessions. Successful moral status degradation influences the nature of the entire array of social control initiatives against NRMs. The violations alleged are so fundamental and massive that protestations of innocence may be summarily rejected. Contented NRM members are dismissed as brainwashed, civic projects are deemed public relations stunts, and organizational affiliates are derisively labeled front groups. Institutions not directly involved in the conflict are encouraged to find occasions for invoking sanctions when opportunities arise, and a climate of hostile public opinion is created that is conducive to expansion of social control authority (Bromley and Breschel 1989).

Some NRM apostates have been able to fashion extended careers as public figures. As the NRM controversy expanded and the ACM linked together a diverse array of movements as cults, former members began identifying themselves as generic cult experts. Through this tactic they are able to adjust to the shifting fortunes of specific movements, new sources of controversy, or changing public interest. For the most part these careers also are quite transitory as they lack career development possibilities, and there has been a continuing flow of members out of NRMs, which creates burgeoning supply of individuals to compete for available role opportunities. Through the 1970s and 1980s there was a continuing flow of opportunities to present testimony at church gatherings, public hearings on the cult problem, cult education programs sponsored by high schools and colleges, interviews with journalists, and ACM conventions. Occasionally, apostates extended their careers by mixing apostate and whistleblowing activity through participating in civil legal proceedings against NRMs. Particularly where plaintiffs have been able to link moral condemnation and personal captivity narratives to bases of legal action, principally infliction of emotional distress, merging apostate testimony and trial testimony has become possible. These trials often span months or even years, thereby in effect creating an extended career. Pre-trial or post-verdict settlements offer apostates a more secure economic base. The greatest career stability for apostates has derived from counseling-related activities as families mandate exit-counseling or individuals seek a means of resolving personal ambivalence. Initially, exit-counselors offered services based simply on their personal experiences. As this niche has developed, former NRM members have begun seeking professional credentials as therapists, with a specialization in what they define as cult-precipitated disorders (Hassan 1988). These apostate careers have demonstrated considerable longevity as practitioners possess greater credentials, legitimacy, and an economic base, and the role can be broadened to incorporate more conventional counseling practice (Brown 1991).

CONCLUSIONS

The central argument of this chapter is that apostasy is a specific form of leavetaking that occurs in situations in which an organization is deemed Subversive. Under these conditions, the high level of tension and power imbalance between organization and surrounding society strongly influences the way in which organizational exit is effected. The argument is developed by identifying three types of organization—Allegiant, Contestant, and Subversive—and three corresponding forms of exit role—defector, whistleblower, and apostate. This is not a general theory of leavetaking but rather a theory of contested exit in the context of differing degrees of organizational control.

The typological presentation of the argument presents a variety of issues. For example, it would be interesting to examine the careers of individuals who attempt to construct an apostate role in exiting an Allegiant organization. If the theory developed here is correct, then such individuals should encounter considerable opposition and limited support in acting out that role. It would also be instructive to study organizations that exhibit mixed type characteristics. It is empirically possible, and indeed likely, that different components of complex organizations and organizations that are in the process of change will exhibit such mixtures. Precisely how the politics of exit operate in such circumstances cannot be derived directly from the theory constructed here. The identity work of individuals as they confront organizational control mechanisms is another issue of considerable interest. The list of intriguing issues that derive from this analysis could easily be lengthened, which means there is considerably more work to be done. However, even as a preliminary statement, the theory developed here is important in distinguishing different types of exit, and different types of contested exit in particular. The way in which contested exits are controlled and by whom plays a significant role in the capacity of organizations to preserve or alter their social niches. To follow out this line of thought is to inquire how it is that some organizations successfully employ power to create and defend their legitimacy and, alternatively, how other organizations can be marginalized and discredited. Since religion is inextricably linked to the exercise of power because it involves both the re-presentation and re-creation of the logic of the social order, this is a foundational issue in the sociology of religion.

REFERENCES

Ammerman, Nancy. 1990. *Baptist Battles*. New Brunswick, NJ: Rutgers University Press.

Armstrong, Karen. 1981. *Through the Narrow Gate*. New York: St. Martin's Press.

Barker, Eileen. 1988. "Defection from the Unification Church: Some Statistics and Distinctions." Pp. 166–84 in *Falling from the Faith*, edited by David Bromley. Newbury Park, CA: Sage.

Becker, Howard. 1963. *Outsiders*. New York: Free Press.

———. 1958. "The Fate of Idealism in Medical School." *American Sociological Review* 23:50–56.

Beckford, James. 1985. *Cult Controversies*. London: Tavistock.

Black, Donald. 1993. *The Social Structure of Right and Wrong*. San Diego: Academic Press.

Bok, Sissela. 1982. *Secrets: On the Ethics of Concealment and Revelation*. New York: Pantheon Books.

Boswell, John. 1981. *Christianity, Social Tolerance, and Homosexuality*. Chicago: University of Chicago Press.

Braithwaite, John. 1985. "White Collar Crime." *Annual Review of Sociology* 11:1–25.

Bromley, David. Forthcoming. "Disclaimers and Accounts in Cases of Catholic Priests Accused of Pedophilia." In *Wolves Among the Fold*, edited by Anson Shupe. New Brunswick, NJ: Rutgers University Press.

————. 1997. "A Sociological Narrative of Crisis Episodes, Collective Action, Culture Workers, and Countermovements." *Sociology of Religion* 58:105–40.

————. 1994a. "Constructing Subversion: A Comparison of Anti-Religious and Anti-Satanic Narratives." Pp. 49–76 in *Anti-Cult Movements in Cross-Cultural Perspective*, edited by Anson Shupe and David Bromley. New York: Garland.

————. 1994b. "The Satanism Scare in the United States." Pp. 49–64 in *Le Defi Magique, Volume II (Satanisme, Sorcellerie)*, edited by Jean-Baptiste Martin and Massimo Introvigne. Lyon, France: Presses Universitaires de Lyon.

————. 1988a. "Deprogramming as a Mode of Exit from New Religious Movements: The Case of the Unificationist Movement." Pp. 166–84 in *Falling from the Faith*, edited by David Bromley. Newbury Park, CA: Sage.

————. 1988b. "Economic Structure and Charismatic Leadership in the Unificationist Movement." Pp. 335–64 in *Money and Power in the New Religions*, edited by James Richardson. Lewiston, NY: Edwin Mellen Press.

Bromley, David, and Edward Breschel. 1992. "General Population and Institutional Elite Perceptions of Cults: Evidence from National Survey Data." *Behavioral Sciences and the Law* 10:39–52.

Bromley, David, and Anson Shupe. 1993. "New Religions and Countermovements." Pp. 177–98 in *Handbook on Cults and Sects in America*, edited by David Bromley and Jeffrey Hadden. Greenwich, CT: Association for the Sociology of Religion, Society for the Scientific Study of Religion, and JAI Press.

————. 1979. "Atrocity Tales, the Unification Church, and the Social Construction of Evil." *Journal of Communication* 29:42–53.

Brown, J. David. 1991. "The Professional EX-: An Alternative for Exiting the Deviant Career." *The Sociological Quarterly* 32:219–30.

Cetnar, William. 1982. "I Was a False Witness." Pp. 31–37 in *Escape from Darkness*, edited by James Adair and Ted Miller. Wheaton, IL: Victor Books.

Coser, Lewis. 1954. "The Age of the Informer." *Dissent* 1:249–54.

Curb, Rosemary, and Nancy Manahan. 1985. *Lesbian Nuns: Breaking Silence*. Tallahassee, FL: The Naiad Press.

Curtis, Beverly. 1977. "One Mormon's Journey to Christ." *Moody Magazine* (July–August):37–38.

Daichman, Graciela. 1990. "Misconduct in the Medieval Nunnery: Fact, Not Fiction." Pp. 97–117 in *That Gentle Strength*, edited by Lynda Coon, Katherine Haldane, and Elisabeth Sommer. Charlottesville: University of Virginia Press.

DellaCava, Frances. 1975. "The Process of Leaving a High Commitment Status." *Sociological Inquiry* 45:41–50.

Ebaugh, Helen Rose. 1988a. *Becoming an EX: The Process of Role Exit*. Chicago: University of Chicago Press.

————. 1988b. "Leaving Catholic Convents: Toward a Theory of Disengagement." Pp. 100–121 in *Falling from the Faith*, edited by David Bromley. Newbury Park, CA: Sage.

Ebersole, Gary. 1988. "Experience/Narrative Structure/Reading: Patty Hearst and the American Indian Captivity Narratives." *Religion* 18:255–82.

Emerson, Robert, and Sheldon Messinger. 1977. "The Micro-Politics of Trouble." *Social Problems* 25:121–34.

Felstiner, William, Fichard Abel, and Austin Sarat. 1980–1981. "The Emergence and Transformation of Disputes." *Law and Society Review* 15:631–54.

Gardiner, John, and David Olson. 1974. *Theft of the City*. Bloomington: Indiana University Press.

Goldner, Fred, R. Richard Ritti, and Thomas Ference. 1977. "The Production of Cynical Knowledge in Organizations." *American Sociological Review* 42:539–51.

Gruss, Edmond Charles. 1970. *Apostles of Denial*. Nutley, NJ: Presbyterian and Reformed Publishing Co.

Harshbarger, Dwight. 1973. "The Individual and the Social Order: Notes on the Management of Heresy and Deviance in Complex Organizations." *Human Relations* 26:251–69.

Hassan, Steven. 1988. *Combatting Cult Mind Control*. Rochester, VT: Park Street Press.

Hirschman, Albert. 1970. *Exit, Voice, and Loyalty*. Cambridge: Harvard University Press.

Hoge, Dean. 1991. "Changes in the Priesthood and Seminaries." Pp. 67–84 in *Vatican II and U.S. Catholicism*, edited by Helen Rose Ebaugh. Greenwich, CT: Association for the Sociology of Religion, and JAI Press.

Jacobs, Janet. 1989. *Divine Disenchantment*. Bloomington: Indiana University Press.

James, Gene. 1980. "Whistle Blowing: Its Nature and Justification." *Philosophy in Context* 10:99–117

Jehenson, Roger. 1969. "The Dynamics of Role Leaving: A Role Theoretical Approach to the Leaving of Religious Organizations." *Journal of Applied Behavioral Science* 5:287–308.

Jenkins, Philip. Forthcoming. "Beyond Reproach: Creating a Culture of Clergy Deviance." In *Wolves Among the Fold*, edited by Anson Shupe. New Brunswick, NJ: Rutgers University Press.

Johnson, Sonia. 1981. *From Housewife to Heretic*. New York: Doubleday & Co.

Kanter, Rosabeth. 1972. *Commitment and Community*. Cambridge: Harvard University Press.

Katz, Jack. 1975. "Essences as Moral Identities: Verifiability and Responsibility in Imputations of Deviance and Charisma." *American Journal of Sociology* 80:1369–90.

Kavanagh, J. 1967. *A Modern Priest Looks at His Outdated Church*. New York: Trident Press.

Kray, Ed. 1972. *Enemy in the Streets*. Garden City, NY: Doubleday.

Levine, Saul. 1984. *Radical Departures*. San Diego: Harcourt Brace Jovanovich.

Lewis, James, and David Bromley. 1987. "Cult Information Disease: A Misattribution of Cause?" *Journal for the Scientific Study of Religion* 26:508–22.

Marx, Gary T. 1974. "Thoughts on a Neglected Category of Social Movement Participant: The Agent Provocateur and the Informant." *American Journal of Sociology* 80:403–42.

Melton, J. Gordon. 1989. *The Encyclopedia of American Religions*. Volume 2. Detroit: Gale Research.

Miller, Leslie. 1990. "Violent Families and the Rhetoric of Harmony." *British Journal of Sociology* 41:263–88.

Murnighan, J. Keith. 1981. "Defectors, Vulnerability, and Relative Power: Some Causes and Effects of Leaving a Stable Coalition." *Human Relations* 34: 589–609.

Nelson, Lynn, and David Bromley. 1988. "Another Look at Conversion and Defection in Conservative Churches." Pp. 47–61 in *Falling from the Faith*, edited by David Bromley. Newbury Park, CA: Sage.

O'Day, Rory. 1983. "Intimidation Rituals: Reactions to Reform." Pp. 169–80 in *Or-

ganizational Influence Processes, edited by Robert Allen and Lyman Porter. Glenview, IL: Scott, Foresman.

Perrucci, Robert, Robert Anderson, Dan Schendel, and Leon Trachtman. 1980. "Whistle-Blowing: Professionals' Resistance to Organizational Authority." *Social Problems* 28:149–64.

Reichman, Nancy. 1992. "Moving Backstage: Uncovering the Role of Compliance Practices in Shaping Regulatory Policy." Pp. 244–68 in *White-Collar Crime Reconsidered*, edited by Kip Schlegel and David Weisburd. Boston: Northeastern University Press.

Richardson, James, Jan van der Lans, and Frans Derks. 1986. "Leaving and Labeling: Voluntary and Coerced Disaffiliation from Religious Social Movements." *Research in Social Movements, Conflict, and Change* 9:97–126.

Robbins, Thomas, and David Bromley. 1992. "Social Experimentation and the Significance of American New Religions: A Focused Review Essay." Pp. 1–28 in *Research in the Social Scientific Study of Religion*, edited by Monty Lynn and David Moberg. Greenwich, CT: JAI Press.

Rothbaum, Susan. 1988. "Between Two Worlds: Issues of Separation and Identity after Leaving a Religious Community." Pp. 205–28 in *Falling from the Faith*, edited by David Bromley. Newbury Park, CA: Sage.

Schmuck, Terry. 1977. "Set Free by the Truth." *The Discerner* 9:10–12.

Scott, James. 1985. *Weapons of the Weak*. New Haven, CT: Yale University Press.

Shupe, Anson. 1995. *In the Name of All That's Holy*. Westport, CT: Praeger.

Shupe, Anson, and David Bromley. 1980. *The New Vigilantes*. Beverly Hills, CA: Sage.

———. 1978. "Continuities in American Religion: Witches, Moonies and Accusations of Evil." *Society* 15:75–76.

Shupe, Anson, David Bromley, and Edward Breschel. 1989. "The Legacy of Jonestown and the Development of the Anti-Cult Movement." Pp. 153–78 in *Jonestown*, edited by Rebecca Moore and Fielding McGehee. Lewiston, NY: Edwin Mellen Press.

Shupe, Anson, David Bromley, and Donna Oliver. 1984. *The Anti-Cult Movement in America*. New York: Garland Publishers.

Simon, David, and D. Stanley Eitzen. 1990. *Elite Deviance*. Boston: Allyn and Bacon.

Sipe, Richard. 1991. *A Secret World*. New York: Brunner/Mazel.

Strauss, Murray, Richard Gelles, and Suzanne Steinmetz. 1980. *Behind Closed Doors*. Garden City, NY: Doubleday.

Tanner, Sandra. 1960. *Out of Darkness, Into the "Sonlight."* Salt Lake City: The Author.

VanDerBeets, Richard. 1972. "The Indian Captivity Narrative as Ritual." *American Literature* 43:548–62.

Weigert, Andrew. 1991. *Mixed Emotions*. Albany: SUNY Press.

Weinstein, Deena. 1977. "Bureaucratic Opposition: The Challenge to Authoritarian Abuses at the Workplace." *Canadian Journal of Political and Social Theory* 1: 31–46.

Weisband, Howard, and Franck Thomas. 1975. *Resignation in Protest*. New York: Penguin Books.

Wiley, Jerry. 1979. "Post-Guyana Hysteria: State of California Occupies Headquarters of the Worldwide Church of God." *Liberty* (May/June):1–3.

Wong, Mary Gilligan. 1983. *Nun: A Memoir*. San Diego: Harcourt Brace Jovanovich.

Worthing, Sharon. 1979. "The State Takes Over a Church." *The Annals* 446:136–48.

Wright, Stuart. 1988. "Leaving New Religious Movements: Issues, Theory, and Re-
    search." Pp. 143–65 in *Falling from the Faith*, edited by David Bromley. New-
    bury Park, CA: Sage.
———. 1984. "Post-Involvement Attitudes of Voluntary Defectors from Controversial
    New Religious Movements." *Journal for the Scientific Study of Religion* 23:172–
    82.
Zablocki, Benjamin. 1996. "Reliability and Validity of Apostate Accounts in the Study
    of Religious Communities." Paper presented at the annual meetings of the As-
    sociation for the Sociology of Religion, New York.
Zald, Mayer and Michael Berger. 1978. "Social Movements in Organizations: Coup
    d'Etat, Insurgency, and Mass Movements." *American Journal of Sociology* 83:
    823–61.

Part III

The Apostate Role
and Career

Chapter 3

Apostasy and the Management of Spoiled Identity

Armand L. Mauss

In his work on apostates Lawrence Foster alludes to the psychological struggle common to the role of "apostate," a role which (with cognate roles like "ex-") has been examined by several sociologists in recent years (e.g., Bromley 1988; Ebaugh 1988; Richardson 1977; Wright 1988). Foster observes that "rather than moving on to make a new and more happy life for themselves, career apostates tend to define themselves more in terms of what they are against than what they are for. Yet their personal ambivalence also may reflect an ambivalence at the heart of the movement with which they maintain such an intense love–hate relationship" (1994, p. 355). The social psychology of apostasy is also a concern of the present chapter, but first it will be useful to review briefly the organizational context which Bromley (this volume) has proposed as the general framework for such an analysis. Then perhaps we can better understand the links between the organizational and the social-psychological levels of analysis.

THE ORGANIZATIONAL CONTEXT

Three organizational ideal-types are proposed in Bromley's framework: Allegiant, Contestant, and Subversive. Although he has in mind religious organizations in particular, he notes in passing that this typology could be generalized to any number of other societal sectors, including industry, politics, and indeed other voluntary organizations besides religion. What distinguishes these three organizational types from each other is the *degree* of tension between them (respectively) and the host society, the Allegiant type having the least tension and the Subversive the most tension. One notices immediately the parallel here with the classical church–sect formulation, with churches, of course, "allegiant" by definition, and various sects (or cults) "subversive" to greater or lesser degrees. Corresponding with each organizational type is a different type of "exiter" or leavetaker: Those who opt to depart from Allegiant organizations Bromley calls "defectors;" those from Contestant organizations are "whistleblowers;" and only those from Subversive organizations are considered actual "apostates" in Bromley's terminology.

The apostate role is typically not only the most acrimonious of the three types, but in its fullest sense it requires an external, oppositional organization or coalition to embrace the apostate and to lend credence and legitimacy to the typical "captivity narrative" explaining both the erstwhile affiliation and the eventual departure of the apostate. In fact, to some extent all three exit types often involve external support: Competitors to Allegiant organizations (e.g., other religious denominations) can be expected to provide aid and comfort for defectors; official or self-appointed monitoring or regulatory agencies for whistleblowers from Contestant organizations; and, as just noted, oppositional or enemy coalitions for apostates from Subversive organizations. While these three types of organizations and exiters can be used heuristically, they actually constitute a *tension continuum* with the surrounding host society, as Bromley points out. Such a continuum, in turn, implies some mixture of both organizational and exiting types in real life, as well as some potential for change across time in the relationship of any given organization to its host environment.

The same organization at the same time, furthermore, might generate "defectors" under some circumstances, as though it were a typical Allegiant organization, but under other conditions generate "whistleblowers," like a Contestant organization. Take, for example, two different scenarios involving the American Catholic Church: The departure of a celibate priest from the Catholic priesthood to a married state in the "competing" Anglican or Episcopal priesthood would seem to represent a "defector" simply migrating from one Allegiant organization to another. On the other hand, a Catholic parent or group of parents, dissatisfied with their efforts to achieve redress of their grievances about priestly pedophilia, might qualify as "whistleblowers" in a Contestant organization when they turn to outside law enforcement or other agencies for support, especially if they end up by leaving the church.

Either implicit or explicit in Bromley's scheme are at least four additional continuous variables (besides the degree of tension): (1) the extent of *internal control* which an organization has over the *construction of the narrative* of the exiter's departure, with organizations at the Allegiant end of the continuum having the most control and those at the other end the least control; (2) the existence and relative power of outside *oppositional organizations* and coalitions, which are minimal at the Allegiant end and greatest at the other (Subversive) end; (3) the amount and kind of *personal anguish* involved for the exiter, which might be low or non-existent for the mere defector but for the full-blown apostate an acrimonious struggle with stigma under severe stress (a matter to receive much more attention later in this chapter); and (4) the *changing*

relationship across time of a religious (or other) organization with its host society, as a sect, cult, or other such Subversive organization gradually reduces
its tension with the society and becomes more Allegiant or church-like. In the
American Catholic Church we can find a familiar example of this transformation
across time from a Subversive or "alien" religious import in the nineteenth
century to an Americanized Allegiant church (indeed, the largest denomination),
or at least something between Contestant and Allegiant.

An especially good example of this complexity from American history is the
Mormon Church, which possessed all the classic characteristics of a Subversive
organization throughout the nineteenth century but underwent an accommodation with American society throughout the twentieth, or at least until the later
decades of the twentieth, when some evidence began to emerge in the church
of a deliberate retrenchment policy intended to recover some of the lost tension
with the surrounding society (Mauss 1994). Late in the twentieth century, the
Mormons (like the Catholics) would thus probably fall on the Bromley continuum somewhere between Allegiant and Contestant, perhaps closer to the latter;
another way of describing the situation might be to view the Mormons as more
Allegiant for some purposes and more Contestant for others. (It should be emphasized here that we are discussing the *North American* setting; virtually everywhere else in the world Mormons would still be at the Subversive point on the
continuum, or perhaps in Latin America, somewhere between Subversive and
Contestant).

The history of exiting from the Mormon Church seems to parallel the changing history of its relationship with American society in about the way that one
would expect from the conceptual framework discussed above. Nineteenth-
century Mormon history is replete with tales of colorful apostates in the full
Bromley sense, exiters who left under conditions of great stress and acrimony
into the waiting arms of a thriving anti-Mormon enterprise (e.g., Launius and
Thatcher 1994). These apostates, of course, provided wonderful grist for the
mass media mills of the time and were highly influential in shaping and maintaining the subversive national image of Mormonism (see e.g., Bitton and Bunker 1983). Perhaps predictably, mass apostasies tended to occur during periods
of special crisis in the church, just prior to each major migration, of which we
shall have more to say later on.

Some apostates during the nineteenth century, both before and after the settlement of Utah, eventually gravitated into various schismatic alternatives to
mainstream Mormonism. However, only the Reorganized Church of Jesus Christ
of Latter Day Saints (RLDS), officially established in Missouri around the
founding prophet's eldest son in 1860, survived in any meaningful sense
(Shields 1982). A few schismatic groups during Mormonism's twentieth-century
assimilation have also proved quite durable (Baer 1988; Bradley 1993), in line
with the Stark and Bainbridge (1985) observations about sectarian schism as a
product especially of reduced tension with the surrounding society (see also

Mauss 1994). However, the focus of this chapter is upon apostasy at the individual level, and not upon schism or collective apostasy, so no further analysis of that process will be offered here.

What does need to be observed, however, is that as twentieth-century Mormonism moved increasingly down the Bromley continuum from its earlier Subversive character, its public exiters were less often apostates in the fullest sense of that term and more often resembled whistleblowers or even mere defectors, although, to be sure, one can see examples of all three exiting types. Well-known examples of defectors from the early twentieth century would include Virginia Sorensen, Vardis Fisher, Nels Anderson, and other members of the so-called "lost generation" of early-twentieth-century Mormon intellectuals and literati, who simply left the church, and often Utah as well, without much fanfare and usually without formal excommunication or other degradation ceremonies traditionally imposed on Mormon apostates (Geary 1977). More recent examples of public leavers or defectors would be Obert C. Tanner and Sterling M. McMurrin, both of whom stayed in Utah, gaining great prominence at the University of Utah and in public service (Newell 1995). Neither of them ever made common cause with anti-Mormons; and the church, for its part, never took formal action against them, perhaps wishing to avoid the bad publicity that their public martyrdom would have brought. More extensive discussion of illustrative individual cases of different kinds of Mormon exiters will be reserved for later in this chapter.

THE STRUGGLE WITH SELF

With that elaboration on Bromley's scheme, let us now see how the organizational or macrosocial level of analysis might be connected to the social-psychological level, which is of special interest in this chapter. To begin with, the potentially exiting individual, whatever the personal or psychological origin of that potential, encounters a specific social situation with a particular mix of variables that are both organizational and personal, including the tension between his/her religious group and the society; the resistance or cooperation likely to be encountered in the organization as s/he works out the departure narrative; and the availability of a satisfactory and supportive "destination" for that departure.

In addition, certain more proximate social-psychological variables will be present, just as they are in the conversion process itself. These would include the amount of resistance or support likely to be encountered from significant others such as family members and closest friends, both within and without the organization; the amount of "investment" that s/he has made in the organization, including both material and human capital; and the salience or centrality of organizational membership to the fundamental definition of self (Gecas and Burke 1995). The mix of all these variables, and perhaps others too, will provide the basis for a cost/benefit (or risk/benefit) assessment to be made before the exiting actually occurs. The mix of such variables, furthermore, changes across time, not only in the historical and organizational sense outlined above, but also in the individual sense of where the person stands in the life cycle, since a potential exiter has more at stake at some stages of life than at others.

The connection between the organizational and the individual levels of analysis, however, is perhaps best understood through the notion of *self-concept*, defined by Stryker (1980) as a hierarchical set of identities, each of which is tied to roles within the social structure, an idea convergent with earlier applications of role theory to both conversion and defection (but see Gecas and Burke 1995, pp. 42–44 for a broader definition of self-concept). Individuals have multiple identities, and "one's identities are active agents which influence one's behavioral choices, . . . provid(ing) behavior with meaning, goals, and purpose." In this conceptualization, "the greater one's commitment premised on an identity, the greater will be the salience of the identity;" and in turn "the salience of an identity directly influences the behavioral choices . . . in any given situation" (Gecas and Burke 1995, p. 45; also Foote 1951; Stryker 1980, 1991). Persons thus "modify, adjust, and negotiate their behavior and its meanings to control reflected appraisals (in order to) make them more congruent with and verify the meanings of their identities" (Gecas and Burke 1995, p. 45; see also Swanson 1988). Of course, all of this is reminiscent (and to some extent derivative) of the work of Erving Goffman (1959, 1963), who portrayed much of human behavior as attempting to control the presentation of self, and/or as defense against a "spoiled identity" in the face of stigmatizing efforts by significant others. In situations carrying a potential for stigma, the individual is likely to react in ways calculated to defend the self.

Various self-states and self-processes might be sources of motivation for individual behavior, including the quest for self-esteem, self-efficacy, or self-verification (Gecas and Burke 1995, pp. 46–49). Of these, I propose that self-verification is especially salient in understanding the career of the apostate or whistleblower (and, perhaps to a lesser extent, that of the mere leaver or defector). The self-verification theory of Swann (1983) is paralleled by the ideas of E. T. Higgins and others, who, in effect, turn self-verification on its head as *self-discrepancy* theory (Higgins 1987, 1989; Higgins et al. 1985). In this theoretical formulation, each person strives for self-verification, failure in which produces different forms of "self-discrepancy."

The two typical forms of self-discrepancy (or inconsistency) are (1) the discrepancy between *actual* self and the *ideal* self; and (2) that between the *actual* self and the *ought* self. The actual self is simply *whatever one thinks one is*, as inferred from the reflected appraisals of others, or from comparisons with reference groups, with significant others, or from other sources. The ideal self comprises the attributes one *wishes* to have; and the ought self comprises attributes one *feels socially or morally obliged* to have.[1] The emotional responses to the two kinds of discrepancies differ. The first kind of discrepancy (actual/ideal) can produce depression, while the actual/ought produces "social anxiety

(accompanied by) social avoidance, distress, and fear of negative evaluation''
(Gecas and Burke 1995, p. 49). In dealing with a somewhat similar issue of
self-verification versus self-discrepancy, Weigert (1991) points to ''the ambivalent self,'' a product of contradictory messages and social expectations which
undermine one's sense of self-authenticity (Gecas 1994, p. 144). Weigert identifies two common forms taken by the effort to resolve ambivalence and achieve
authenticity: the existential response and the eschatological.

In Gecas's interpretation (1994, p. 147) of Weigert, the *"existential* response
acknowledges the difficulties and moral ambiguities of modern life, yet stoically
tries to make the best of it as a free and responsible person,'' which in Higgins's
terms, I would suggest, might be seen as a resolution of the actual/ideal discrepancy. This ''existential'' resolution of the discrepancy seems an apt description of the response of *either* the ''defector'' or the ''whistleblower,'' as
Bromley calls them. The difference between these two would be that for the
defector, who just walks away, the actual/ideal discrepancy occurs at the level
of *personal* ideals, such as intellectual integrity, where self-authenticity requires
simply a recognition by the exiter that s/he has lost faith or lost commitment to
key beliefs of the erstwhile religion. For the whistleblower, the discrepancy
occurs at the level of *social* ideals, where self-authenticity has been threatened ̄
by a conscience made to feel increasingly guilty from looking the other way,
or even covering up the unethical or immoral conduct of one's co-religionists
or religious leaders. To the extent that this kind of discrepancy is perceived also
in the reflected appraisals of significant others, there would seem to be the
potential for stigma in Goffman's terms.

''(Weigert's) *eschatological* resolution, by contrast,'' says Gecas, ''seeks escape from modern ambivalence by embracing a (typically) religious fundamentalist doctrine offering a simplified moral universe and providing a mythic
framework for interpreting and living in modern society'' (Gecas 1994, p. 147).
Of course, the resolution need not always be fundamentalist in nature, for other
kinds of ''(m)oral crusades (or) political activism can have authenticating consequences for participants, assuming that their commitment to the cause is sincere'' (Gecas 1994, p. 146). In any case, the eschatological resolution suggested
by Weigert seems to me an apt description of the way that Bromley's typical
''apostate'' would resolve an actual/ought discrepancy (as per Higgins), with its
''social anxiety'' and ''fear of negative evaluation'' (or stigma) increasingly
experienced by a disillusioned believer on the way to apostasy. Perhaps that
helps to explain the common pattern by which apostates leave one kind of
fundamentalist or ''high-tension'' religion only to throw in with an oppositional
group that is equally uncompromising. Yet, as Goffman indicates (1963, p. 114):

The problems associated with militancy are well known. When the ultimate political
objective is to remove stigma . . . , the individual may find that his very efforts can
politicize his own life, rendering it even more different from the normal life initially

denied him—even though the next generation of his fellows may greatly profit from his efforts by (gaining greater acceptance).

While Goffman's (1963) classical formulation does not use the terminology of self-verification, self-discrepancy, or self-authenticity, one can nevertheless see such concepts implied in the individual's struggle to prevent a "spoiled identity" in stigmatizing (or potentially stigmatizing) situations. Every individual "acquires identity standards which he applies to himself in spite of failing to conform to them, (so) it is inevitable that he will feel some ambivalence about his own self" (pp. 106–7). Furthermore, during the period of commitment to his or her religious community (i. e., prior to encountering issues of discrepancy or inauthenticity in his religious life),

the individual may (have) deeply involve(d) his ego in his identification with a particular part, establishment, and group, and his self-conception as someone who does not disrupt social interaction or let down social units which depend upon that interaction. When a disruption occurs, then, we may find that the self-conceptions around which his personality has been built may become discredited. (Goffman 1959, p. 243)

The process of exiting thus carries a *double* risk of stigmatization, for "pre-stigma acquaintances, being attached to a conception of what he once was, may be unable to treat him either with formal tact or with familiar full acceptance," while his "post-stigma acquaintances (i.e., after his exit as whistleblower or apostate) may see him simply as a faulted person" (Goffman 1963, p. 35). That is, even the new associates in an external or oppositional group might be slow to grant full acceptance, for the newly exited person has a lot to live down from his unsavory past involvements. At the same time, the individual himself or herself retains the ambivalence about self suggested above:

Given the ambivalence built into the individual's attachment to his stigmatized category, it is understandable that oscillations may occur in his support of, identification with, and participation among his own. There will be "affiliation cycles" through which he comes to accept the special opportunities for in-group participation or comes to reject them after having accepted them before. There will be corresponding oscillations in belief about the nature of his own (new) group and the nature of . . . (his previous group). (p. 38)

Despite his focus mainly at the social-psychological level, Goffman also links this level back again to the social-organizational one, for "(i)t is only to be expected that this identity ambivalence will receive organized expression in the written, talked, (and) acted . . . materials of representatives of the (exiting category)" (1963, p. 108). To begin with, the stigmatized condition itself inclines "members of a particular stigma category . . . to come together into small social groups whose members all derive from the category, these groups themselves being subject to overarching organization to varying degrees" (1963, pp. 23–

24). Furthermore, "(t)he relationship of the stigmatized individual to the informal community and formal organizations of his own kind is . . . crucial. This relationship will, for example, mark a great difference between those whose differentness provides them with very little of a new 'we,' and those . . . who find themselves part of a well-organized community . . . , (and) it is largely in relation to this own-group that it is possible to discuss the natural history and the moral career of the stigmatized individual" (pp. 38–39).

Of course this new "own-group," as Goffman calls it, is conceptually very close to, if not identical with, the external "oppositional group" to which the true "apostate" migrates in Bromley's terminology (and the same might be said of the budding sectarian schism where the apostasy is collective). The "whistleblower" type, too, might find refuge to a greater or lesser extent in such external group support. Among the obvious functions of these "own-groups" is providing support for the negotiation of a new "definition of the situation" to help the individual resist stigmatizing assaults on his or her identity (Goffman 1959, pp. 252–55). Another function is collaboration and validation for the apostate as s/he works out the retrospective accounts of the apostate career, including how s/he came "to the beliefs and practices that he now has regarding his own kind and (the) normals. A life event can thus have a double bearing on (the) moral career, first as immediate objective grounds for an actual turning point, and later (and easier to demonstrate) as a means of accounting for a position currently taken" (1963, pp. 38–39).

To summarize this section, the theoretical framework proposed here goes something like this: We can take it as given that certain macro-social or organizational variables are strongly implicated in the process by which exiters from a given religious community depart as either leavers (defectors), whistleblowers, or apostates. The likelihood that an exiter will take on the apostate role (as compared to one of the other types) is enhanced to the extent that (1) there is high tension between this religious community and the host society; (2) there is an external oppositional group (including a schismatic sect) to which the exiter can migrate; and (3) certain other organizational variables discussed earlier. Yet organizational or structural conduciveness does not help much to explain motivation at the individual level.

For this we need to turn to social-psychological explanations that find such motivation in the efforts of individuals to manage or prevent "spoiled" or stigmatized identities through resolving certain kinds of "self-discrepancies." Any kind of discrepancy carries some potential for stigma, perhaps especially that kind characterized by Higgins as the "actual/ought" discrepancy, in which the individual perceives or anticipates disapproval in the reflected appraisals of significant others in the religious community where membership has bestowed such "role primacy" (Wright in this volume). Any kind of discrepancy carries also a threat to the individual's "self-authenticity," in Weigert's terms. One way of dealing with such threats is to change reference groups, so that the thoughts and acts felt as discrepant in the original religious community are resolved through verification and authentication in the new oppositional context; such also provides the collaboration and support which will help the apostate (or whistleblower) create a retrospective account of his or her career. Indeed, as Stuart A. Wright points out (Chapter 5 this volume), the apostate's newly transformed identity tends to become the most salient one in his/her emerging role-identity hierarchy.

ILLUSTRATIVE CASES OF MORMON EXITERS

Whether despite or because of its history of monolithic solidarity, the Mormon Church has always generated a variety of apostates, whistleblowers, and defectors. Many of these have formed themselves into schismatic sects across the years (Shields 1982), but many others have simply dropped out and taken their religious allegiance back to more traditional religions—or, as has been equally often the case, to no particular religion at all (Albrecht et al. 1988). As indicated earlier, Mormon exiters during the nineteenth century were much more likely than those in the twentieth to be apostates in the full sense defined by Bromley, though some of these might have begun as whistleblowers. The nineteenth-century conditions facilitating apostasy and whistleblowing included the important structural factor of high tension between the Mormons (including their various schisms) and the host society, along with the related factor of a plethora of perpetually indignant oppositional groups in the society, especially those associated with mainstream Protestantism of the time. Yet, as we have also argued here, certain social-psychological experiences among actual and potential exiters seem to have played some part in key instances of apostasy. These experiences produced for at least some of the exiters a kind of acute identity crisis in the form of self-discrepancies, ambivalence about self-authenticity, or even a sense of spoiled identity.

The Nineteenth-Century Context

As the Mormon polity and mode of governance evolved from a fairly primitive, egalitarian form toward a more authoritarian system centralized around the prophet, the potential for defection increased correspondingly, especially among a membership converted from the surrounding context of universalism and Jacksonian republicanism. This potential turned into veritable waves of apostasy, particularly at three critical junctures in early Mormon history. These were (1) the mid-1830s when the church generally, and some of its members individually, suffered severe economic setbacks in Kirtland, Ohio, eventually exacerbated by the national Panic of 1837 (Backman 1983; Hill 1980); (2) the overlapping or partly contemporaneous Missouri persecutions during the late 1830s, when Mormons from Kirtland attempted during a five-year period to establish a Zion or divinely ordained homeland but were chased out of four different counties by severe persecution (LeSueur 1987); and (3) the mid-1840s, when their founding prophet was assassinated and they were chased from the city of Nauvoo, Illinois, which they had built from a swamp (Flanders 1965). Since these three crises were times of especially heightened tension with the outside, it is understandable that they would also be especially productive of apostates. Once the Mormons fled west from Illinois and established their final Zion in remote Utah, the external tension and oppositional groups were much less immediate, both geographically and politically, and the rate of apostasy declined correspondingly until late in the century, when pressure from the federal government mounted again over the issues of polygamy and theocracy (Alexander 1986).

An illustration of how we might apply "self-discrepancy theory" in analyzing apostate experiences from the nineteenth century can be seen in the case of *William E. McLellin*, who joined the church in 1831 and its Quorum of Twelve Apostles in 1835. He showed a certain social insensitivity from the very beginning, periodically asserting a claim to superior intellectual ability and literary attainment. Such an "ideal self," however, was often in contrast to the "reflected appraisals" of his Mormon colleagues, which pointed instead to an "actual self" with "more learning than sense," as Joseph Smith reported (Howard 1994, p. 77).

Two personality traits in particular seem to have complicated McLellin's turbulent relationship with his Mormon colleagues: a noteworthy "faculty for misjudging his social environment" (Howard 1994, p. 77); and a constant quest (seemingly desperate at times) to obtain respect and prestige in his standing among successive reference groups in the fledgling and fractious Mormon movement of the time. These traits seemed to set McLellin up for a series of identity crises with a recurring pattern. First he would reach out in almost sycophantic fashion to attach himself to a leader or mentor, thereby ingratiating himself and gaining leadership in the new movement. His acceptance would be signalled by some sort of public acknowledgment and approval from the leader (sometimes speaking for God), which McLellin would then overinterpret as according him an exalted spiritual status. At first he would publicly commit himself to follow the leader and his teachings to the end of time, thereby expressing the convergence he aspired to achieve between his "ought" and his "actual" selves. However, he would soon alarm his newly found leader (and other followers) with some spontaneous and ill-advised abuse of their confidence, causing them to turn against him with public criticism, thereby opening a discrepancy between the two "selves" just mentioned; thereupon McLellin would move on to another leader.

This cyclical pattern first showed itself in McLellin's conversion to Joseph Smith's main Mormon movement in late 1831, when he declared Smith to be "a man of God . . . a Prophet, Seer, and Revelator to the Church of Christ" and asked the prophet to inquire of God's will concerning his future life. Smith responded with a revelation commending McLellin for his repentance and reception of the gospel, urging continued repentance and vigilance against temptation, and promising him "a crown of eternal life" (Howard 1994, p. 77; see also the LDS Church *Doctrine and Covenants*, Section 66). With this strong endorsement from his colleagues and from God, McLellin was soon sent on a mission, from which, however, he suddenly returned in a matter of weeks to get married. This was only one instance of many in which he failed to carry out his prophet's instructions, prompting another revelation in which even God pronounced Himself as "not well pleased with my servant William E. McLellin," and demanded that McLellin repent of his many failings under threat of excommunication (Howard 1994, p. 78).

Having thus been shamed, McLellin seriously considered leaving the church several different times, beginning in late 1835; but he could not seem to tear himself away from his religious commitments and investments as a Mormon convert. "That push-pull relationship with the church would become a part of McLellin's life ever after" (Howard 1994, p. 79), thereby revealing the classical ambivalence of which Goffman, Weigert, and others have written. Yet, as the financial setbacks of the Kirtland community exposed the ineptitude of the Mormon leaders in economic matters, McLellin's embarrassment and disagreements with the church leadership became more public. His colleagues in the leadership reacted with public chastisements and eventually with excommunication in 1838. In the process, he was periodically and publicly stigmatized as a troublemaker and enemy to God's people, which doubtless presented him with a discrepancy between his "ought self" as a devout and loyal disciple and his "actual self" as renegade in the eyes of his erstwhile brethren. As one of the twelve apostles, furthermore, he shared in the public shame and stigma surrounding the economic collapse brought on by Smith and the other leaders in Kirtland. Like many other prominent Mormon leaders of the Kirtland period, McLellin distanced himself from the financial scandal by leaving the town and denouncing Joseph Smith as a fallen prophet. For awhile he even participated in some of the persecutions experienced by Mormon refugees who had fled to Missouri from Kirtland (Howard 1994, p. 80).

After a short time away from Mormonism in an attempt to establish himself as a physician, McLellin soon sought out a schismatic faction led by George M. Hinkle, and was pleased to accept ordination as an apostle under Elder Hinkle's leadership of "the true, the only true church of God now on the earth" (Howard 1994, p. 81). Hinkle, however, soon charged McLellin with apostasy for reneging in various ways on his commitments to that group and cut him off. Meanwhile, the main Mormon body had moved from Missouri to Nauvoo, Illinois, and was experiencing a major succession crisis upon the assassination of Joseph Smith. McLellin arrived in Nauvoo in late 1844 and threw his lot with a faction that had opposed Joseph Smith as a fallen prophet even before the assassination. At last, it seemed, McLellin would now be able to help put the church right and vindicate himself in the process.

The main (but ultimately unsuccessful) contender against Brigham Young for the mantle of succession was Sidney Rigdon, a leader ever since the early 1830s in Kirtland, Ohio. McLellin began a public campaign for Rigdon, promising "to stand by him in all righteousness before God, while he stands as a man of God to plead with the world" (Howard 1994, p. 83). In accord with the familiar pattern, McLellin was made part of the leadership of Rigdon's emerging Church of Christ in early 1845, which undertook, in a series of public resolutions, to vindicate itself by excoriating Joseph Smith and Nauvoo Mormonism. This effort, of course, provided vindication as well for McLellin's own ongoing campaign to close the discrepancy between his "ought" and "actual" selves which had existed ever since his first falling-out with Smith in Kirtland. For several months, McLellin travelled and preached tirelessly for Rigdon's church, enjoying in the process a number of divine revelations of his own predicting a glorious future for his relationship with Rigdon. Yet he soon fell out with this new church, apparently over his demand, *contra* Rigdon's policy, that the church should move back to Kirtland. Rigdon then denounced McLellin as an apostate "from the church and kingdom of the living God, who (is) lifting up (his) puny arms against the work of the Almighty" (Howard 1994, p. 86), once again opening McLellin's old wounds and his recurring "actual/ought" self-discrepancy.

Over the next three decades, McLellin's career as a professional apostate went through this same cycle several times more. After leaving Rigdon, he turned next to David Whitmer in Missouri, trying unsuccessfully to get the latter to lead a new Mormon movement; then he attached himself for awhile to the schism of James J. Strang in Wisconsin; sought (but did not receive) a place in the emerging Reorganized LDS Church formed in 1860 under "young Joseph" (son of the slain prophet); and finally, for a few months in 1869, participated with the Granville Hedrick faction back in Independence, Missouri. McLellin's initiatives with Whitmer and with the RLDS proved abortive, but with the others he went through the familiar cycle of enthusiastic conversion, acceptance of leadership, failure and disaffection, and finally acrimonious apostasy, unsuccessful to the very end in his quest for permanent reconciliation between his "ought" and "actual" selves (and perhaps also his "ideal" and "actual" selves). He died in 1883, having spent his final years in an extensive letter-writing campaign "intent on setting the record straight" (Howard 1994, p. 97).

The Twentieth-Century Context

Examples of outright apostasy in the Bromley sense are not so easy to find in the twentieth-century Mormon Church. To be sure, one still sees dissent aplenty, and even some major sectarian schisms in this century. Since the historical tension between the church and the society has largely dissipated, one might expect fewer actual apostates. Yet the tension has by no means disappeared, so we should also expect at least some celebrated cases of whistleblowers, as well as plenty of mere leavers (defectors). Furthermore, as a destination for potential apostates and whistleblowers, there remains a visible anti-Mormon

enterprise, not only in the United States but in Europe (Introvigne 1994), somewhat in parallel to the Cult Awareness Network (which itself certainly makes
room for anti-Mormons as well as anti-cultists). This anti-Mormon enterprise is
found partly in specialized organizations like Ed Decker's "Ex-Mormons for
Jesus;" but it is also to be found in certain congregations, or even in entire
denominations, of the evangelical Christian spectrum. Any dedicated Mormon
apostate or whistle-blower can find places to turn for aid and comfort. Yet, even
so, there does not seem to be the proliferation of apostates that occurred in
nineteenth-century Mormonism, at least not if we are referring to those who
achieve careers as exponents of anti-Mormon organizations.

One clear exception to that generalization, which stands out in large part
precisely because it is unique, is the Utah Lighthouse Ministry of *Jerald and
Sandra Tanner* in Salt Lake City (Foster 1994). The Tanners were both lifelong
Mormons before leaving the church in the late 1950s for evangelical Protestantism, specifically the Christian and Missionary Alliance. Since at least 1964,
when Jerald quit his job as a machinist to devote himself to anti-Mormon publishing, the Tanners' ministry (once called Modern Microfilm Company) has
become a major source of newsletters, pamphlets, books, and copies of historical
documents, all intended to undermine the truth claims of Mormonism by exposing doctrinal fallacies, historical inaccuracies, and corrupt organizational
practices, whether past or present.

Interestingly enough, however, the Tanner case, by its very singularity, illustrates the difficulty in maintaining visible apostate careers when a successful
movement like Mormonism moves increasingly in the Allegiant direction. Although modern Mormonism certainly has its enemies, they are no longer numerous or powerful enough to constitute a large oppositional market for products
like those of the Tanners. Indeed, from the viewpoint of Mormon leaders, perhaps the most vexing uses made of the Tanner materials have been by those
curious subscribers *within* the Mormon fold (or marginal to it), who simply
want access to controversial documents and information that the leaders themselves try to keep out of circulation! Yet the Tanners have earned a certain
grudging respect in Utah for their sincerity and integrity: Although they
sometimes use inflammatory rhetoric and naive reasoning, they have usually
substantiated their claims carefully, and they have avoided tabloid scandal-
mongering for its own sake (unlike the Ex-Mormons for Jesus). Furthermore,
the Tanners were among the first to suspect fraud in Mark Hofmann's "discov-
eries" of certain debunking "historical documents" from early Mormonism,
and to say so publicly (Sillitoe and Roberts 1988; Turley 1992).

Even with the articles by Foster (1984, 1994) and the disclosures by themselves (Tanner and Tanner 1982), we have very little biographical information
on the Tanners. Jerald Tanner apparently was intellectually a highly curious
young man whose disillusionment with Mormonism's truth claims began while
he was still a teenager. In associating themselves with the sentiments of a certain
fellow apostate, the Tanners reveal the depth of their own "actual–ideal" self-

discrepancy: "(N)othing really matters in life but the truth. (Having felt) that they had found the truth, and (having given) it their heart, mind, and strength, then (they) found themselves in error. And when you have been deceived on such a scale, you want others to know about it" (quoted in Foster 1994, p. 359). Then again, in the words of Sandra Tanner (quoted in Foster 1994, p. 346), "Mormonism is claiming they are *The* Church that God's directing, as opposed to all the other ones just doing it on manmade ability. So when you make that kind of a distinction, one expects a better performance record . . . I expect their history to conform with the kinds of claims they make for it" (emphasis in the original).

In what the Tanners reveal about their Mormon upbringing (Foster 1994, p. 347), there are intimations not only of this kind of "actual–ideal" self-discrepancy, but also of the "actual–ought" discrepancy resulting from an inability (or unwillingness) to conform to the social expectations of the Mormon reference group. Jerald seemed bitter about never having been able to find satisfying social relationships with Mormons. His family life was filled with stress and apparently isolated from many positive aspects of Mormon culture. Furthermore, he and his father both drank heavily, in clear contravention of the orthodox Mormon health code, and so did many of Jerald's boyhood Mormon friends. All of this would have put Jerald in a very ambiguous position socially, contributing to a feeling of ambivalence about his self-authenticity, and creating a painful discrepancy between the actual self and the ought self (as per Higgins). This actual–ought discrepancy would carry the risk of stigma from the moral judgments of his co-religionists, while the actual–ideal discrepancy, discussed above, would suggest the sense of having been "taken in" or "made a sucker," a perhaps less conspicuous but still painful sense of stigma. Both kinds of discrepancies would cry out for resolution, and the Tanners' apostate career seems to have provided that resolution in spades.

These two apostate vignettes, one from the nineteenth and one from the twentieth century, are intended not as "the explanations" for the careers of the apostates in question but merely as indications of how social-psychological theory could be joined to structural theory to offer a somewhat fuller explanation for the apostate phenomenon than either kind of theory could offer separately. Yet it is important to keep in mind that not all forms of exiting are contested. What we might call "non-negotiated leavetaking" occurs especially in Allegiant organizations but might occur all across the continuum. The less contested the exit, the less serious the identity problem created for the exiter. Thus one can well imagine that correspondingly less intense self-discrepancies would be involved for the defectors and the whistleblowers than for apostates. Both of these other kinds of exiters are more common than apostates in the modern Mormon Church; and though not all exiters stay away permanently, about half of them do. Preliminary survey data (Albrecht et al. 1988) indicate that most Mormon exiters, whether periodic or permanent, cite reasons of "lifestyle" or social belonging that might suggest self-discrepancies, but we would need in-depth interview data to get a fuller picture. In any case, the frequency of exiting has become so common in Utah that the Protestant mainline there has formed the Society of St. Chad to help "transitional" Mormons make the journey from Mormonism to other denominations.

An indication that the Mormon Church itself has recognized an appreciable increase in sheer defection (or uncontested exiting), as opposed to apostasy, was an official decision late in the century to dispense with the formal excommunication process for defectors. Traditionally, the only way in which a defector (or any exiter) could get his/her name removed from church records was to submit to a formal excommunication court (even if in absentia), a process which not only stigmatized unnecessarily the friendly defector but tied up enormous amounts of clergy time and record-keeping in an essentially meaningless ritual. Since about 1980, however, Mormons who want to relinquish their membership need only send a "letter of resignation" to local clergy—an interesting and pragmatic organizational concession to the changing composition (and increasing numbers) of Mormon exiting types in the modern era.

Late-Twentieth-Century Whistleblowers and Growing Mormon Tension with Society

If it is true, however, that Mormon defectors are fairly common these days, and that true Mormon apostates are rather rare, there remains the middle category of whistleblowers, which have been the most conspicuous type of Mormon exiter since midcentury, at least. As typical with whistleblowers, few if any have intended at the beginning to work their way entirely out of the church, though many have ended up that way through the formal excommunication process. Even after reaching the outside, however, Mormon whistleblowers have generally not found the external organizational support that would make possible new careers as whistleblowers (to say nothing of apostate careers). It might be useful to consider briefly a couple of these whistleblower cases in order to provide some concreteness to these generalizations.

Fawn McKay Brodie is often considered part of Mormonism's "lost generation" of literati, most of whom left Utah and the church during the first half of the twentieth century (Geary 1977). Consisting mostly of novelists, a few like Brodie were also historians discovering for the first time the many discrepancies in official Mormon histories. While many of this generation became alienated from Mormonism during their literary careers, their alienation usually did not become widely known, so their departure from the church was more in the nature of simple defection rather than apostasy per se. A few, such as Juanita Brooks, even retained some church ties and activity. Not so with Fawn Brodie, author of a celebrated and controversial 1945 biography of Joseph Smith, the founding Mormon prophet (Brodie 1945).

Written in the genre of psychohistory, and resembling a historical novel as much as a biography, this work constituted an incisive debunking of Smith's prophetic claims, and derivatively of the most fundamental truth claims of Mormonism. It was, in other words, a major whistleblowing enterprise from a well-placed insider: Brodie was from the prominent McKay family. Her uncle was the senior-most apostle and was to become president of the church a few years later. It was widely (but incorrectly) suspected that she had used her family connections to gain access to "incriminating" historical documents from the church archives. Given the prominence both of her family and of her book, it is not surprising that she was formally excommunicated from the church in early 1946.

Brodie's life story (e.g., Bringhurst 1994a, 1994b) offers plenty of clues pointing to self-discrepancies of both the actual–ideal and the actual–ought types. An intellectually precocious young woman who graduated from the University of Utah at the age of 19, she found her university experience a serious challenge to the idealized understanding she once had had of her religious heritage. Indeed, even before college she found ambiguities in her religious ideals: Her father was very devout and essentially unsympathetic with the questions she raised as a youngster. She was closer to her mother, who apparently had doubts of her own but was not willing to rock the family boat by articulating them explicitly. Brodie accordingly received somewhat mixed messages about what constituted her actual self as far as religious identity was concerned; yet she grew up as an active and apparently committed Mormon.

Her actual–ought discrepancy developed as she associated for the first time with non-Mormon and ex-Mormon peers at the university, and as she came increasingly under the influence of her mother's brother on the faculty there. Already a defector from Mormonism himself, this "favorite uncle" (as she thought of him) encouraged Fawn in her religious questioning and eventually mentored her in the production of a major research paper, which debunked the widespread public notion that the church welfare program had made Mormons largely independent of federal assistance during the depression. This was Brodie's first whistleblowing effort, but it was published under a pseudonym to avoid upsetting the family, as though to postpone the painful process of resolving the ambiguity in her self-concept; for the "ought self" of her upbringing was confronting an emerging "actual self" increasingly uncomfortable with obligatory Mormon ways.

The resolution of this discrepancy eventually took the form of replacing her earlier ought self with one derived from the heterodox family members and non-Mormon reference groups of her college environment. When she left for graduate work at the University of Chicago in that condition, her Mormon past soon dropped away. "It was like taking off a hot coat in the summertime," she reported (Bringhurst 1994b, pp. 110–11), and she acquired a whole new identity, one which she soon solidified by marriage to a Jewish fellow student at Chicago. Far away from the stigma as "black sheep" in both family and church, she finally felt free to begin research for the book that would "blow the whistle" on Mormon truth claims and eventuate in her complete and public break with the church and people of her youth.

Yet Brodie never made common cause with any anti-Mormon enterprises, which were no longer numerous or powerful in any case. Brodie's whistleblowing was not over theological issues as such, which might have attracted her to the Protestant anti-Mormons (the basic premise of her book, indeed, seems atheistic); nor was her whistleblowing over legal issues like nineteenth-century polygamy and theocracy, or (as with Sonia Johnson later) over the transversing of church/state boundaries, which might have given her an incipient anti-Mormon audience of a more political kind. Brodie's attack, rather, was more in the nature of an exposé against the *cultural and intellectual* respectability which Mormons had tried so hard to achieve during the first half of the twentieth century. Implicitly, her book asks how any but a bunch of simpleminded country bumpkins could be taken in by the frauds of Joseph Smith. In producing the book, furthermore, Brodie seems to have been urged on at least as much by cultural critics of the Mormons in Utah and in the eastern literary establishment (the "cultural regulators" of the time) as by any animus of her own (Bringhurst 1994a, 1994b). In any case, by heaping its prizes and accolades on her book, the eastern literary establishment provided the external verification that seemed to legitimate retroactively the path Brodie had chosen and the new identity she had created.

Sonia Johnson, a generation later, became a whistleblower in the more typical fashion envisioned by Bromley (Pottmyer 1994). She came to be known primarily for her *From Housewife to Heretic* (1981), in which she chronicled her evolution from the first of these roles to the second. This evolution was portrayed as the inevitable result of an act of conscience, namely, her public exposé of the illegal intervention of Mormon Church leaders into the political campaign against ratification of the Equal Rights Amendment (ERA) in the 1970s. In the classic tradition of post-hoc biographical constructions, this book depicts a young woman chafing under patriarchal oppression as she grew up in a devout Utah Mormon home, later playing the dutiful wife in following her good Mormon husband from place to place in his career. Somewhat in contrast, however, her personal correspondence and other papers, covering a much longer period, tell the story of a much more conventional Mormon girl and woman, coming only late to a feminist consciousness, and coping with the heartache of infidelity in a husband who was very far from the conventional Mormon mold (Kellogg 1996).

Whenever and however her feminism finally bloomed, it was eventually given public expression through her association with a small group of Mormon feminists in northern Virginia, where she and her family had come to live in 1976. During the next two years, she was strongly "converted" to feminism, and, as eventual president of "Mormons for ERA" (White 1985), Johnson became increasingly vocal and visible publicly, not only as an advocate for the ERA but also as a critic of her church's stealthy and circuitous political interventions (Pottmyer 1994). Her activities included not only participation in various demonstrations, but even testifying before the Senate Judiciary Committee under the hostile questioning of Senator Orrin Hatch of Utah. Eventually, she joined the National Organization for Women (NOW) and travelled to various states under NOW auspices to advise pro-ERA forces on how best to counter their Mormon opponents. Late in 1978, an anti-ERA lobbying organization was formed in Virginia by Mormons acting ostensibly as individuals, but it failed to register as a lobbying group under state law, a lapse which Johnson was instrumental in making public. By this time, she had "blown the whistle" more than once.

In her various public activities and speeches over a two-year period, Johnson eventually crossed a rather ambiguous line in the minds of church leaders between "loyal opposition" and outright disloyalty. Late in 1979 she was called before a church court and excommunicated for teaching false doctrine and other similarly vague charges. After her book came out, she enjoyed a few years of celebrity in feminist circles, including an unsuccessful candidacy as national president of NOW, and also as U.S. presidential candidate for the fledgling Citizens Party. She was in some demand around the country on the speakers' circuit, too. Her notoriety, however, did not last long, for the country soon turned its attention from the failed ERA to other issues and elected a conservative national administration. No longer at home in either the Mormon or the feminist enterprises, Johnson could not turn back in any direction, and as time went on her radicalization grew apace; she burned a number of important social bridges with her church friends, her family, and even other feminists. Her marriage had already collapsed in divorce during the very period of most intense struggle with the church. Even a later lesbian relationship failed after a few years. Eventually, she left everything and everyone behind for the seclusion of a vaguely lesbian commune in New Mexico (Pottmyer 1994).

As revealed in her own books and speeches, and in articles written even by her friends, Sonia Johnson's career was rife with self-discrepancies of all kinds. An accomplished woman with a doctoral degree, she was also a conventional woman with a husband and four children. Her "actual" self must often have been under pressure as she weighed the ambivalent "oughts" of her professional identity versus her domestic identity. The potential for the stigma of failure was always present in one of those identities or the other, especially with a husband who often failed to meet the responsibilities of his own obligatory roles. Later on, when she acquired her "actual" identity as a feminist, she soon found that it was incompatible with her "ought" identity as a faithful Mormon woman, despite her continuing service and activity in the church up to the point of her excommunication.

She had rather naively believed that her church leaders would cease their opposition to ERA if only she and other Mormon feminists could show them the fundamental compatibility between feminism and the Mormon heritage; or, that failing in such "internal" lobbying, she might be able to stop the misguided political efforts of her leaders through pressure from the outside. Rather than achieving thereby the desired self-verification, Johnson instead suffered a series of stigmatizing experiences, first in being publicly castigated by a powerful co-religionist (Orrin Hatch); then in being shunned by other Mormons she had always considered friends; then in being dumped by her husband, not because he disagreed with her feminist ways but in favor of one or more other women; and finally, in her widely publicized excommunication, again at the hands of local leaders whom she had always regarded as friends.

Having felt betrayed by her own people for her conscientious whistleblowing efforts intended for their own good, Johnson found external support in politically liberal groups like NOW that verified her efforts to merge her actual and ought selves. Even that support, however, proved transitory, and her candidacy for the NOW presidency was rebuffed by a large margin, as was, of course, her candidacy for the presidency of the United States. It was as though she had outlived her usefulness and been cast aside, a common fate of whistleblowers, as Bromley reminds us. She seems to have experimented with one kind of identity after another, each time cutting more ties with her Mormon past in a continuing quest for a stable and verified identity. Perhaps by now her quest has been achieved, but "from housewife to lesbian communard" was a long, hard journey!

CONCLUSION

To recapitulate briefly: Bromley postulates three different ideal types of exiters, each corresponding to a different organizational type and a different form of external opposition to the religious community which the exiters are leaving. Exiters are true *apostates* only to the extent that they have access to oppositional organizations which will sponsor their careers and validate the retrospective biographical accounts of their outrageous experiences during their sojourns in the erstwhile religion. A second type of exiter is the *whistleblower*, who differs from the apostate in a naive original intention to set things right in a religious community to which s/he basically feels loyal, but who finds such efforts unappreciated and comes to depend increasingly on the support and validation of different kinds of outside sponsorship from regulatory, civic, mass media, or other ostensibly "neutral" organizations—in contrast to the focused "anti-" or oppositional organizations supporting apostates. Finally, the third and the least acrimonious type of exiter is the *defector*, who negotiates with the leaders or principals of the religious community the terms of departure which are non-stigmatizing to the defector and which leave the legitimacy of the religion intact. To the extent that outside organizations are involved, they simply stand ready to welcome the defector into a new religious fold that will be more compatible with his/her evolving self-concept and belief system.

Of course, the availability and access to outside organizations will be a function partly of the degree and nature of the cultural tension between the religious community and the host society: The greater the tension, the greater the likelihood of dedicated oppositional organizations which can harbor and sponsor apostates; the greater also the likelihood that regulatory, mass media, and other civic organizations will take an interest in the claims of whistleblowers. Since cultural tension is realistically best conceived as a "continuous variable," the Bromley typology actually constitutes a continuum with the two extremes and the center marked, respectively, by the three types. This implies the presence of "mixed types along the continuum as an empirical matter. It also implies that all three types can be found at any point along the tension continuum, but that the *mixture* of types will favor the *predominance* of apostates at one extreme, of mere defectors at the other extreme, and of whistleblowers in the middle.

A logical extension of these implications is that as the degree of tension between a religious community and the host society changes across time, so the "mix" of the three types of exiters from that community will also change. This idea has been illustrated here in the case of the Mormons: In the nineteenth century, when the Mormons were generally considered a highly subversive and degenerate religious cult, those who exited were especially likely to be apostates who could find support and careers in any number of outside organizations hostile to Mormonism. Then, during the early twentieth century, as Mormons made a conscientious and largely successful effort to conform to normative American ways, the proportion of exiters in the apostate category seems to have diminished in favor mainly of defectors. Various schismatic sects occurred, but one rarely heard of apostate Mormon individuals in the early twentieth century. Even the exceptional cases of the Tanners and Ed Decker et al. occurred later.

These exceptions, coming as they did after mid-century, must be considered in light of the argument made elsewhere (Mauss 1994) that since mid-century the Mormon Church has entered a "retrenchment" phase in a more or less deliberate effort to re-assert doctrinal and behavioral boundaries between Mormons and others, with a concomitant increase in cultural tension with American society. To the extent that such an argument has validity, we should expect apostates to appear again now and then. However, since the retrenchment in question comes nowhere near a return of Mormonism to its nineteenth-century disrepute, we would not expect apostates to be common. Much more common would be incipient or actual whistleblowers, with a continuing but much quieter contingent of mere defectors. The recurring and unprecedented appearance of Mormon whistleblowers since 1960 over the race issue, and later over feminist issues, and still later over the limits of ecclesiastical authority (Mauss 1996), testifies to the plausibility of this explanation, at least in the Mormon case, for the waxing and waning of apostates, as opposed to whistleblowers and other types of exiters.

Finally, a major argument of this chapter has suggested the need for considering the microcosmic along with the macrocosmic level of explanation for the different types of exiting. However useful and plausible Bromley's structural or macrocosmic conceptualization may be, with its various possible modifications and elaborations, exiting ultimately occurs at the *individual level*. Self-verification theories of identity in social psychology can complement organizational explanations by postulating the different kinds of "self-discrepancies" that contribute to the decisions of exiters to seek resolutions for their dissonance in new careers with new reference groups.

Any of the discrepancies might be involved for any of the exiters, perhaps even in an additive way. However, the "actual–ought" self-discrepancy postulated by Higgins seems especially severe and thus especially likely to be involved in the apostate case and perhaps to a lesser extent in the whistle-blower case. The "actual–ideal" discrepancy seems to fit the defector case especially, though it could also apply in the whistle-blower case. Since the actual–ought discrepancy reflects the potential exiter's resistance to the socially obligatory elements in the life of the religious community, it also carries the highest risk of stigma and thus of "spoiled identity." The resolution of that discrepancy can perhaps be most readily achieved by changing the nature of the "ought" through changing reference groups, which is the typical strategy of the apostate in Bromley's sense. Future theorizing and research can doubtless enrich our explanations for exiting at both the organizational and the social-psychological levels.

NOTES

I am indebted to my WSU colleague, Professor Viktor Gecas, for critical guidance and suggestions on this manuscript.

1. The content of the *ought* self, while apparently originating primarily in perceived social obligations ("other-ought"), might also have a personal component ("self-ought").

REFERENCES

Albrecht, Stan, Marie Cornwall, and Perry Cunningham. 1988. "Religious Leave-Taking: Disengagement and Disaffiliation among Mormons." Pp. 62–80 in *Falling from the Faith*, edited by David Bromley. Beverly Hills, CA: Sage.

Alexander, Thomas. 1986. *Mormonism in Transition: A History of the Latter-day Saints: 1890–1930*. Urbana: University of Illinois Press.

Backman, Milton. 1983. *The Heavens Resound*. Salt Lake City: Deseret Book Co.

Baer, Hans. 1988. *Recreating Utopia in the Desert*. Albany: SUNY Press.

Bitton, Davis, and Gary Bunker. 1983. *The Mormon Graphic Image, 1834–1914*. Salt Lake City: University of Utah Press.

Bradley, Martha. 1993. *Kidnapped from that Land: The Government Raids on the Short Creek Polygamists*. Salt Lake City: University of Utah Press.

Bringhurst, Newell. 1994a. "Fawn McKay Brodie: Dissident Historian and Quintessential Critic of Mormondom." Pp. 279–300 in *Different Visions*, edited by Roger Launius and Linda Thatcher. Urbana: University of Illinois Press.

———. 1994b. "Juanita Brooks and Fawn Brodie: Sisters in Mormon Dissent." *Dialogue: A Journal of Mormon Thought* 27: 105–27.

Brodie, Fawn. 1945. *No Man Knows My History*. New York: A. A. Knopf.

Bromley, David, ed. 1988. *Falling from the Faith*. Beverly Hills, CA: Sage.

Ebaugh, Helen. 1988. *Becoming an EX*. Chicago: University of Chicago Press.

Flanders, Robert. 1965. *Nauvoo: Kingdom on the Mississippi*. Urbana: University of Illinois Press.

Foote, Nelson. 1951. "Identification as the Basis for a Theory of Motivation." *American Sociological Review* 26:14–21.

Foster, Lawrence. 1994. "Apostate Believers: Jerald and Sandra Tanner's Encounter with Mormon History." Pp. 343–65 in *Differing Visions*, edited by Roger Launius and Linda Thatcher. Urbana: University of Illinois Press.

———. 1984. "Career Apostates: Reflections on the Works of Jerald and Sandra Tanner." *Dialogue: A Journal of Mormon Thought* 17:35–60.

Geary, Edward. 1977. "Mormondom's Lost Generation: The Novelists of the 1940s." *Brigham Young University Studies* 18:89–99.

Gecas, Viktor. 1994. "In Search of the Real Self: Problems of Authenticity in Modern Times." Pp. 139–54 in *Self Collective Behavior and Society*, edited by Gerald Platt and Chad Gordon. Greenwich, CT: JAI Press.

Gecas, Viktor, and Peter Burke. 1995. "Self and Identity." Pp. 41–67 in *Sociological Perspectives on Social Psychology*, edited by Karen Cook, Gary Fine, and James House. Boston: Allyn and Bacon.

Goffman, Erving. 1963. *Stigma: Notes on the Management of Spoiled Identity*. Englewood Cliffs, NJ: Prentice-Hall.

———. 1959. *The Presentation of Self in Everyday Life*. Garden City, NY: Doubleday.

Higgins, E. Tory. 1989. "Self-Discrepancy Theory: What Patterns of Self-Beliefs Cause People to Suffer?" *Advances in Experimental Social Psychology* 22:93–136.

———. 1987. "Self-Discrepancy: A Theory Relating Self and Affect." *Psychological Review* 94:319–40.

Higgins, E. Tory, R. Klein, and T. Strauman. 1985. "Self-Concept Discrepancy Theory: A Psychological Model for Distinguishing among Different Aspects of Depression and Anxiety." *Social Cognition* 3:93–136.

Hill, Marvin. 1980. "Cultural Crisis in the Mormon Kingdom: A Reconsideration of the Causes of the Kirtland Dissent." *Church History* 49:286–97.

Howard, Richard. 1994. "William E. McLellin: 'Mormonism's Stormy Petrel.' " Pp. 76–101 in *Differing Visions*, edited by Roger Launius and Linda Thatcher. Urbana: University of Illinois Press.

Introvigne, Massimo. 1994. "The Devil Makers: Contemporary Evangelical Fundamentalist Anti-Mormonism." *Dialogue: A Journal of Mormon Thought* 27:153–69.

Johnson, Sonia. 1981. *From Housewife to Heretic*. Garden City, NY: Doubleday.

Kellogg, Heather. 1996. "Shades of Gray: Sonia Johnson's Life Through Letters and Autobiography." *Dialogue: A Journal of Mormon Thought* 29:77–86.

Launius, Roger, and Linda Thatcher, eds. 1994. *Differing Visions: Dissenters in Mormon History*. Urbana: University of Illinois Press.

LeSueur, Stephen. 1987. *The 1838 Mormon War in Missouri*. Columbia: University of Missouri Press.

Mauss, Armand. 1996. "Authority, Agency, and Ambiguity: The Elusive Boundaries of Required Obedience to Priesthood Leaders." *Sunstone* 19:20–31.

———. 1994. *The Angel and the Beehive*. Urbana: University of Illinois Press.

Newell, L. Jackson. 1995. "Sterling Moss McMurrin: A Philosopher in Action." *Dialogue: A Journal of Mormon Thought* 28:1–17.

Pottmyer, Alice. 1994. "Sonia Johnson: Mormonism's Feminist Heretic." Pp. 366–89 in *Differing Visions*, edited by Roger Launius and Linda Thatcher. Urbana: University of Illinois Press.

Richardson, James, ed. 1977. *Conversion Careers*. Beverly Hills, CA: Sage.

Shields, Steven. 1982. *Divergent Paths of the Restoration Movement*. 3d ed. Bountiful, UT: Restoration Research.

Sillitoe, Linda, and Allen Roberts. 1988. *Salamander: The Story of the Mormon Forgery Murders*. Salt Lake City: Signature Books.

Stark, Rodney, and William Bainbridge. 1985. *The Future of Religion*. Berkeley: University of California Press.

Stryker, Sheldon. 1991. "Exploring the Relevance of Social Cognition for the Relationship of Self and Society." Pp. 19–41 in *The Self-Society Dynamic*, edited by Judith Howard and Peter Callero. New York: Cambridge University Press.

———. 1980. *Symbolic Interactionism*. Menlo Park, CA: Cummings.

Swann, W. B. 1983. "Self Verification: Bringing Social Reality into Harmony with the Self." Pp. 33–66 in *Psychological Perspectives on the Self*, edited by Jerry Suls and A. G. Greenwald. Hillsdale, NJ: Erlbaum.

Swanson, Guy. 1988. *Ego Defenses and the Legitimation of Behavior*. New York: Cambridge University Press (ASA Rose Monograph Series).

Tanner, Jerald, and Sandra Tanner. 1982. *Mormonism: Shadow or Reality?* Salt Lake City: Modern Microfilm Co.

Turley, Richard. 1992. *Victims: The LDS Church and the Mark Hofmann Case*. Urbana: University of Illinois Press.

Weigert, Andrew. 1991. *Mixed Emotions*. Albany: SUNY Press.

White, O. Kendall. 1985. "A Feminist Challenge: 'Mormons for ERA' as an Internal Social Movement." *Journal of Ethnic Studies* 13:29–50.

Wright, Stuart. 1988. "Leaving New Religious Movements: Issues, Theory, and Research." Pp. 143–65 in *Falling from the Faith*, edited by David Bromley. Beverly Hills, CA: Sage.

Chapter 4

Standing at the Cross-Roads: The Politics of Marginality in "Subversive Organizations"

Eileen Barker

This chapter is concerned with a category of persons who have remained at best neglected, at worst unrecognized, by scholars and others interested in describing and explaining contemporary NRMs. I am referring to those who, having once been fully fledged, core members of an NRM, are now operating at the margins of the movement. It is argued that such persons add a further dimension to the debate about the politics of religious apostasy, providing, as they do, an alternative position and function for disaffected members of NRMs that are in tension with the rest of society. Furthermore, by operating at the margins of the movement, these members contribute to the emergence of a new dynamic in the internal structuring and culture of the movement, as well as in its relations with the external social environment.

Most discussions by scholars and others interested in new religions make a relatively simple distinction between members (who may be subdivided into new converts, rank-and-file members and leaders) and ex-members (who may be called past members, apostates, defectors, or some other name denoting that they once were, but are no longer, a member of the NRM in question). But whatever the internal divisions or particular terms used for persons in each of the two categories, it is usually made clear to which of the two (member or ex-member) any particular individual belongs. This distinction would certainly seem to be the case in the majority of contributions to this volume, in which an individual tends to be seen (at least analytically) as unambiguously in or out of the movement at any particular time.

That a clear distinction is usually drawn between members of an NRM and the rest of society is not surprising, as the new religions with which we are concerned are commonly seen, both by themselves and by outsiders, as the kinds of organizations that are "in a state of high tension with their surrounding environment." That is, they belong to that category of movement which Bromley would call a Type III "Subversive" organization, and are typically of the opinion that "He that is not with me is against me," with, thus, a sharp distinction being drawn between "us" and "them"—by both us and them. What I am suggesting is, however, that relatively early in the development of any NRM, following an initial period before any institutionalization has set in, there emerges a variety of positions at the social boundaries of the movement. These positions offer individuals an alternative to the stark "with us or against us" stance, and can function both to heighten and to reduce the tension between the movement and its surrounding environment.

One can detect two main categories of persons who straddle the "them" and "us" distinction. For the sake of clarity, I shall call one category *peripheral* and the other *marginal*.[1] The status of peripheral membership will have been instigated by, and is, thus, officially recognized and sanctioned by, the leadership of the movement. Marginal membership, on the other hand, does not exist as an officially recognized status. While the peripheral member is characterized as being positively inclined toward the movement, but not sufficiently committed to make the sacrifices demanded by full membership, the marginal member is committedly questioning at least some of the movement's beliefs and/or practices. While peripherals might be expected to contribute to a lessening of tension between friend and foe ("them" and "us"), the existence of marginals can undermine the "us"ness in ways that can appear to threaten the integrity of a movement.

PERIPHERAL MEMBERS

Most religions have various levels of membership, ranging from the fully committed who, like priests or nuns, devote their entire lives to the movement, to loosely affiliated associates who make an occasional visit or contribution. Other things being equal, it is likely that the variety of levels of membership and the difficulty in establishing exactly who is or is not a member will be greater the longer a religion has been in existence and the closer it approximates to one of Bromley's Type I (Allegiant) organizations. Nonetheless, any organization might establish one or more categories of associate membership—even a movement which is relatively new, which celebrates the equality of a "priesthood of all believers," and/or which would be classified as a Type III (Subversive) organization.

The status of peripheral membership of an NRM will usually have been instituted by the leadership in order to accommodate and, perhaps, to make use of individuals who share the movement's beliefs but are unable or unwilling to make the degree of commitment expected of core members. Often the main distinction between them and core members is that the latter are more likely to be engaged in some kind of missionary activity. There are exceptions, but peripheral members are unlikely to live with core members or to do full-time work for the movement; they may, however, be a source of extra (in some cases, considerable) financial support. While they have a positive orientation toward the movement, peripheral members are likely to exhibit this in a less fanatical and/or aggressive manner than that frequently displayed by core members—there is, in other words, less tension between peripheral members and society than there is between core members and the rest of society.

We can find examples of peripheral members in all three of the NRMs that Bromley uses as examples of Subversive organizations. As early as the late 1960s, the International Society for Krishna Consciousness (ISKCON) was inviting members of the local Indian community to its Temples and it has long recognized what is known as a "Congregation" or "Sanga" (associate) membership; in the late 1970s, Sun Myung Moon, the founder of the Unification Church, introduced a "Home-Church" membership; in 1989, David Berg, the founder of The Family, introduced the status of "TSer."

Peripheral members need to be distinguished from "sympathizers," who have done little more than sign a piece of paper suggesting that they share some of the movement's ideals or objectives—possibly no more than agreement on a single issue such as "world peace" or "the restoration of family values"—by the fact that they would identify themselves and be identified as a follower of the religion in question rather than another or no religion.[2] The distinction is, however, by no means always an easy one to make. When Berg introduced the status of TSers in 1989, this was the second of six concentric circles of discipleship which he identified. Those within the third circle, consisting of Catacombers (young probationary or part-time members) and "Live-outs," would fall into the peripheral membership category, but those within the fourth,[3] the fifth, and the sixth circles would not. The point to be noted here is that even a movement as clearly in tension with the surrounding society as The Family was in 1989 could have a series of more or less committed members and several identifiable circles of supporters who were non-members. A further point that can be made is that a single title can span the full range of core, peripheral, and sympathizers. For example, "Patrons," who contribute money to ISKCON, may be fully initiated members (although not resident in a Temple), but they might be little more than "sympathizers" who define themselves broadly as Vaishnavas, but rarely visit an ISKCON temple.

If peripherals were once core members, their shift to peripheral membership will have been negotiated openly and their status will be recognized by the movement, by non-members and, importantly, by the individuals themselves. Of the three NRMs mentioned in the previous paragraph, The Family has probably the highest proportion of members who have moved from core to periphery—sometimes at their own behest, sometimes on the orders of the leadership. There are also those who had left the movement altogether but have been drawn back into it when they came to believe that peripheral status was a more attractive option than either full-time missionary commitment or life in "The System"—the name given by The Family to the outside society.

Unification Home-Church members have tended to be persons who have never been attracted to the lifestyle of full membership. While 80 percent of the core Unificationists whom I studied in the late 1970s were under 30 years old at the time they joined the movement, 80 percent of the Home-Church members were over 30; while less than 7 percent of the core Unificationists were married at the time of joining, only a fifth of the Home-Church members had *not* been married; while core members were disproportionately male, Home-Church members were disproportionately female. The Home-Church members were less well educated and, on average, of a somewhat lower socioeconomic status, but came from a wider range of backgrounds than the core members. At the time of the study, I observed that:

The existence of the Home-Church members indicates that the Unification Church can appeal to a constituency wider than that from which the full-time Moonie is drawn, but . . . it succeeds in doing so only as long as it does not demand the kind of unquestioning devotion and sacrificial life style that the young, unmarried [core] Moonie is prepared to give (Barker 1984, p. 210).

Members of ISKCON's congregation, who may provide support of both a financial and political nature to the movement, tend to be distinguished from core devotees in the West in that they have been ethnic Asians, using Temple facilities for worship as ISKCON has provided one of the few opportunities in predominantly Christian societies for the traditional ritual and teaching of Vaishnava Hinduism. There is, however, a growing proportion of Caucasian congregation members, especially in Eastern Europe and the former Soviet Union. Even in the West, it has become far more difficult to distinguish between core and peripheral members within ISKCON. Living in the Temple is no longer considered an essential prerequisite for being a "real" devotee, and the vast majority of members now live as householders, many in nuclear families, working in some outside job, but following the basic precepts of the movement.

The main point to be made about peripheral membership is not so much the financial assistance that peripheral members give to their movement but the political help they might give through bridging a gap between members and non-members. The fact that they are associated with and have more knowledge of their NRM than most non-members, yet, at the same time, lead more "ordinary" lives and have more contact with the outside environment than most core members means that, to some extent at least, peripheral members can act as intermediaries between the movement and outsiders. TSers frequently make television appearances and speak to the media in support of The Family; they have also provided temporary homes to some core members' teenage children who have been uncertain whether or not they want to stay in the movement. An example of the lobbying support given to ISKCON by its congregational members is to be found in the saga of Bhaktivedanta Manor (Nye 1996). Unification Home-Church members have played an important role in mediating between parents and their (adult) children who have joined the movement, thus easing, in at least some instances, one of the most trenchant sources of tension between an NRM and its immediate social environment.

But although the lives and identity of peripheral members are bound up with the movement and they are regarded as friends and supporters by the core membership, peripheral members are unlikely to be trusted with full details of the movement's beliefs and practices. I have talked to many Unification Home-Church members who are amazingly ignorant of some of the more esoteric practices and beliefs of the movement. Members of ISKCON's congregation who worshipped at one of the Temples in the early 1980s were unlikely to be aware of the scandals associated with the movement in the period following Prabhupada's death. And while The Family distributes one set of its literature, at one time known as "Mo Letters," to all levels of its membership, there are other letters, designated DO (Disciples Only), which contain more contentious statements (and employ some of the more explicitly sexual language utilized by David Berg and, more recently, his wife, Maria), and which are not distributed to TSers.[4]

Thus it is that the sanctioned existence of a peripheral membership can blur the relatively strong boundary to be found in Type III organizations between members and *non-members*. The blurring takes a radically different form, however, when we turn to the "marginals," who challenge the boundary between members and *ex-members*.

MARGINAL MEMBERS

While one may join an NRM as a peripheral member, one does not join as a marginal member. When marginal members join a Type III new religion, they will have thought of themselves and been thought of by others as core members. The customary battle cry of a Subversive organization being "You are either with us or against us," the hierarchy cannot easily acknowledge, let alone sanction, members who question the beliefs and practices for which the movement stands. Nonetheless, there are usually at least some who will be occupying an ambiguous, unacknowledged and/or unrecognized position at the margins of even the most ideal-typical Subversive movement.

When, at some period in their adult lives, the marginals converted to their NRM, they would have done so because they believed that the movement could offer them something that the outside society could not or did not offer them. At the time of their conversion, they are likely to have believed that whatever it was that the movement was offering them was important enough for them to dedicate their lives to it; their commitment would have been such that the most significant criterion for identifying themselves and others was membership in the movement—whether they were one of "us" or one of "them."

There are, of course, many reasons why people might join one of the variety of NRMs to be found in contemporary society. The initial reason for joining could have been that they had been searching for a religious explanation for their existence on earth, and/or a spiritual life in which they could develop a deeper relationship with God or dedicate themselves to devotion to Krishna. It may have been that they had believed they could contribute to the building of the Kingdom of Heaven on earth or to the making of a better world, and/or that they could be one of the elect at the time of the millennium. It could be that they felt they had met a group of like-minded people with whom they could develop sincere and deep friendships, or a community that would follow the kind of lifestyle (be it ascetic or hedonistic, this-worldly or other-worldly) which they themselves would like to follow. It is possible that they believed that the movement could reveal esoteric techniques with which they would develop their true potential, discover "the God within," or progress in their careers and find true health, wealth, and happiness. On encountering the movement, they may simply have felt that they had "come home."

The reason why members shift to the margins will vary, but it is likely to be the result of some profound disagreement with *part* of the NRM. At the same time, they are also likely to believe that their movement—its beliefs, practices, or members—still has something to offer. It may be that the marginal remains convinced that the founder is the Messiah, or that he has revealed The Truth, but that the movement is being destroyed by a corrupt, second-level leadership— or s/he may even believe that the founder has become corrupted and strayed from the truth which he (or possibly she) once proclaimed. On the other hand, it may be that the beliefs are no longer convincing (perhaps a millennial date has passed without any obvious proof that something significant happened), but that the once literally held beliefs can still provide a goal—a direction—toward which people can aspire and which is superior to that found in any of the other religions or ideologies available in the wider society. Alternatively, it could be that the beliefs are completely rejected, yet the friendships that have been built up over the years prevent the marginal from completely severing ties. In short, something associated with the movement is seen in negative terms, but something else is still seen in positive terms.

The marginals' position is almost bound to have led them to deliberate whether it is better for them to stay within the movement or to leave. The pushes and pulls from the movement may produce a nice balance, and it is then that their experiences and perceptions of the outside society will take on a crucial significance. Sometimes marginals would have left the movement altogether had they not been deterred from doing so by the very circumstances which Bromley suggests function as facilitators for members to exit from Subversive Type III organizations: in the case of marginals, these can militate *against* their making the complete break.

Thus, at the same time as there is a vestigial pull from the movement, there may also be a push from the social environment. An extreme example of "push" arises when parents have been so worried by their child's involvement in what they have come to believe is a dangerous cult which exerts mind control over its members that they accept that the only way to "rescue" their children is to resort to the illegal practice of kidnapping them for "deprogramming," or, more frequently nowadays, to submit them to an "exit-counselor" who attempts to persuade them to leave the movement before they themselves feel ready to leave. Although such efforts have a high "success rate" among relatively new converts, who may well have been about to leave anyway, with longer-term members they not infrequently end in failure, the members returning to the movement feeling betrayed, insulted, angry and/or disillusioned—and more committed than before to staying in the movement, despite their disillusionment (Barker 1983a).

But even marginals who have either vicariously or themselves "tested the water" can be well aware that it is not only the anti-cult organizations which demand a particular narrative of disengagement in which the movement is identified in unequivocally negative terms, and leavers are expected to affirm some variant of the mind-control thesis as an explanation for their apparent lapse from sanity or adherence to social "normality." Relatives and friends may also be seeking exoneration from supposed guilt by this route—they may feel both threatened and fearful that the ex-member is not "really out" unless he or she plays along with the apostate narrative.

Another requirement of the apostate narrative is that ex-members are expected to *return* to their "pre-cult" selves, for there is a widespread acceptance of the proposition that cult membership results in a cult identity which is schizophrenically separate from the "real" (that is, "pre-cult") personality (Hassan 1988, pp. 72–75). They are denied the possibility of seeing their time in the movement as a period of learning and even benefiting, albeit from mistakes as well as from achievements. They are, rather, expected to revert back to the stage that they were at before becoming a member. Given that research has indicated that many young adults join a new religion as a way of getting beyond the "pre-cult" identity with which their (usually well-meaning) parents have burdened them (Levine 1984), it is not altogether surprising that some will choose to stay on the margins rather than return to what they had found an uncomfortable if not an intolerable situation.[5]

In other words, just *because* the outside is in such tension with the NRM, some of the movement's members prefer to create a niche at the margins of the movement within which they endeavor to cope with the internal tensions—tensions both within themselves and between themselves and the core elements of the movement—a situation which, although not easy, seems to them to be more palatable than the apostate role.

Marginal members may be more or less frank with core members, with ex-members, and/or with non-members about their feelings toward the movement and the wider society; and while those at the very margins may continue to be considered core members by some, they may come to be thought of as fringe members by others, and even as ex-members by yet others. Indeed, their own estimation about their position vis à vis the movement could be crystal clear or incredibly muddled and uncertain. The ambiguity of their evaluation of the movement is usually matched by the ambivalence of their feelings toward it.

Thus, the personal, and largely private, narrative of the marginal member differs both from that of the true-believing member at the center of the movement and from that of the true-believing apostate in association with the anti-cult movement, whose narratives give relatively unambiguous—although mirror image—accounts which rarely entertain such phrases as "on the one hand . . . ," "however," or "nonetheless." But unless they make an unambiguous statement that they are no longer members, or the hierarchy decides to ask them to leave, marginal members usually appear to be treated and to act in public as though they were still core members. They are not contained at a sanctioned distance, as are peripheral members; nor have they distanced themselves by exiting as an apostate. By no means do all core members "live in" and/or work for their movement, but in NRMs where that is the norm, marginal members are almost as likely as core members to do so. In situations where there is a choice for core members, the marginal member is more likely to live and/or work "outside," although this is not always the case. They will certainly have a much better idea about what has gone on, and is going on, within the movement than have most peripheral members—or even, in some cases, core members.

As mentioned earlier, one possibility for members whose commitment is wavering is for them to move to the status of peripheral membership, and this is certainly an option that has been taken up by several members of The Family who no longer felt that they could lead a life of demanding and sacrificial total commitment. But by no means all marginals are attracted to this option, for it is not necessarily, or even usually, a desire for less involvement or less commitment that is leading them to question the movement. As marginals they may believe that the peripheral has the worst of both worlds, being betwixt and between, without the benefits of either full membership or full detachment.

It could be argued that there is an ideal-typical personality difference to be found between those who spend some time as a core member of a Type III movement and then become marginals and those who end up as peripheral members. Like most of their friends who are still in the movement (or who have left altogether), the marginal is more likely to be a "strong believer" type. While the peripheral member may be characterized as being generally positive, but less than fully committed about *all* aspects of the movement, the marginal may have a divided heart, but each half will be strongly committed—one-half "Against Us" and the other "For Us" and/or "Against Them."[6] While peripheral members are likely to have an identity that is, to some extent at least, independent of the movement, marginal members are more likely to feel their identity is still intimately tied to the movement. This might seem paradoxical when marginals are characterized as more critical of the NRM than are the majority of peripheral members. If, however, we recognise that many apostates, especially those who have strong connections with the anti-cult movement, would also seem to be defining themselves *in relation to* the NRM—albeit in a negative, oppositional relationship—the situation of marginal members does not appear so strange.

So far as I am aware, there has not yet been any systematic study of marginal members—possibly because many of them are not easily identifiable. From my own studies, however, if I had to hazard one characteristic that might help me to distinguish marginals (or potential marginals) from hard-core members on the one hand and apostates on the other, it would be their sense of humor. Not that all marginals have a strongly developed sense of humor, or that core members and ex-members have none, but, taken as a whole, I suspect that one will find more clowning, jokes, quips, and laughter in marginal circles than in other parts of "the cult scene." And this is not, perhaps, surprising when one considers that a sense of humor can be associated with a sense of irreverence, and with an ability to look around corners, recognizing the familiar in the unfamiliar and the ridiculous in the familiar. Related to that is an ability to tolerate and even celebrate paradox and to distance oneself from the safety of psychological certainties.

Two further points might be made: First, humor can be a valuable means of survival in a situation where "straight talk" is dangerous for the individual. To say what one thinks in an exaggerated form with a smile can relieve personal frustrations without being taken too seriously. The Fool is a classic role in which it is permitted to air what could lead to expulsion or worse were it said by others. But humor can also be a dangerous political weapon to wield against a movement that takes itself too seriously. Jokes can undermine authority and lead to a questioning of that which is held to be sacred. Both the Fool and the Type III organization need to take the two-edged sword of humor pretty seriously.

ISOLATED INDIVIDUALS, GROUP, AND NETWORK DYNAMICS

Thus far, the discussion has focused on some of the pushes and pulls operating on individuals who move to the boundaries of Type III NRMs. The fact that these are "Subversive organizations" in tension with the surrounding environment means that the movements frequently exhibit certain characteristics which can enable us to understand further the social processes that affect the development of the marginal status—and how such a development will, in turn, affect the dynamics of the organization as a whole.

Although the theme of this chapter is to question the myth that there is always a clear-cut distinction between members and non-members of movements which are in tension with their social environment, it is not being denied—indeed, it is undoubtedly true—that much of the rhetoric of the movements proclaims that the distinction exists, and that the membership forms a group which is separated from the rest of society by a strong, unambiguous boundary, and that differences within the group and any variety which might exist in the outside society fade into insignificance *when membership or non-membership is under consideration.*

"We," the insiders, are assumed to be homogeneously good and godly, while "they," the inhabitants of the wider society, are assumed to be homogeneously bad, satanic, and "other." The tension is, moreover, kept aflame by the fact that the movement's opponents, particularly the popular media and those associated with the anti-cult movement, have a similar image of the movement, except that they see *it* as being on the evil and/or satanic side of the boundary while they themselves are the good and/or godly "us."

The greater the tension with the outside, the more the internal diversity needs to be controlled. Not only will a clear distinction be made between members and non-members, keeping the two socially as well as definitionally separate, but a number of devices will be employed to prevent the development of close ties between members—even in movements where the rhetoric is that of close and equal relationships between the "brothers" and "sisters" of a united religious or spiritual family. It is not unusual for the movements to impede the establishment of close bonds between a husband and wife. Constant mobility—both geographical and social—also militates against the development of close friendships.

The movements tend, moreover, to promote a mass culture, in which only commonly shared knowledge (beliefs, opinions, and practices) initiating from, and approved by, the leadership can be expressed. At the apex of the hierarchy, Type III NRMs frequently have a leader who is wielding charismatic authority and who is, thereby, granted the right to tell his (occasionally her) followers what to think and what to do. Although it is rare, completely successful, charismatic authority carries considerably more sway and covers considerably more aspects of the followers' lives than do other types of authority—but any type of authority is, by definition, power (the ability to get others to do what one wants) that is legitimate in the eyes of those subservient to the power. In some disturbing experiments involving the apparent application of electrical shocks, Stanley Milgram (1974) demonstrated how an authority figure can convince a not inconsiderable minority of people that they should agree to do things which they would not dream of doing on their own account.

The culture constantly reinforces the positive aspects of the movement while emphasizing the negative aspects of the external social environment. Any questions and complaints from members about what goes on within the movement are publicly interpreted as evidence that it is the questioner/complainer, not the movement, who is in the wrong—thus both deterring individuals who might see things differently from voicing their own opinion, and leading them to doubt their own perception in the face of an apparently unanimous verity. Solomon Asch (1959) has demonstrated how frequently people will agree to judgements about which there seems to be group consensus, when they would have come to a quite different decision had they not been subjected to the group judgement. He found that, under perfectly "normal" conditions, peer pressure could lead about one-third of his subjects to suppress their independent evaluations, sometimes coming to doubt the evidence of their own eyes. This was most likely to occur when there appeared to be *no one* who shared the subject's perception. If, however, there was even one other person disagreeing with the group, then the influence of the majority verdict all but evaporated.

Control is further enforced in the form of a hierarchical structure with communication and authority being mediated vertically so that each individual relates mainly to others who are clearly defined as being in a position of superiority or inferiority—and who are, thereby, socially distanced. The concentration of this patterning of relationships between unequal inferiors and superiors (what Unificationists refer to as Cain and Abel relationships), and the imposition of a milieu in which only the group ethos can be safely voiced, means that there is a *relative absence of networking*—that is, individuals relating to each other on a *horizontal* level according to their *own* particular interests.

"Pioneer" marginals will, thus, tend to be isolated from each other. Sometimes married couples, or two or three very close friends, may risk sharing confidences and relocate themselves at the margins together, but, at least in the early stages of a movement, it is relatively rare for first-generation members to migrate from the core to the margins as part of a group—they are much more likely to move by themselves; the decision will be a personal one; and it will probably be a lonely decision too, for they will find it difficult to identify others who have similar doubts—and one marginal's questions are not necessarily those of another marginal.

But the rhetoric, definitions, structure, and culture projected by the hierarchy have a certain fragility. Just as the so-called mind-control techniques are not nearly as effective as the movements' opponents claim and as the movements would undoubtedly like (Barker 1989, ch. 2), so the suppression of a relatively independent and uncontrolled system of relationships between members is not as effective as the leadership would wish. If (as is almost bound to be the case) a sufficient number of decisions are made by semi-disaffected individuals to move away from the core, the marginals can begin to recognize each other as such, and they will start to exchange experiences, doubts, and hopes. At first these exchanges will be tentative, on a one-to-one basis, but eventually the marginal members can develop a network of people sharing a number of common interests.

Thus it is at the margins, rather than at the core of the movement, that a network is most likely to develop—it emerges through the patterned interactions of individuals who have distanced themselves from the core of the movement and who are looking for relationships that are not filtered through the official authority structure, and for a definition of a reality that is, at times at least, at odds with that promulgated by the leadership.

It is in the very nature of a network that, unlike a group held together by a clear boundary, a mass culture, and a hierarchical structure, it does not interact as a corporate entity. The network is a system of relationships in which individuals, on their own behalf, interact with other individuals. But a network of marginals cannot exist on its own, in a vacuum. It needs to be connected with others—core members, peripheral members, ex-members, and non-members—who act as resources to feed the network with information that can reinforce or question both what the marginals perceive as positive aspects of the movement, and what they see as negative aspects.

First, without some kind of interaction between core and marginal members, the marginals could hardly continue to be seen as members at all. Some core members may be suspicious of individual marginals and treat them with caution, with a mutual exclusion of confidences; but others, while aware that marginals are not always in complete agreement with everything connected with the movement, consider them to be, in the final analysis, "one of us" and will not shun them in the way that the non-member or ex-member would be shunned. It is, moreover, possible that a long-standing member who has contributed much to the movement in the past is seen not so much as being owed something by the movement, but as worthy of being treated with a certain degree of respectful caution by the hierarchy, given that he or she may well be in possession of information which it is prudent to keep within the movement.

Second, the marginal member might network with peripheral members, and, through them, become more familiar with ways of thinking that are less "them/us" than those of the core membership. The peripheral members might also introduce the marginals to persons in the category of non-members. It may be, however, that the marginals have relatively little contact with the peripherals, possibly because the latter do not have the strength of feeling or degree of experience and knowledge that the marginal convert who has moved from the core has. In several ways they can see the peripheral members' interests as being peripheral to their own interests.

Third, marginals may have contact with ex-members whom they knew and with whom they have had close relationships. Although they may exchange information with apostates, it is unlikely that most of these ex-members would have a strong involvement in anti-cult activity, partly because anti-cultists tend to be uninterested in having any kind of relationship with members of NRMs (be they core or marginal members) except for the purpose of removing them from the movement; and partly because the marginal member is likely to be suspicious of ex-members who opt for the apostate narrative and deny those things which he or she still considers to be positive and worth preserving. Those ex-members with whom the marginal does have contact are likely to agree with much of the marginal's position and will help to reinforce this in their mutual creation and maintenance of a "plausibility structure" (Berger and Luckmann 1967). Furthermore, it is not unknown for ex-members to provide marginal members with material support that the NRM itself does not offer, or actually refuses, at times of need. It is possible to cite cases when, for instance, ex-members have given impoverished marginals money for medical expenses, or they have employed them in casual work, such as baby-sitting, house-painting, or secretarial assistance.

Fourth, marginals may develop relationships with a variety of non-members.

They may repair broken or severely strained bridges with members of their family. They may also rediscover old friends and start to relate to them as old friends rather than as potential converts. They may discover new friends through their childrens' schools, through working in the "outside" society, and various other avenues. Such contacts expose or reintroduce them to a variety of alternative ways of thinking and living as well as a number of alternative standards by which they can assess the movement's beliefs and practices. While such exposure can lead marginals to increase their questioning and discontent of the movement, it can also function to reinforce a belief that the outside world is not as godly, moral, pure, liberal, or attractive in some other way as is the movement.

A further, somewhat curious and novel, thread connecting the marginal network to the external environment is the relationship that several marginal members have developed with scholars who have studied their movement and who knew them, possibly when they were either true-believing or secretly questioning core members. It may even have been through talking to a sociologist about religion that some of the questions and doubts that had been suppressed (or, as one of my respondents put it, had been "placed in the pending file") were first taken out into the open and critically examined. Politically, the social scientist who knows the movement and yet is not a part of it can play a singular role as a "professional stranger" for marginals who are anxious to blow whistles without, on the one hand, being identified by the core hierarchy, or, on the other hand, giving material to the more anti-cult–oriented media, which could be more damaging than they feel warranted (Barker 1987). The full story of the ways in which social scientists get information from marginal members and act as independent variables affecting the fortunes of both members and NRMs is one that has yet to be told (Barker 1995a). Carter (Chapter 11 this volume) explores some of the methodological issues involved.

SECOND-GENERATION MARGINALS

One of the characteristics of *new* new religious movements is that the membership, almost by definition, consists of people who have converted into the movement. Thus far, it has been these first-generation members upon whom this chapter has focused. It should, however, be noted, that within a couple of decades of the foundation of any movement, it is probable that there will be a new generation of young adults who have been born into the movement. It should also be noted that there are several marked differences between them and those who had made the decision to convert from the "outside."

For second and subsequent generations, core membership is almost invariably a birthright. They will have been brought up with the taken-for-granted expectation that this is where their identity and, probably, their future lies. By no means do all those born into the movement share the strong commitments and passions of first-generation members—many seem more like peripherals in that their feelings about the movement are relatively undifferentiated and lukewarm. However, throughout most of their childhood and early adolescence, the question of their social identity is unlikely to have figured prominently among their concerns, even if, at an "outside" school or when mixing with non-members, they may have denied, or at least kept quiet about, their membership in the movement (for, let us remember, we are talking about movements which are in tension with the rest of society). It is true that there are new religions which, like many old religions, ask their children to make a personal statement of faith and commitment when they reach a certain age, and it is then that they will be admitted into full membership of the believing community—but they will always have been a part of the social group; their *rite de passage* is not "from them to us" in the way that the *rite de passage* of a convert will have been, and, unlike the marginal convert, their knowledge of living on the "outside" will not be firsthand.

Questioning or disobedience in which second-generation children indulge will be seen as being naughty, willful, or wicked behavior *within* the context of the movement, rather than as "satanic invasion," betrayal, or one of the distancing accounts that may be used to explain recalcitrant behavior by converts. Second-generation members are, moreover, unlikely to be expelled (although they may occasionally be handed over to a non- or ex-member parent or grandparent). There is thus a sense in which second-generation members can play at the boundaries of the movement in ways that are not available to those who have converted into the movement—especially during a zealously "them" versus "us" period.

While a sizable proportion of second-generation members will grow up to accept and delight in the beliefs and practices in which they have been brought up, and others will rebel and leave as soon as possible, there are also those who will move to the margins of the movement; but they are likely to do so by a significantly different route from that of the convert marginal, and the marginal structures and cultures within which they function will, at least in the early stages, also be different, for, while the first-generation marginals are likely to operate initially as individuals then, later, as a network, second-generation marginals are more likely to operate as a group.

Young people in all spheres of life typically confide in friends of their own age who have undergone the same or similar experiences; secrets from parents and other adults are commonly shared among children, who soon learn to identify informers and skillfully to avoid revealing confidences to the "tell-tale-tits." Unlike the converts, children born into the movement may thus be brought up with others with whom they can construct and maintain an alternative reality that supports subterfuge, questioning and, indeed, an undermining of the definitions of social and spiritual reality which are presented by those with official authority within the movement. When second-generation members do move toward the margins, they tend, consequently, to do so with trusted peers.

THE GROWTH OF MARGINAL NETWORKS

Marginal networks flourish more easily under some conditions than under others. Other things being equal, the more effectively authoritarian a regime is, the less likely it is that horizontal networking will prosper. The reporting of actual and potential dissidents, sophisticated techniques of surveillance such as those employed by Sheela at Rajneeshpuram (Fitzgerald 1986; Milne 1986) and numerous other well-documented means of control (Barker 1992), tend either to suppress overt expressions of dissatisfaction, or to lead to the disgruntled individual leaving the movement altogether. On the other hand, if a religion is sufficiently laid-back, it becomes difficult to see what is the core and what the boundary—not that this is likely to be a characteristic of Type III organizations in tension with the wider society; it is more frequently observed in Type I or II denominations and/or churches.

Further *ceteris paribus* generalizations might be made: Marginal networks become stronger and increasingly visible with the passage of time. Many of the changes that commonly take place in new religions create an environment in which the role, if not the officially sanctioned status, of marginal membership can more easily develop (Barker 1995b). As converts grow older, they tend to mature; experience results in initial enthusiasms being replaced by a more judicious outlook. As already mentioned, members of second and subsequent generations, who cannot easily leave or be expelled before adulthood, and who cannot easily be isolated from their peers, may move to the margins in small, self-supporting groups. Charismatic leaders die. If the movement expands in numbers and spreads geographically, authority has to be mediated through a number of different channels, some of which may not function in the manner ordained by the top leadership. And, as was suggested in relation to the introduction of peripheral membership, expansion may also mean that some kinds of compromise are made to recruit from a wider pool of potential converts than the original, more self-selecting pool.

Once a critical number of marginals are exchanging ideas that are not those accepted by the official hierarchy, others will be encouraged to approach them more openly than they would those who seem always to toe the party line; the "Solomon Asch syndrome" of fearing to be the only person out of step is overcome; it becomes progressively easier for closet marginals to "come out" and risk exploring their own doubts or questions, which, in turn, reinforce and/or become added to the bank of beliefs and practices that may be subjected to scrutiny. As the evidence accumulates that misgivings are not due merely to the ill-informed or subversive fantasies of ignorant or disloyal individuals, not only is a culture at odds with that constructed by the official leadership elaborated and refined, but further developments emerge to support the growth of the network. Semi-underground newspapers may start to circulate and, more recently, modern technology, particularly the Internet, is used to promote the exchange of views between individuals who are separated by thousands of miles—a far cry from whispered confidences exchanged in dark corners between individuals nervous of being seen talking together.

Of course, the development of marginal politics does not necessarily, or even probably, progress without numerous difficulties, and there can be serious reversals in the fortunes of an expanding network. The leadership is unlikely to suffer overt criticisms without some attempt to suppress or contain what it may (quite accurately) see as a growing threat to its authority and interests. Individual members may be expelled. The Family, ISKCON, and the London Church of Christ are examples of movements that have seen sudden and dramatic purges of those sections of their membership which were deemed to have strayed too far from the movements' ideals. *The Round Table*, a semi-underground newsletter which provided a forum for the exchange of views among dissident Unificationists, was allowed to flourish for a short period, but was put to sleep somewhat unceremoniously after too many members of the leadership had come under attack. Recently, the contributors from one country to an international Internet web site that entertains critical appraisals of Unification beliefs and practices fell strangely silent.

Nonetheless, as the alternative versions of reality are circulated, they become increasingly difficult for the official hierarchy to counter, and the membership becomes increasingly difficult to control. And, let it be remembered, marginal members do want to bring about change. They are not content to passively accept merely part of the movement and ignore the rest. They are, by definition, persons who care strongly about their movement. They care about and want to preserve whatever it was that they believed to be positive, and they care about and want to change whatever it is that they see as negative.

As marginals become more certain that their complaints are justified, they can be strengthened in their resolve to do something, individually or with others. Marginality becomes a unionized phenomenon. A new political arena has emerged. Sometimes it is internal pressure that is put on the hierarchy, who may make virtue out of necessity, adapt and/or introduce reforms. Members of the network learn from each others' successes and failures and a collective wisdom for dealing with some of the more intransigent aspects of the movement may develop. Corporate whistleblowing becomes a real possibility. Some marginals may now cross the boundary and formally announce themselves to be ex-members, maintaining the support of the network, equipped with resources and a narrative that they could not have obtained from either the core members or the non-members alone. Individual grievances can become a class action.

CONCLUDING REMARKS

The thrust of this chapter has been that disaffected members of organizations in a state of tension with their social environment are not limited to the alternative roles of, on the one hand, core membership or, on the other hand, apostasy. Despite the rhetoric of Type III new religions, their opponents, and, quite often, social scientists, there are usually at least two types of membership that fudge the boundary between the movements and the rest of society.

Peripheral membership offers a status officially sanctioned by the movement's leadership which allows persons not to commit themselves to the full rigors of the movement's beliefs and/or practices. Marginal membership is an unofficial position occupied by those who have misgivings about part of the movement's beliefs and/or practices, and who want to distance themselves intellectually and, perhaps, psychologically from the core membership, but are still sufficiently attracted to at least part of the movement to wish not to adopt the apostate role. The path to marginal membership of those who converted to the movement differs radically from that of members born into the movement.

The existence of both peripheral and marginal membership has a number of intended and unintended consequences for the individual and for the movement, affecting both its internal structure and culture and its relationship with the external environment. Marginal membership tends to give rise to an emergent, unofficial and possibly underground network of horizontal relationships which draw on a number of resources both within and outside the movement. The network creates and sustains a structure and culture that differ from and will, to a greater or lesser degree, be in opposition to the vertical hierarchy and mass culture promoted by the movement's leadership. Under certain conditions, it is possible for the network to play a political role both within the movement and in the movement's relationship with the wider society with considerably greater effect than the peripheral member, the lone whistleblower or, perhaps, the angry apostate.

Much more work of a comparative nature needs to be done on the development and consequences of borderline memberships of Type III NRMs. This chapter has been written in an attempt to point out that, first, their many-dimensional existence should be more widely recognized; second, the processes involved in their development should be charted in further detail; third, the role they play in providing a halfway house for disaffected members and creating changes in both the internal and external environments into which marginals may later move should be examined in considerably more detail. Finally, it is hypothesized that the roles of both peripheral and marginal membership can, but do not always, play a significant role in bringing the Type III organization nearer Type II or even Type I organizations; then, with a lessening of the tensions between the movements and the rest of society, there emerges a whole new set of dynamics within the politics of apostasy.

NOTES

I would like to express my gratitude to the British Academy for help with funding my research on changes in new religions.
1. These ideal types (in the Weberian sense) are drawn from firsthand empirical re-

search into a substantial number of NRMs, but it should be stressed that reality cannot be pushed into such tight Procrustean beds. Real-life members of such types frequently merge imperceptibly into another type, and many, many more subcategories could be elaborated. Given the restrictions of space, my aim here is merely to alert the reader to an aspect of empirical reality that does not seem as yet to have been sufficiently recognized.

2. Thus, members of the Unification-sponsored Professors Academy for World Peace may well be Catholics, Lutherans, Buddhists, or Jews and would qualify as "sympathizers," but not as peripheral members of the Unification Church itself; on the other hand, most members of CARP, the student branch of the Unification Church, would qualify as peripheral members.

3. The fourth circle consisted of DFers (persons who regularly received the *Daily Food* booklets, consisting basically of Bible stories and other "faith-inspiring stories").

4. The suspicion that TSers might pass on information to non-members, which is not without foundation, has been made explicit in some DO letters. See, for example, "Trimming Down to a Gideon's Band" ML #2527, 7/89, and "Loving Jesus" Maria #314 DO 3033 12/95 para 73.

5. An interesting case study is "John," who has now reached middle age, having joined his Type III NRM some 20 years earlier. He has worked full-time for the movement throughout that period, and has spent the last seven years in foreign countries, attempting to promote the ideals he believes that the movement stood for when he joined it, but which he now believes it no longer pursues. When talking to other members (be they core, marginal, or peripheral), he declares that he now considers himself to be a member of the Church of England. He is, however, adamant that his parents, who have fiercely opposed his membership of the movement, should not learn that he is no longer a core member.

6. The concept of strong believer is not the same as that of Hoffer's (1951) true believer, who embraces a complete package with a fervent devotion. The true believer is more likely to be a core member or an apostate. What is being suggested here is that it is possible for persons capable of a strong commitment to be "split" in their commitment. One way of trying to convey the distinction that is being made here might be to talk of moderate fanatics (peripherals) and fanatic moderates (marginals), but I do not wish to imply that the state of high tension between a Type III NRM and the surrounding environment is necessarily due to the movement having fanatic beliefs and/or practices—or indeed, that only fanatics join and leave such movements. It is possible to observe a variety of other distinguishable types of persons in the movements.

REFERENCES

Asch, Solomon. 1959. "Effects of Group Pressure upon the Modification and Distortion of Judgements." Pp. 174–83 in *Readings in Social Psychology*, edited by E. E. Maccoby, T. M. Newcomb, and E. L. Hartley. London: Methuen.
Barker, Eileen. 1995a. "The Scientific Study of Religion? You Must Be Joking!" *Journal for the Scientific Study of Religion* 34:287–310.
———. 1995b. "Plus ça change . . .". *Social Compass* 422:165–80.
———. 1992. "Authority and Dependence in New Religious Movements." Pp. 237–55 in *Religion: Contemporary Issues*, edited by Bryan Wilson. London: Bellew.

————. 1989. *New Religious Movements: A Practical Introduction.* London: HMSO.

————. 1987. "Brahmins Don't Eat Mushrooms: Participant Observation and the New Religions." *LSE Quarterly* (June):127–52.

————. 1984. *The Making of a Moonie: Brainwashing or Choice?* Oxford: Basil Blackwell; reprinted by Gregg Revivals, Aldershot, 1993.

————. 1983a. "With Enemies Like That . . . Some Functions of Deprogramming as an Aid to Sectarian Membership." Pp. 329–44 in *The Brainwashing/Deprogramming Controversy*, edited by David Bromley and James Richardson. New York: Edwin Mellen Press.

————. 1983b. "Doing Love: Tensions in the Ideal Family." Pp. 35–52 in *The Family and the Unification Church*, edited by Gene James. New York: Rose of Sharon.

Berger, Peter, and Thomas Luckmann. 1967. *The Social Construction of Reality.* London: Allen Lane.

Douglas, Mary. 1970. *Natural Symbols.* London: Barrie & Rockliff.

Fitzgerald, Frances. 1986. *Cities on a Hill.* New York: Simon & Schuster.

Hassan, Steve. 1988. *Combatting Cult Mind Control.* Wellingborough, England: Aquarian Press.

Hoffer, Eric. 1951. *The True Believer.* New York: Harper & Row.

Levine, Saul. 1984. *Radical Departures.* San Diego: Harcourt Brace Jovanovich.

Milgram, Stanley. 1974. *Obedience to Authority.* New York: Harper & Row.

Milne, Hugh. 1986. *Bhagwan: The God that Failed.* London: Caliban Books.

Nye, M. 1996. "Hare Krishna and Sanatan Dharma in Britain: The Campaign for Bhaktivedanta Manor." *ISKCON Communications Journal* 4:5–23.

Chapter 5

Exploring Factors That Shape the Apostate Role

Stuart A. Wright

Despite popular literature and lurid media accounts targeting highly sensationalized stories of rescued or recovering "ex-cultists," empirical studies of defectors from new religious movements (NRMs) generally indicate favorable, sympathetic, or at the very least, mixed responses toward their former groups (Barker 1984, 1988; Beckford 1985; Galanter 1989; Goldman 1995; Levine 1984; Lewis 1986; Skonovd 1981; Solomon 1981; Taslimi, Hood, and Watson 1991; Wright 1984, 1987, 1988, 1991; Wright and Ebaugh 1993). Indeed, high attrition rates have produced large pools of defectors (Barker 1987, 1988; Bird and Reimer 1982; Bromley 1988; Gelberg 1987; Levine 1984; Skonovd 1981; Wright 1987; Wright and Ebaugh 1993), yet relatively few go on to level scurrilous accounts against their former groups, finding careers as vocal, public detractors. This raises an important sociological question: What separates vituperative, public detractors from sympathetic, indifferent, or quietly disenchanted ex-members? Why do some leavers turn unfavorable experiences into a moral campaign while others resolve them with considerably less trouble and conflict?

There are important sociological variables that can help to explain these divergent response patterns. Other things being equal, former members of NRMs express varying degrees of sympathy or antipathy contingent upon selected social factors, indicating a more complex explanation of post-involvement attitudes and behaviors than is often assumed. In this chapter I offer a comparative analysis of the research literature on groups of ex-members or "exes" (Ebaugh 1988) examining the sympathy–antipathy dimension as a function of two sets of variables, divided into *structural* (role primacy, imputed cultural value of exited groups) and *processual* (mode of exit, location of new social networks). Herein it is argued that constellations of these key variables promote a richer understanding of the situated meanings, roles, and reactions of apostates.

DEFINING THE APOSTATE ROLE

Before proceeding, it is critical to the argument that a distinction be made between the typical *leavetaker* and the *apostate*. The *leavetaker* may be defined as one who decides to terminate his or her commitment and disaffiliate in a non-public act of personal reflection and deed. The decision to leave may involve different levels of anguish, equivocation, or strategy but the leavetaker does not assume a public role of hostile recrimination in the wake of departure. In the transition to a new role and status, the leavetaker effectively integrates the biographical experience of prior religious involvement into a larger, wholistic concept of self shaping one's identity. Indeed, the former commitment is often defined as a necessary or meaningful episode in the individual's spiritual and socioemotional development. For example, 67 percent of defectors from three NRMs in a previous study conducted by the author reported that they were "wiser for the experience" (Wright 1987, pp. 87–88). Similarly, Skonovd found that defectors from eight different NRMs reported successful academic and career pursuits, and many others "indicated that they developed a high level of self-control" which allowed them "to concentrate attention and energy on any goals they chose" (1981, p. 175). Levine (1984), who studied over 800 youthful converts to extremist groups, found that 90 percent left within two years of joining and used their experiences to navigate through a turbulent, post-adolescent identity crisis. "Most important," he states, "they (were) able to resume the sorts of lives their parents had hoped for them and to find gratification and significance in the middle-class world they had totally abjured. In short, they (were) able to use their radical departure in the service of growing up" (1984, p. 15). Jacobs' study of deconversion from NRMs found that in the initial phase of disengagement leavers experienced various emotions, such as guilt, fear, and anger. But during the reintegration phase ex-members "accli-mate(d) to his or her new independent status through the adoption of a more positive worldview in which the future is deemed exciting while the past is perceived as a valuable but painful lesson in life's disappointments" (1989, p. 120). Goldman also reports that the experience of ex-members of one NRM, the Shiloh communal movement, was "a critical influence" that was deemed both "positive and extensive" (1995, p. 351). She notes that "The personal importance attached to their past membership is underscored by the fact that most respondents (62%) would like to do something like Shiloh again" (1995, p. 347; see also Taslimi, Hood, and Watson 1991). In all of these studies, researchers indicate ways in which problem-solving strategies in post-NRM life are shaped by prior movement participation. Previous beliefs are reformulated, revised, and made to fit the defector's new social location and worldview, as well as provide a salient filter for fashioning a new life-course. While leavers may experience emotional pain or disillusionment initially, they often become reflective and philosophical about these experiences, and they are likely to accept responsibility and accountability for their choices. Generally, the leavetaker tends to fall toward the sympathetic end of the continuum.

The *apostate*, on the other hand, is defined as a defector who is aligned with an oppositional coalition in an effort to broaden a dispute, and embraces a posture of confrontation through public claimsmaking activities. In effect, the apostate carves out a moral or professional career as an ex, capitalizing on opportunities of status enhancement afforded the individual through organizational affiliation with the oppositional group(s). The post-involvement identity of the apostate is negotiated within the interactional context of a countermovement coalition and subsequently packaged for public consumption as the "wronged" person. The new identity serves to launch the new career of the moral entrepreneur who becomes engaged in a mission to expose the evils of the suspect group—one which features the characteristics of a "Subversive" organization (Bromley, Chapter 2 in this volume). The newly constructed role places the apostate in a position that is diametrically opposed to one's former beliefs and commitment. The apostate seeks to polarize the former and present identities, accentuating a personal transformation akin to conversion. Indeed, the intensity and zeal in which the apostate embraces the new moral vision, seeks atonement through public confession and testimony, and makes salvific claims of redemption, at least suggests that the ex-member's new affiliation may be analyzed as a type of quasi-religious conversion in its own right. Herein, exiting a deviant career to become an apostate is given meaning to the extent that social and moral distance between the two worlds can be maximized. It is typically characterized as a darkness-to-light personal transformation.

With regard to new religions specifically, apostates frequently develop an occupational or professional role within the anti-cult movement (ACM) as a deprogrammer, counselor, exit therapist, conference speaker, administrative officer, or some combination of the above (see Giambalvo 1992; Hassan 1988; Ross and Langone 1988; Ryan 1993; Tobias and Lalich 1994, p. 60), insuring a sort of institutionalization of apostasy. According to exit counselor Carol Giambalvo, "Exit counselors are usually former cult members themselves" (1992, p. 3). The industry of anti-cultism, spearheaded by key interest groups or movement organizations (MOs) such as Cult Awareness Network (CAN) and The American Family Foundation (AFF), attests to this institutionalization.

A better understanding of apostasy can be achieved by exploring our definition in terms of two constructs, *narrative* and *role*.

APOSTASY AS NARRATIVE

Captivity Narrative

For the apostate, one's previous involvement in a NRM is readily dismissed or discredited as a pseudo-conversion resulting from deceptive "mind control" practices. The account is formulated in a *captivity narrative* (Bromley, Chapter 2 in this volume) emphasizing the alleged manipulation, entrapment, and capture of the idealistic and unsuspecting target. Personality factors or defects may be identified as contributing to heightened vulnerability of some individuals, including dependency needs, unassertiveness, gullibility, low tolerance for ambiguity, cultural disillusionment, naive idealism, undiscerning desire for spiritual meaning, and susceptibility to trance-like states (Ross and Langone 1988, p. 32; Tobias and Lalich 1994, pp. 27–28). For the most part, however, the captivity narrative stresses the potent, *external* forces of group pressure, alternately called "brainwashing," "thought reform," "mind control," or "coercive persuasion" (Clark et al. 1981; Galanti 1993; Hassan 1988; Lifton 1961, 1985; Ofshe and Singer 1986; Schein et al. 1961; Singer 1979, 1986, 1995; Singer and Ofshe 1990; Zimbardo and Anderson 1993). With some minor variation, the captivity narrative follows a very familiar pattern. Carefully orchestrated, behavioral conditioning practices induce ego-destruction and overstimulation of the nervous system, resulting in a diminished capacity for rational decision making, radical personality change, impaired psychological integration, dissociation, split personality, and other mental disturbances converging to manufacture and sustain the pseudo-conversion. Personal accountability is excused since no exercise of choice or free will is made in joining. The new convert is held mentally captive in a state of alternate consciousness due to "trance-induction techniques" such as meditation, chanting, speaking in tongues, self-hypnosis, visualization, and controlled breathing exercises (Langone 1995; Ross and Langone 1988; Singer 1979, 1995; Tobias and Lalich 1994, p. 39). With trance-induction techniques destroying the individual's natural ego-defenses, and exacerbated by information control, language manipulation, confession sessions, demands for purity and group primacy, the cultist is reduced to performing religious duties in slavish obedience to the whims of the group and its authoritarian or maniacal leader.

Warfare and Hostage-Rescue Motifs. The captivity narrative provides a rationale for the *warfare* and *hostage-rescue* motifs, central themes in ACM ideology. Since converts are defined as psychological captives or "hostages" to cultist mind-control techniques, circumstances call for a "rescue" strategy. The analogy of Chinese communist brainwashing practices employed against P.O.W.s during the Korean War, and later by Russian communists during the Cold War years (see Lifton 1961; Schein et al. 1961) is frequently evoked in anti-cult literature (Clark et al. 1981; Ford 1996; Hassan 1988; Singer 1979, 1995). The hostage-rescue motif constructs the conflict between new religions and their detractors as "warfare," invoking the "discourse of war" (Wagner-Pacifici 1994) and attendant militarization themes designed to establish an image of an "enemy" with evil intent. Military symbols, speech, and metaphor are employed to describe the "battle" against cults, wherein cult members are seen as "enemies" of freedom, or the state, and cultists are inflicted by the psychological horrors of war atrocities and P.O.W. camp experiences—battle fatigue, combat trauma, psychosocial manipulation, isolation, sleep deprivation, and post-traumatic stress syndrome. Exit therapist Wendy Ford, for example, offers the following analogy to parents of ex-cultists: "It can help to realize that like a veteran returning home from a war, he has been somewhere you have not been, exposed to the horrors of a trauma you can only imagine. For all your years of experience, you have not been in his war" (1996, p. 1).

One frequently finds allegations of stockpiled weapons, boot camp conditions of living, military-like regimens of discipline, and other "totalistic" organizational features. Consistent with the framing of the conflict in this manner, NRM leaders may be cast as "terrorists," and cult residences become "compounds" or "bunkers." Agents of the countermovement coalition are cast as heroic warriors or soldiers, endangering their own lives to save the embattled hostages. Rescue efforts that require forcible intervention on the part of deprogrammers are conducted in covert-style operations, involving surveillance and infiltration of enemy camps, and typically entail abduction, kidnapping, and harrowing escapes from behind enemy lines in order to emancipate the brainwashed hostages.

The "warfare mentality," however, can be dangerous, because in conditions of war, the goal is to destroy or annihilate the opponent (Wagner-Pacifici 1994, p. 142). One of the psychological effects of labeling an opponent as the "enemy" is that it dehumanizes him and reduces inhibitions to harm or inflict violence (Grossman 1995, p. 161). In military training, psychological conditioning entails dehumanizing the enemy and contributes to the making of a more effective soldier in combat precisely because it reduces inhibitions to kill. According to military psychologist Dave Grossman, "If your propaganda machine can convince your soldiers that their opponents are not really human, but are 'inferior forms of life,' then their natural resistance to killing their own species will be reduced" (1995, p. 161). That is why during wartime, it is common to hear the enemy defamed by pejorative terms ("gook," "slopehead," "kraut"). This process achieves moral and cultural distance between the parties and heightens the likelihood of aggression. Perhaps the most dramatic example of how the warfare mentality has produced lethal and destructive consequences was the military-like assault by federal agents on the Branch Davidian sect outside Waco, Texas in 1993 (Wright 1995).

Not surprisingly, ACM efforts to cast the cult conflict in terms of warfare has resulted in numerous "casualties" involving harmful and illegal actions (Bromley 1983; Kelley 1977; Lemoult 1978; Robbins 1988; Robbins et al. 1985; Shepherd 1983). Recently, deprogrammer Rick Ross and Cult Awareness Network (CAN) were found guilty by jury trial of the abduction and involuntary deprogramming of Jason Scott, a Pentecostal convert to the Life Tabernacle Church, in U.S. District Court in Washington. The jury awarded compensatory and punitive damages to Mr. Scott in the amount of $4.9 million for violating his civil rights (*Scott vs. Ross et al.* 1995). In 1991, Scott was assaulted by Ross and his accomplices, wrestled to the ground, dragged to a nearby house, handcuffed, spirited away by his "rescuers" and thrown into the back of a van. Scott told jurors that he was pinned down by his kidnappers, his ankles tied with a nylon strap, duct tape was wrapped around his face from ear to ear, and he was told to "stop praying and shut up." The court upheld the decision in an appeal by Ross and CAN, and the judge stated in his 15-page order that the defendants' "seeming incapability of appreciating the maliciousness of their conduct towards Mr. Scott" made the large reward "necessary to enforce the jury's determination on the oppressiveness of the defendants' actions and deter similar conduct in the future."

However appropriate a warfare mentality is for the military under combat conditions, the same cannot be said of domestic conflicts in civil society. James Aho's insightful work on the "sociology of the enemy" is instructive: "With the subject of enemies we stand before what seems to be a form of collective psychosis" (1994, p. 12). According to Aho, the pursuit of an enemy arises out of the impulse to rectify a perceived violation of oneself: One typically justifies such actions based on a socially constructed sense of *victimization*. "It is primarily as a victim . . . that he understands his military posturing. Like those of people everywhere and always, his is a 'just' war, carried out in 'self-defense,' engaged in 'reluctantly' and only as a 'last resort' " (Aho 1994, pp. 11–12). Wars are rationalized as moral campaigns to erase "evil" and champion justice in order to conceal the darker side of aggression. The risk such campaigns take, however, is the "danger of becoming demonic oneself. For it can, if taken incorrectly, be considered an apology for moral relativism, nihilism, and ultimately for cynicism of the sort congenial to fascism" (Aho 1994, p. 13).

Apostasy as Role Behavior

Apostasy is also learned as a function of *role-taking*. It is important to understand that the apostate role has been carefully crafted as a part of the social structure of the ACM and it exists independently of any individual's incumbency. In effect, ownership of the role belongs to the organization. Consequently, the potential apostate must perform the appropriate role or "social script" defined by the organization. The social actor's performance then will be judged by his or her ability to remain faithful to that script.

Survivor/Victim Role. One particularly effective dramatization of the script by the ACM has been the recasting of the ex-member as a "victim" or "survivor" (Langone 1993; Goldberg and Goldberg 1982; Jenkins and Maier-Katkin 1991). The victim/survivor role shares similarities with the "sick" role analyzed by Parsons and others, and can best be understood in the context of a "medicalization of deviance" approach (Conrad and Schneider 1992). Parsons and Fox (1952) have noted that the designation of a person as "ill" changes the obligations that others have toward the person and the his/her obligations toward them. The sick person requires special treatment and becomes an object of compassion and welfare; a person to be "helped" rather than punished. Gusfield (1996, p. 175) observes that "The sick person is not responsible for his acts. He is excused from the consequences which attend the healthy who act the same way.'' Thus, deviance considered *willful* tends to engender harsher and more punitive reactions by society, while deviance in the form of illness or sickness tends to be defined as *unwillful*, generating more sympathetic responses (Conrad and Schneider 1992, p. 32). Parsons (1951) contends that there exists for the sick person a culturally available "sick role" which functions to conditionally legitimate the deviance of illness and funnel the sick into the reintegrating domain of physicians. For sickness, then, medicine is the appropriate institution of social control and physicians operate as social control agents.

Anti-cult therapists contribute significantly to the construction of the "victim" role for ex-members of NRMs. Paul Martin, director of an exit-counseling/rehabilitation center in Ohio, states:

In coming to grips with what has happened to the ex-cultist, it is quite helpful to employ the victim of trauma model. According to this model, victimization and the resulting distress it causes are due to the shattering of three basic assumptions that the victim held about the world and the self. These assumptions are the belief in personal invulnerability, the perception of the world as meaningful, and the perception of oneself as positive. The former cult member has been traumatized, deceived, conned, used, and often emotionally and mentally abused. . . . Like other victims of such things as criminal acts, war atrocities, rape and serious illness, ex-cultists often reexperience the painful memories of their group involvement. (1996, p. 3)

Michael Langone, in his book *Recovery from Cults*, compares "ex-cultists" to other "victims of abuse": "When they leave, for whatever reason, they will tend, as do victims of other forms of abuse, to believe that they left because something was wrong with *them*" (1993, p. 11). Langone lionizes the role of the anti-cult therapist as one who helps the victim come to understand his or her victimization (mind control) at the hands of a ruthless cult. "(E)x-cultists must be educated about the dynamics of cult control and exploitation, not only so they can recover from the adverse effects of their cult experience, but also so they will know what kind of help they require" (p. 11). Langone goes on to suggest that many ex-cultists are languishing aimlessly in the wrong kinds of counseling by well-intentioned but uninformed psychotherapists who do not understand the insidious effects of mind control. "Ex-cultists are not merely misguided or troubled seekers," Langone contends. "They are victims" (p. 12). Langone's implicit repudiation of conventional therapy and thinly disguised promotion of a specialized "cult counseling" accentuates the marginality of anti-cult clinicians. Robbins observes that "Such 'counselors' are usually not well integrated into professional psychotherapy" (1988, p. 93; see also Sullivan 1984).

Psychiatrists, therapists, and social workers form an important component of the ACM coalition since as "helping professionals" they provide lucrative counseling services to this population. The literature on exit-counseling is framed in terms of medicalization replete with terms like "recovery," "rehabilitation," and ''healing'' in describing work with ex-members. By casting the apostate as a ''victim'' of cult-induced mental illness, exit therapists and anti-cult counselors parlay their institutional authority and position into venues of social control over disfavored groups. The ''treatment'' of ex-members isn't simply a reintegration function for the sick; it is a powerful niche from which to wage a political campaign against NRMs; therapists become social control agents with private enforcement powers. For the apostate, alliance with respected institutional forces enables the disgruntled ex-member to transform personal grievances into a *social* problem.

FACTORS INFLUENCING THE SYMPATHY–ANTIPATHY DIMENSION

I now return to the initial research question raised at the beginning of the chapter: What separates caustic, public detractors from sympathetic, stoic, or indifferent ex-members of NRMs? In Chapter 3, Mauss (this volume) explores the identity construction and maintenance dynamics of apostasy. Here, I want to examine four factors that shape responses of leavers which are particularly relevant to our discussion of the apostate role. These are divided into *structural* and *processual* factors.

Structural Factors

Role Primacy. All of us occupy and perform roles in the social structure. In fact, we occupy multiple roles or ''role sets,'' juggling many responsibilities and duties simultaneously. However, some roles are certainly more important than others. We can refer to roles given highest priority in role sets as *role primacy*. Role primacy corresponds with the concept of ''master status'' around which we build identity, recognition, and power in relation to other statuses and roles (Merton 1957). Ebaugh (1988) has analyzed the extent to which the ''centrality of the role'' affects role exits. She found that since one central role is valued more highly and carries greater weight, leaving it has more devastating consequences. ''By contrast, other roles are more peripheral to self and can be abandoned with little personal trauma or sense of loss (Ebaugh 1988, p. 36). She cites Goffman's concept of ''role distance'' which denotes activities an individual performs with little emotional or psychological investment. Extending this idea, I suggest that role primacy is a factor in the development of apostasy. This holds true of both former and present role configurations of apostates. It is worth noting that even the new role adopted by the apostate is defined in reference to the previous one (''ex-cultist''), a revealing nomenclature which Ebaugh refers to as ''role residual'' (Ebaugh 1988; Wright and Ebaugh 1993). The term ''apostate,'' of course, is a designation assigned by others, not one adopted by the defector.

Before disengagement ensues, the individual's primary role or master status tends to be defined as strictly a religious one. One of the most common objections by critics of new religions has been the adoption of a singularly important, socially restrictive emphasis on the religious role by the devotee, to the exclusion of other roles and relationships, particularly those involving family and friends (Clark et al. 1981; Hassan 1988; Langone 1993; Ross and Langone 1988; Tobias and Lalich 1994). Some critics have even expressed concerns that the lack of diverse, heterogenous roles and interaction within the larger society impedes development of a healthy mental state. Indeed, the defining features of a "totalistic" religious organization are that it encourages exclusivity, separatism, single-mindedness, total commitment, and deep religious faith. Clearly, these characteristics are endemic to role primacy. Consequently, the extremely important value placed on this role makes justification of one's departure more difficult to manage, posing a dilemma for the social actor that other, less significant or peripheral roles would not. How does one explain such total immersion in a religious group if the individual has come to the conclusion that it was a mistake and that he or she does not wish to continue participation any longer?

Certainly, one way of resolving the dilemma and absolving oneself of accountability is to embrace an explanation of psychological manipulation and mind control that allegedly caused the behaviors in question. Assuming an apostate role serves a *restitutive* function, entailing a type of atonement or making amends for excluding and upsetting family members and friends. Studies reveal that converts' families and kin report a wide range of emotional wounds during cult involvement, including feelings of shame, guilt, rejection, abandonment, acute distress, and a sense of failure (Beckford 1985; Kaslow and Sussman 1982; Langone 1993; Markowitz 1993; Ross and Langone 1988; Tobias and Lalich 1994). Latent guilt for emotional pain inflicted on kin and significant others requires the offender to repay his or her debt. The rules regulating the "emotional economy" (Clark 1991) of the group (i.e., the method for dispersing the emotional resources necessary for maintaining connectedness) have been violated, exhausting the offender's "sympathy margin" or "sympathy credits." The failure to reciprocate to others' emotional gifts or concern breaks a fundamental rule in the emotional economy, according to Clark. Having accumulated a large amount of "sympathy debt" while absorbed in an exclusivist sect, the prodigal returnee will likely feel the weight of his or her sins and find it necessary to atone in dramatic fashion. In exchange terms, the social group demands reparation equal to the offense. Consequently, the disgruntled ex-member pursues the apostate role with the same vigor and intensity that characterized his or her former commitment. Although most ex-members of NRMs do not become apostates, we may hypothesize that the pervasive feature of role primacy in such groups increases the likelihood that leavers will assume apostate roles. Where affiliation involves less dedication, or more inclusive roles, it is less likely that violations of family and friendship bonds will occur. Hence, the compelling need to repair emotional damage lessens the likelihood of becoming an apostate.

Social Value of One's Former Group. Some role exits are more likely than others to find social support or approval. For example, becoming an ex-convict or ex-alcoholic are role realignments that society views favorably, signifying a positive transition to a more valued status or place (Cordilia 1983; Denzin 1987; Norris 1976; Room 1977; Trice and Roman 1996). Exits from a stigmatized role linked to social deviance—crime and illness—are lauded, signified by the terms "rehabilitation" and "recovery," respectively. Other role exits, however, rate low on the social approval scale (divorced person, ex-nun, transsexual), indicating passage from an acceptable status to a less valued one (Ebaugh 1977, 1988; San Giovanni 1978; Vaughn 1986). Ebaugh refers to this property as the "social desirability" of role exiting (1988, p. 39). The process of carving out an identity as an "ex" is highly influenced by the imputed social value of one's former group.

Bromley, in the introductory chapter of this volume, offers a structural analysis of this process. He suggests that different types of organizations or groups (Allegiant, Contestant, Subversive) determine how society will perceive disputes producing conflict and defection. Defectors' narratives find varied levels of sympathy or antipathy largely dependent on the degree to which they possess *legitimacy* (i.e., they are defined by other salient organizational actors as constituting the appropriate structural solutions to the functions they perform) and *effectiveness* (i.e., they possess the capacity to manage successfully the social relations within their spheres of authority). These conditions reflect the amount of social tension that exists between the organizational type and the surrounding environment or host culture. *Allegiant* organizations (medical/therapeutic, educational, professional associations) enjoy low tension with surrounding society, making disputes and defectors' claims more difficult to muster. The dispute settlement process is structured and managed by the organization autonomously, which gives it control and ownership of the problem. *Contestant* organizations generally include commercial businesses or enterprises which register moderate levels of legitimacy and social tension. Disputes that arise usually involve external third parties, such as regulatory agencies, that adjudicate competing claims and grievances. Contestant organizations do not enjoy the same degree of control over dispute settlements as Allegiant organizations, but because they possess considerable legitimacy, there is a strong tendency toward "dispute narrowing" and negotiated settlements that limit organizational liability. Disaffected members ("whistleblowers") may find some support in alliances with regulatory agencies because they are cast as reflecting public-minded spiritedness and community interests. *Subversive* organizations (NRMs, radical political groups, cultural fringe groups) share few common interests with other organizations in their environment, creating high tension and broad oppositional coalitions. These organizations have few allies, virtually no organizational legitimacy, and therefore face continuous opposition and social control efforts designed to suppress or destroy them. Dispute settlements are controlled subtantially by oppositional coalitions engaged in the process of "dispute broadening," analogous to deviance amplification (Hall et al. 1978) whereby human acts or events are made to seem more threatening than they really are. Opponents develop a countersubversion ideology (Davis 1960; Robbins and Anthony 1979), usually involving some form of conspiracy theory, that is constructed to legitimate expanded control over these groups. Opponents' efforts at social control are strengthened by alliances with apostates; the latter use the organizational resources of oppositional groups to air personal disputes and grievances in a more public forum.

Bromley's typology sheds light on how some types of groups—those that are culturally disvalued—are more likely to produce role exiters that fall toward the antipathetic end of the continuum. The imputed value of Subversive organizations is low, social tensions are pervasive, and oppositional coalition resources are readily available and enthusiastically offered to conflicted leavers who have disputes with their former groups.

Processual Factors

Mode of Exit. Exiting involves differing levels or degrees of *voluntariness* (Ebaugh 1988; Wright 1984, 1987, 1988; Wright and Ebaugh 1993). Purely voluntary defectors may be defined as those who leave without aid or intervention by oppositional forces. On the other hand, purely involuntary defectors refers to those who have undergone coercive deprogrammings. Early studies found the distinction between voluntary and involuntary defectors to be fairly clear because the options to intervention or extraction were confined largely to the method of forced deprogramming. Deprogrammings were more common up until the mid-1980s when they ran into serious legal challenges (Richardson 1991; Robbins 1988). These early studies revealed a marked difference between voluntary and involuntary defectors regarding post-involvement attitudes and responses. Defectors who left on their own were much more likely than deprogrammed ex-members to give reflective and sympathetic narratives about their former groups (Barker 1984; Levine 1984; Lewis 1986; Skonovd 1981; Solomon 1981; Wright 1984, 1987). Findings suggested that through the process of deprogramming, a mediated, packaged explanation (brainwashing) was adopted wholesale by deprogramees, accounting for sharp differences with voluntary leavers regarding the sympathy–antipathy dimension.

The issue of voluntariness became more complex as the ACM began to shift its strategy to less coercive interventions through professionalization, a process in which research and the roles of psychiatrists, psychologists, and social workers became more salient (Robbins 1988, p. 6). The development of the role of medical personnel as social control agents gave rise to exit therapy/exit-counseling, a non-coercive form of intervention (Hassan 1988). However, even these forms have been occasionally assisted by some coercive deprogrammings, and the degree to which intervention has been "voluntary" remains a subject of some debate (Wright and Ebaugh 1993). For example, some forms of exit-counseling take place only after disaffection or disaffiliation (Rothbaum 1988).

In other cases, the imposition of therapy is clearly foisted on the committed but unsuspecting devotee in a manner that belies the meaning and intent of the term "counseling" (Hassan 1988, pp. 123–24; Schwartz and Kaslow 1982, pp. 24–25; Tobias and Lalich 1994, pp. 60–61).

More recent studies indicate these differences still hold generally, but that the issue of voluntariness has become more difficult to determine. Disaffected or troubled members may agree to voluntarily speak with an exit-counselor. Other members report being pressured by their families to see an exit therapist. Still others report being surprised by an unannounced visit from a counselor/ex-member accompanied by a family member. There have been various forms of trickery or deception practiced by panicked parents or kin in an effort to dissuade the convert. It is not clear how most exit therapists feel about complicity in such matters, but it is certain that some find it necessary, even though they may have some reservations about the ethical implications of the practice. One prominent exit-counselor and ex-Moonie, Steven Hassan, gives the following account to justify complicity in a clearly non-voluntary intervention.

After a failed intervention, . . . (families) have two choices. They can back off, telling the member that they've done all they can. . . . Or they can choose to attempt a *covert intervention*. A covert intervention is the most difficult to accomplish successfully. It is an attempt to counsel the cult member without his knowing that the family is trying to help him re-evaluate his involvement. It is tricky to find a pretext for me to meet the individual and gain enough time to do much good. . . . Covert interventions involve deception, something I accuse cults of doing, which makes me uncomfortable. However, I am not trying to make someone into my follower; once my job of presenting information, laying out alternatives, and counseling is accomplished, it is up to the individual to make use of the experience. (Hassan 1988, pp. 123–24, emphasis added)

Hassan's account illustrates the problem in simplistically categorizing exit-counseling strategies as voluntary. Some aspects of coercion may be employed in so-called voluntary "re-evaluation" methods and rationalized or masked as a necessary evil. The defector may or may not be aware of the extent to which this cognitive "re-evaluation" can function as a rite of passage leading to the apostate career. The heightening of anxiety conveyed through deviance amplification and alarmist rhetoric in the dissuasion process may convince the wavering cult member to adopt a new identity and vocation. Unlike the defector who leaves without such benefits of "counseling," the apostate is afforded career opportunities through which redemption is achieved and a new purpose and meaning is found. If the individual has already defected in a contested exit, an alliance with oppositional forces serves the interests of both parties and one is less likely to find any elements of coercion in the exit-counseling process.

Location of New Social Networks. Studies show that social networks play an important part in both conversion (Lofland 1966; Lofland and Stark 1965; Snow and Phillips 1980; Snow et al. 1986; Stark and Bainbridge 1980) and deconversion/disengagement processes (Goldman 1995; Lewis 1986; Robbins 1988;

Solomon 1981; Wright 1987, 1988). Social relocation and affiliation with new social groups can provide a distinctly different perspective or worldview. The disengagement process is not complete until the individual is socially relocated and supported by a new plausibility structure that separates and insulates the ex-member from the previous role identity and belief system (Wright 1987, pp. 75–76). What distinguishes leavers from apostates is the type of social group or network in which the defector affiliates. Apostates align themselves with oppositional coalitions, which accounts for embellished counter-subversion narratives (Robbins and Anthony 1979) and the proliferation of "atrocity tales" (Bromley, Schupe, and Ventimiglia 1983). According to Robbins, "Some data on recriminatory testimonies arise from very specialized 'network samples' of ex-devotees who have become involved in a social network of deprogrammers, counselors, ex-convert support groups and 'concerned' (or 'anti-cult') organizations. Many ex-converts do not claim to have been largely passive victims of mind control. Those who *do* make this claim are more likely than others to have undergone deprogramming and/or to have had contact with counselors, rehabilitation groups, deprogrammers, ex-convert support groups, and organizations concerned with cult problems" (1988, p. 74). Apostate "support groups" such as FOCUS (Hassan 1988) and similar networks are described in Goldberg (1993), Goldberg and Goldberg (1982), Langone (1990, 1993), Martin (1996), Singer (1979, 1986), and Tobias and Lalich (1994).

J. David Brown (1996) has conducted research on "professional exes" who have exited their deviant careers by replacing them with occupations in professional counseling. Focusing on substance abuse counseling, Brown cites studies that show the majority of counselors in this field are former substance abusers. Building on Ebaugh's role-exiting work, he offers a four-stage process outlining the professional ex phenomenon, providing an analysis that is relevant to our study of apostates. The first stage in the process of becoming a professional ex is *emulation of one's therapist*. Brown states that "The emotional and symbolic identification of these ex-s with their therapists during treatment, combined with the deep personal meanings they imputed to these relationships, was a compelling factor in their decisions to become counselors" (1996, p. 441). He describes the development of an emotional bond between therapist and client as a process of "surrender" to the therapist who "enacted a powerfully charismatic role in (the) professional ex's therapeutic transformation. Their (therapists) 'laying on of verbal hands' provided initial comfort and relief from the ravaging symptoms of disease" (p. 441). Counseling as a profession came to symbolize a "sacred quest" for divine grace while counselors were seen as embodiments of the sacred outcome. Brown invokes Weber's (1963) theory of charisma to evaluate the counselor-patient relationship, suggesting that the therapist inspires absolute trust and devotion by virtue of special healing powers and knowledge. "Within the therapeutic relationship," Brown states (1996, p. 441),

professional ex-s perform a priestly function through which a cultural tradition passes from one generation to the next. While knowledge and wisdom pass downward (from professional ex- to patient), careers build upward (from patient to professional ex-). As bearers of the cultural legacy of therapy, professional ex-s teach patients the definition of the situation they learned as patients. Indeed, part of the professional ex-mystique resides in once having been a patient.

Professional exes are devotees responding to counselors' "proselytizations" as a promissory note for salvation and redemption. In this sense, Brown says that the clinic or treatment center is transformed into a "moral community of single believers" involving rituals and practices that sustain adherents' mental and emotional states.

Stage two of the process is referred to as the *call of the counseling career*. At this phase, professional exes recognize that "(b)ehaviors previously declared morally reprehensible are increasingly understood within a new universe of discourse as symptoms of a much larger disease complex. This recognition represents one preliminary step toward grace" and so professional exes "must dedicate themselves to an identity and lifestyle that ensure their own symptoms' permanent remission" (1996, p. 442). Assuming a career as a professional ex fulfills two functions: (1) it provides a context of moral meanings and structure from which to maintain a constant vigilance over potentially recurring symptoms, and (2) offers an outlet for redemption by internalizing as a moral mission the spiritual duty (counseling career) of helping both oneself and others. One's past experience as an ex uniquely endows the individual with special qualifications, providing professional and moral differentiation from other counselors whose therapeutic skills are merely mundane and ordinary. "Professional ex-s embrace their deviant history and identity as an invaluable, therapeutic resource and feel compelled to continually reaffirm its validity in an institutional environment" (p. 442–43).

Stage three of the process involves *status-set realignment*. Here Brown observes what I earlier referred to as "role primacy." Professional exes find that their transformed identity becomes the most salient in the status set or "role identity hierarchy." Role realignment is engineered in order to be consistent with the new self-image. "Association with an institutional environment and an occupational role gives the professional ex- a new sense of place in the surrounding community, within which form new self-concepts and self-esteem, both in the immediate situation and in a broader temporal framework" (1996, p. 444).

Finally, stage four is referred to as *credentialization*. While entry into a professional occupation usually requires specialized knowledge acquired at institutions of higher learning, the moral and experiential qualifications of the ex permit "legitimate claims to the 'entitlements of their stigma' (Gusfield 1996), including professional status. Their monopoly of an abstruse body of knowledge and skill is realized through their emotionally lived history of shame and guilt as well as hope and redemption secured through therapeutic transformation" (1996, p. 445). Moreover, challenges to their beliefs about how they or their patients should enact the rites associated with recovery are condemned since such challenges can be dismissed as "profane," emanating from the uninitiated. Here, Langone's implicit repudiation of conventional therapists who fail to understand the complex dynamics of "mind control" is relevant.

Research indicates that apostates are more likely to be linked to interventions such as deprogrammings or exit therapy. Giambalvo's observation that "Exit counselors are usually former cult members themselves" (1992, p. 3) is well taken. Like former substance abusers, most exit therapists and cult counselors are not professional exes. We can now add a more refined observation to the above statement: *exit counselors are usually apostates.* Consequently, when the mode of exit involves exit-counseling, therapy, or rehabilitation, connecting the ex-member to anti-cult social networks which operate as "moral communities of single believers," the likelihood of apostasy is increased. In effect, the exit-counseling enterprise functions as a charismatic community for re-socialization and therapeutic transformation, as well as a central mechanism for recruiting, cultivating, and promoting apostates.

CONCLUSION

This chapter advances several key arguments. First, it postulates that apostasy is a unique phenomenon constituting a distinct type of religious defection. The apostate is a defector who is aligned with an oppositional coalition in an effort to broaden a dispute, and embraces public claimsmaking activities to attack his or her former group. Unlike typical leavetakers whose responses range from indifference to quiet disenchantment, the apostate assumes a vituperative or hostile posture and pursues a moral campaign to discredit the group. Moreover, the apostate carves out a professional career as an ex, building vocational opportunities and capitalizing on grievances to enhance a newly acquired status. Other chapters in this volume, most notably Chapters 9 and 10, analyze the way in which the apostate role changes with the character of movement-countermovement conflict.

Second, it is argued that apostasy can be better understood in terms of *narrative* and *role*. The apostate, it is revealed, follows a predictable pattern or formula for post-involvement explanations of adherence to the disvalued group. This formulaic explanation is described as the "captivity narrative," which emphasizes the alleged manipulation, entrapment, and capture of the idealistic but unwitting target of sinister "cult" practices. The convert is held mentally captive in a state of alternate consciousness engineered though so-called "trance-induction techniques" (meditation, chanting, speaking in tongues, self-hypnosis, visualization, controlled breathing exercises). Trance-induction techniques work to diminish natural ego-defenses, impair psychological integration, and produce a "brainwashing" effect, reducing the cultist to slavish obedience, stilted affect, psychotic episodes, nervous breakdowns, delusions of grandeur, regression to childlike behavior, paranoia, and suicidal thinking. The captivity narrative also provides a rationale for the "warfare" and "hostage-rescue" motifs in which a discourse of war is invoked to describe conflicts between new religions and their detractors; cults are likened to P.O.W. camps and deprogrammings are cast as heroic hostage-rescue efforts.

Third, the argument is made that individuals are disposed to apostasy as a function of structural and processual factors. Structural factors include role primacy and the social value of one's former group, while processual factors include mode of exit and location of new social networks. *Role primacy* is endemic to totalistic religious organizations, diminishing other roles (familial, occupational) which, in turn, engenders conflict and feeds parental support of anti-cultism. As reparation for emotional damage inflicted on family and kin, the apostate role serves a restitutive function in the social structure. *The social value of one's former group* is a critical factor influencing apostasy in that different types of organizations determine how society will manage disputes involving disgruntled ex-members. Subversive organizations, such as NRMs, have few institutional allies, possess low levels of legitimacy, and face broad oppositional coalitions which diminish their control over dispute settlements. Thus, oppositional forces tend to be successful in dispute-broadening efforts that cultivate and promote the apostate role. *Mode of exit* refers to the degree of voluntariness in the disengagement process. Purely voluntary defectors are not likely to express hostile attitudes toward their former groups while those experiencing "exit-counseling" are more likely to become vituperative, public detractors. *Location of new social networks* is offered as a factor to explain the distinction between leavers and apostates. It is shown that apostates align themselves with oppositional coalitions which account for recriminatory testimonies. In particular, anti-cult networks operate as "moral communities," counselors perform priestly functions as charismatic healers, and the exit-counseling enterprise serves as a mechanism for recruiting and training apostates. Taken together, these variables explain heightened antipathetic responses of ex-members and account for the development of the apostate as a distinct social type.

REFERENCES

Aho, James. 1994. *This Thing of Darkness*. Seattle: University of Washington.
Ammerman, Nancy. 1995. "Waco, Federal Law Enforcement, and Scholars of Religion."
    Pp. 282–98 in *Armageddon in Waco*, edited by Stuart Wright. Chicago: University
    of Chicago Press.
Barker, Eileen. 1988. "Defection from the Unification Church: Some Statistics and Dis-
    tinctions." Pp. 166–84 in *Falling from the Faith*, edited by David Bromley. New-
    bury Park, CA: Sage.
————. 1987. "Quo Vadis? The Unification Church." Pp. 141–52 in *The Future of New
    Religious Movements*, edited by David Bromley and Phillip Hammond. Macon,
    GA: Mercer University Press.
————. 1984. *The Making of a Moonie*. London: Blackwell.
Beckford, James. 1985. *Cult Controversies*. London: Tavistock.

Bird, Frederick, and Bill Reimer. 1982. "Participation Rates in New Religious and Para-Religious Movements." *Journal for the Scientific Study of Religion* 21: 1–14.

Bromley, David G., ed. 1988. *Falling from the Faith.* Newbury Park, CA: Sage.

———. 1983. "Conservatorships and Deprogramming: Legal and Political Prospects." Pp. 267–94 in *The Brainwashing/Deprogramming Controversy*, edited by David Bromley and James Richardson. New York: Edwin Mellen.

Bromley, David, Anson Shupe, and Joseph Ventimiglia. 1983. "The Role of Anecdotal Atrocities in the Social Construction of Evil." Pp. 139–60 in *The Brainwashing/ Deprogramming Controversy*, edited by David Bromley and James Richardson. New York: Edwin Mellen.

Brown, J. David. 1996. "The Professional Ex-: An Alternative for Exiting the Deviant Career." Pp. 439–47 in *Deviance: The Interactionist Perspective*, edited by Earl Rubington and Martin Weinberg. Boston: Allyn & Bacon.

Clark, Candace. 1991. "Sympathy in Everyday Life." Pp. 193–203 in *Down to Earth Sociology* (6th ed.), edited by James Henslin. New York: Free Press.

Clark, John, Michael Langone, Robert Schacter, and Roger Daly. 1981. *Destructive Cult Conversion.* Weston, MA: American Family Foundation.

Conrad, Peter, and Joseph Schneider. 1992. *Deviance and Medicalization.* Philadelphia: Temple University Press.

Cordilia, Ann. 1983. *The Making of an Inmate.* Cambridge, MA: Schenkman.

Davis, David Brion. 1960. "Some Themes of Counter-Subversion: An Analysis of Anti-Masonic, Anti-Catholic, and Anti-Mormon Literature." *Mississippi Historical Review* 48:205–24.

Denzin, Norman. 1987. *The Recovering Alcoholic.* Beverly Hills, CA: Sage.

Ebaugh, Helen Rose. 1988. *Becoming an Ex.* Chicago: University of Chicago Press.

———. 1977. *Out of the Cloister.* Austin: University of Texas Press.

FBI. 1991. Advanced Hostage Negotiation School, San Antonio, TX, August.

Ford, Wendy. 1996. "The Role of the Family." *AFF News* 2(2):1, 3.

Fyfe, James. 1995. Testimony before Senate Judiciary Committee Hearing on Waco, October 30.

Galante, Jeri-Ann. 1993. "Reflections on 'Brainwashing.' " Pp. 85–103 in *Recovery from Cults: Help for Victims of Psychological and Spiritual Abuse*, edited by Michael Langone. New York: W. W. Norton.

Galanter, Marc. 1989. *Cults: Faith, Healing and Coercion.* New York: Oxford University Press.

Gelberg, Steven. 1987. "The Future of Krishna Consciousness in the West: An Insider's Perspective." Pp. 187–209 in *The Future of New Religious Movements*, edited by David Bromley and Phillip Hammond. Macon, GA: Mercer University Press.

Giambalvo, Carol. 1992. *Exit Counseling: A Family Intervention.* Bonita Springs, FL: American Family Foundation.

Goldberg, Lorna, and William Goldberg. 1982. "Group Work with Former Cultists." *Social Work* 27:165–70.

Goldberg, William. 1993. "Guidelines for Support Groups." Pp. 275–84 in *Recovery from Cults: Help for Victims of Psychological and Spiritual Abuse*, edited by Michael Langone. New York: W.W. Norton.

Goldman, Marion. 1995. "Continuity in Collapse: Departures from Shiloh." *Journal for the Scientific Study of Religion* 34:342–53.

Grossman, Lt. Col. Dave. 1995. *On Killing: The Psychological Cost of Learning to Kill in War and Society*. New York: Little-Brown.

Gusfield, Joseph R. 1996. *Contested Meanings: The Construction of Alcohol Problems*. Madison: University of Wisconsin Press.

———. 1963. *Symbolic Crusade*. Champaign: University of Illinois Press.

Hall, Stuart, Chris Critcher, Tony Jefferson, John Clarke, and Brian Roberts. 1978. *Policing the Crisis*. London: Macmillan.

Hassan, Steven. 1988. *Combatting Cult Mind Control*. Rochester, VT: Park Street Press.

Jacobs, Janet. 1989. *Divine Disenchantment: Deconverting from New Religious Movements*. Bloomington: University of Indiana Press.

———. 1984. "The Economy of Love in Religious Commitment: The Deconversion of Women from Non-Traditional Religious Movements." *Journal for the Scientific Study of Religion* 23:155–71.

Jenkins, Phillip, and Daniel Maier-Katkin. 1991. "Occult Survivors: The Making of a Myth." Pp. 127–44 in *The Satanism Scare*, edited by James Richardson, Joel Best, and David Bromley. New York: Aldine de Gruyter.

Kaslow, Florence, and Marvin Sussman. 1982. *Cults and the Family*. Boston: Haworth.

Kelley, Dean M. 1977. "Deprogramming and Religious Liberty." *Civil Liberties Review* (July/August):23–33.

Langone, Michael, ed. 1993. *Recovery from Cults: Help for Victims of Psychological and Spiritual Abuse*. New York: W. W. Norton.

———. 1990. "Working with Cult-Affected Families." *Psychiatric Annals* 20:194–98.

Lemoult, John. 1978. "Deprogrammed Members of Religious Sects." *Fordham Law Review* 46:599–634.

Levine, Saul. 1984. *Radical Departures*. New York: Harcourt Brace Jovanovich.

Lewis, James. 1986. "Reconstructing the 'Cult' Experience." *Sociological Analysis* 40: 197–207.

Lifton, Robert J. 1985. "Cult Processes, Religious Totalism and Civil Liberties." Pp. 59–70 in *Cults, Culture and the Law*, edited by Thomas Robbins, William Shepherd, and James McBride. Chico, CA: Scholars Press.

———. 1961. *Thought Reform and the Psychology of Totalism*. New York: W. W. Norton.

Lofland, John. 1966. *Doomsday Cult*. New York: Irvington.

Lofland, John, and Rodney Stark. 1965. "Becoming a World-Saver: A Theory of Conversion to a Deviant Perspective." *American Sociological Review* 30:862–75.

Markowitz, Arnold. 1993. "Guidelines for Families." Pp. 285–99 in *Recovery from Cults: Help for Victims of Psychological and Spiritual Abuse*, edited by Michael Langone. New York: W. W. Norton.

Martin, Paul. 1996. "Pitfalls to Recovery." *AFF News* 2(1):1, 3.

Merton, Robert. 1957. *Social Theory and Social Structure*. New York: Free Press.

Norris, J. L. 1976. "Alcoholics Anonymous and Other Self-Help Groups." Pp. 735–776 in *Alcoholism: Interdisciplinary Approaches to an Enduring Problem*, edited by R. E. Tarter and A. A. Sugarman. Reading, MA: Addison-Wesley.

Ofshe, Richard, and Margaret Singer. 1986. "Attacks on Peripheral versus Central Elements of Self and the Impact of Thought Reforming Techniques." *Cultic Studies Journal* 3:2–24.

Parsons, Talcott. 1951. *The Social System*. Glencoe, IL: Free Press.

Parsons, Talcott, and Renee Fox. 1952. "Illness, Therapy, and the Modern Urban American Family." *Journal of Social Issues* 8:31–44.

Richardson, James. 1991. "Cult/Brainwashing Cases and Freedom of Religion." *Journal of Church and State* 33:55–74.

Robbins, Thomas. 1988. *Cults, Converts and Charisma*. London: Sage.

Robbins, Thomas, and Dick Anthony. 1979. "Cults, Brainwashing and Countersubversion." *The Annals* 446:78–90.

Robbins, Thomas, William Shepherd, and James McBride. 1985. *Cults, Culture and the Law*. Chico, CA: Scholars Press.

Room, Robin. 1977. "A Note on Observational Studies of Drinking and Community Response." *Drinking and Drug Practices Surveyor* 13:17–22.

Ross, Joan Carol, and Michael Langone. 1988. *Cults: What Parents Should Know*. Weston, MA: American Family Foundation.

Rothbaum, Susan. 1988. "Between Two Worlds: Issues of Separation and Identity after Leaving a Religious Community." Pp. 205–28 in *Falling from the Faith*, edited by David Bromley. Newbury Park, CA: Sage.

Ryan, Patrick. 1993. "A Personal Account: Eastern Meditation Group." Pp. 129–39 in *Recovery from Cults: Help for Victims of Psychological and Spiritual Abuse*, edited by Michael Langone. New York: W. W. Norton.

San Giovanni, Lucinda. 1978. *Ex-Nuns*. Norwood, NJ: Ablex.

Schein, Edgar, Inge Schneier, and Curtis Barker. 1961. *Coercive Persuasion*. New York: W. W. Norton.

Schwartz, Lita Linzer, and Florence Kaslow. 1982. "The Cult Phenomenon: Historical, Sociological, and Familial Factors Contributing to Their Development and Appeal." Pp. 3–30 in *Cults and the Family*, edited by Florence Kaslow and Marvin Sussman. Boston: Haworth.

Scott, Jason v. Rick Ross et al. 1995. U.S. District Court, Western District of Washington at Seattle, Case no. C94–0079C.

Shepherd, William. 1983. "Constitutional Law and Marginal Religions." Pp. 258–66 in *The Brainwashing/Deprogramming Controversy*, edited by David G. Bromley and James T. Richardson. New York: Edwin Mellen.

Singer, Margaret. 1995. *Cults in Our Midst*. San Francisco: Jossey-Bass.

———. 1986. "Consultation with Families of Cultists." Pp. 270–283 in *The Family Therapist as Systems Consultant*, edited by L. I. Wynne, S. H. McDavid, and T. T. Weber. New York: Guilford Press.

———. 1979. "Coming Out of the Cults." *Psychology Today* 8:72–82.

Singer, Margaret, and Richard Ofshe. 1990. "Thought Reform Programs and the Production of Psychiatric Casualties." *Psychiatric Annals* 20:188–93.

Skonovd, Norman. 1983. "Leaving the Cultic Religious Milieu." Pp. 91–105 in *The Brainwashing/Deprogramming Controversy*, edited by David Bromley and James Richardson. New York: Edwin Mellen.

———. 1981. *Apostasy: The Process of Defection from Religious Totalism*. Doctoral dissertation, University of California, Davis. Ann Arbor, MI: University Microfilms.

Snow, David, and Cynthia Phillips. 1980. "The Lofland-Stark Conversion Model: A Critical Assessment." *Social Problems* 27:430–47.

Snow, David, E. Burke Rocheford, Steven Worden, and Robert Benford. 1986. "Frame Alignment Processes, Micromobilization, and Movement Participation." *American Sociological Review* 51:464–82.

Solomon, Trudy. 1981. "Integrating the 'Moonie' Experience: A Survey of Ex-Members of the Unification Church." Pp. 275–94 in *Gods We Trust*, edited by Thomas Robbins and Dick Anthony. New Brunswick, NJ: Transaction.

Stark, Rodney, and William Sims Bainbridge. 1980. "Networks of Faith: Interpersonal Bonds and Recruitment to Cults and Sects." *American Journal of Sociology* 85: 1376–95.

Stone, Alan A. 1993. *Report and Recommendations Concerning the Handling of Incidents Such as the Branch Davidian Standoff in Waco, Texas*. Report commissioned by U.S. Justice Department.

Strenz, T. 1979. "Law Enforcement Policies and Ego Defenses of the Hostages." *FBI Law Enforcement Bulletin* 48:1–12.

Sullivan, Lawrence. 1984. "Counseling and Involvements in New Religious Groups." *Cultic Studies Journal* 1:178–95.

Taslimi, Cheryl, Ralph Hood, and P. J. Watson. 1991. "Assessment of Former Members of Shiloh." *Journal for the Scientific Study of Religion* 30:306–11.

Tobias, Madeleine Landau, and Janja Lalich. 1994. *Captive Hearts, Captive Minds*. Alameda, CA: Hunter House.

Trice, Harrison, and Paul Michael Roman. 1996. "Delabeling, Relabeling and Alcoholics Anonymous." Pp. 433–39 in *Deviance*, edited by Earl Rubington and Martin Weinberg. Boston: Allyn & Bacon.

Vaughn, Diane. 1986. *Uncoupling*. New York: Vintage.

Wagner-Pacifici, Robin. 1994. *Discourse and Destruction: The City of Philadelphia versus MOVE*. Chicago: University of Chicago Press.

Weber, Max. 1963. *The Sociology of Religion*. Boston: Beacon.

Wright, Stuart. 1995. *Armageddon in Waco*. Chicago: University of Chicago Press.

———. 1991. "Reconceptualizing Cult Coercion: A Comparative Analysis of Divorce and Apostasy." *Social Forces* 70:125–45.

———. 1988. "Leaving New Religious Movements: Issues, Theory and Research." Pp. 143–65 in *Falling from the Faith*, edited by David Bromley. Newbury Park, CA: Sage.

———. 1987. *Leaving Cults: The Dynamics of Defection*. Washington, DC: Society for the Scientific Study of Religion.

———. 1984. "Post-Involvement Attitudes of Voluntary Defectors from Controversial New Religious Movements." *Journal for the Scientific Study of Religion* 23:172–82.

Wright, Stuart, and Helen Rose Ebaugh. 1993. "Leaving New Religions." Pp. 117–38 in *Cults and Sects in America*, edited by David Bromley and Jeffrey Hadden. Greenwich, CT: Association for the Sociology of Religion and JAI Press.

Zimbardo, Phillip, and Susan Anderson. 1993. "Understanding Mind Control: Exotic and Mundane Mental Manipulations." Pp. 104–28 in *Recovery from Cults: Help for Victims of Psychological and Spiritual Abuse*, edited by Michael Langone. New York: W. W. Norton.

Chapter 6

Apostates Who Never Were: The Social Construction of *Absque Facto* Apostate Narratives

Daniel Carson Johnson

Hear the tale of an on-again, off-again novitiate of the Hotel Dieu Nunnery in Montreal who, upon taking the veil, soon learned enough of deceit, debauchery, and murder to be repulsed from the Black Sisters forever—this was *Maria Monk* . . . or was it? Or listen to the story of Monk's contemporary, *Rebecca Reed*. She confronted less in the way of atrocity in the Ursuline Convent on Mt. Benedict in Charlestown, Massachusetts, but she spent enough time there—first as a novice, then as "Sister Mary Agnes"—to come away circulating scathing reports of the practices associated with convent life . . . or did she? Heed the voices of *Mike Warnke* and *Lauren Stratford*: some 30 years ago, we would have found Warnke officiating or Stratford participating in any of a number of secretive rituals conducted by the far-reaching league of satanists . . . or would we have? And weigh the words of *Alberto Rivera*. As the 1960s drew to a close, he was forsaking his Jesuit past and running for his life from the vindictive agents of the Roman Catholic Church . . . or was he?

The literature surrounding instances of apostasy is characterized by continual battles and negotiations over matters of fact. On the one hand, the works produced by high-profile religious leavetakers are riddled with accusations against the organizations that formerly claimed their allegiances. On the other hand, the religious groups thus defamed frequently respond to the claims levied against them with denials and contradictory claims of their own. Where they elect to advance their counterclaims at length, a protracted debate ensues over what really happened (in the particular case in question) and what really happens (more generally). As Bromley suggests in this volume's framing chapter, these kinds of disputatious outcomes are built into the very social structure within which the social form called "apostasy" emerges. They are what makes it necessary for us to speak of a "politics" when considering what might otherwise be construed as a purely personal act of religious leavetaking.

From time to time, the contests of fact that surround instances of apostatizing give rise to a charge that is truly arresting. It is a charge that the avowed apostate was not who he or she claims to have been "back then," and thus is not the authoritative voice he or she claims to be now. In some cases, charges of this sort are backed by a wealth of credible evidence, enough for most objective observers to weigh in with an opinion as to the verity of the tale the apostate told.

To be sure, this is not an area where sweeping judgments sit especially well. For their part, the practitioners of the resurgent cross-disciplinary study of "narrative" are quick to insist that the line separating fact from fiction in the life histories that individuals produce is never clear. Concern with getting behind the story to what *really* happened, they reason, is the residue of an outmoded dualism of subject and object, which must be abandoned if we are to see how seamlessly "narrative fact/fictions" envelop, transcend and, ultimately, *become* lived experience (e.g., Booth 1988; Bruner 1987, 1995; Denzin 1989a, 1989b; Plummer 1990). And even for those who resist following the epistemological paths down which narrative theory would lead them, the politically charged nature of the "apostatic" atmosphere is hardly one that lends itself to clear judgments of facticity. As Zablocki (1996) and Carter (Chapter 11 of this volume) demonstrate, the task of weighing the trustworthiness of the accounts offered by the various players in instances of apostasy demands painstaking efforts of triangulation—efforts that, for all their rigor, still often fail to yield a single story that an objective researcher can tell with any degree of certitude.

Nonetheless, in some cases the evidence is so strong that we can confidently conclude that the very starting point of the apostate's tale is a fabrication. In some cases we can conclude with a reasonable degree of certainty that we are dealing with "apostates who never were."

Not only *can* we reach such a firm conclusion; I contend that, analytically, it makes sense that we *should* do so. A science that strives to understand apostasy as a thoroughly social phenomenon has much to gain by recognizing the members of this curious class of apostates for what they are. Here we are confronted by a series of apostate tales that at their most critical junctures consist of little more than "tissues of falsehood." The presence of such tales presents a challenge to conventional ways of thinking about how political orders give birth to apostasy. They challenge us to consider the political structure of apostasy as something *generative*, something that does more than simply transform lived experience into apostate narrative. In this respect, these tales lead us at least part of the way down paths that we might not be philosophically inclined to follow, demanding a particularized version of the theoretical account that narrative theorists would have us apply more generally. For here we are compelled to consider just how much social dynamics can do to make an apostate of someone who never was, and who otherwise never would be.

This chapter represents at least the beginnings of an effort to do just that. I begin by taking stock of what is lost to us as analyzers of apostate narratives when we come across accounts such as the ones here considered: in short, the presumed rooting of the narrative in historical context or biographical experience. I then detail some of the commonalities of style that nonetheless mark these accounts. Finally, I close by identifying the common sociostructural features that remain to help fashion these narratives along the lines detailed, the constitutive elements of a political order that actively outfits suitable candidates in apostasy's narrative garb.

SEARCHING FOR A NARRATIVE ANCHOR

Anytime we treat the specific tales told by apostates as though they exemplified a distinctive genre of literature, we are assuming that the tales themselves are shaped by factors that transcend the historical particulars of the cases in question. It is only in light of such an understanding that efforts to identify the distinguishing features of the ''apostate narrative'' make any sense at all. Even so, the reader who wonders why a work that passes itself off as non-fiction ended up looking like it did is generally led (by sheer force of habit if nothing else) to weigh the historical particulars first. To the extent that the less case-specific structural factors enter into direct consideration at all, they are viewed as transformative elements rather than generative ones. The net effect that is attributed to them is simply one of their shaping the raw materials of the narrative along the lines that distinguish the broader literary form. As for the raw materials themselves, the presumption is that they have been fixed by historical circumstance. We shall see presently how this presumption manifests itself in conventional ideas about the politics of religious apostasy. Our more immediate task, however, is to demonstrate just how tenuous a presumption it sometimes is.

The reading eye tends to distill two basic components from the presumptively determinative historical circumstances of non-fictional work. On the one hand, there is a specific concern with the details of the real-life protagonist's experience. These elements of a ''biographical history'' are supposedly reflected in what is said of the narrative protagonist, who comes to life as the tale is told. On the other hand, there are the more general details related to the real-world actors and events that touched the life of the historical protagonist. Here again, the reports supplied in the narrative are supposed to reflect (and faithfully so) the particulars of this ''contextual history.''

When we consider apostate literature, however, we observe the potential for purportedly non-fictional accounts to wander from each of the historical anchors to which their readers seek to tie them. While we would hardly claim that the potential for this sort of thing is unique to the apostate narrative, some of what we observe within this literary genre *is* unique in that it approaches the limiting case. It stretches the membrane separating non-fiction from fiction about as far as it can be stretched. For what we find in cases like those of Maria Monk, Rebecca Reed, Mike Warnke, Lauren Stratford, and Alberto Rivera are apostate narratives that are somehow set adrift from the biographical and contextual histories to which they are supposedly tied.

Autobiographical Laxity

As far as the particularities of biographical history are concerned, we must acknowledge that the "deanchoring" that takes place with the construction of apostate narrative is a matter of degree. Apostate accounts are essentially autobiographies, and autobiographies are never perfect works of non-fiction. While we may recoil from the sentiment so starkly expressed by George Bernard Shaw in his own autobiography—"All autobiographies are lies. I do not mean unconscious, unintentional lies: I mean deliberate lies" (1969, p. 1)—there is no denying the fact that autobiographies consist of highly selective, idealized accounts of the lives of the people who write them. For the narrative theorist, it could be no other way: "When someone tells you his life . . . it is always a cognitive achievement rather than a through-the-clear-crystal recital of something univocally given. In the end, it is a narrative achievement. There is no such thing psychologically as 'life itself' " (Bruner 1987, p. 13).

This characterization applies doubly to apostate narratives, which are shaped by something more than just authorial vanity or constructionist endeavors. Beyond the authors' basic concerns that the tales told of them coincide with what Adams (1990) calls their "private mythologies," the autobiographical elements of apostate narratives are further shaped by a concern that the targeted religious groups be painted in the worst possible light. In this respect, every apostate account—even the tamest among them—strives to slacken the lines that tie it to its moorings in "real" biographical history. The only question is, just how much slack can they give themselves?

The case of Rebecca Reed is enough to demonstrate that things can at least advance to where the apostate bestows a new title upon her former self. A defector possessed of a genuine personal history with a given religious group embellishes that history with inventions both small and great. Eventually, she takes on a whole new identity, one not entirely foreign to her acquaintance, but nonetheless different from anything she has actually been. September 11, 1831 (the date of Reed's coming to reside at the convent) becomes August 5 (Moffatt 1835, p. 3); January 18, 1832 (the date of her departure) becomes sometime in February (Moffatt 1835, p. 4; Reed 1835b, p. 166); four months and eight days becomes "Six Months in a Convent." Of greater consequence, the young woman's repeatedly rebuffed pleas to be initiated into the convent (Moffatt 1835, pp. 11–13), become a series of flattery-laced conversations with a warmly embracing Mother Superior, who declares up front that Reed is destined for a religious vocation and "ought to make any sacrifice, if necessary, to adopt the religion of the cross" (Reed 1835a, pp. 54–56, 61–62). More important still, the exasperated Mother Superior's reluctant agreement to admit the woman into the conventual academy for a limited term as a charity pupil (Moffatt 1835, pp. 3, 14–15) becomes a hastily arranged reception into the nunnery as a novitiate, followed a few months later by a secret ceremony in which she takes her vows and dons the habit (Reed, 1835a, pp. 70, 124–25). In this manner, a young woman who spent a few months studying music from a handful of Ursuline nuns, becomes, according to her own court testimony, "Mary Agnes Theresa, Choir Sister."

Yet the drifting of autobiographical apostate narrative from the substance of biographical history can be even more pronounced than this. Sometimes it even goes "all the way," such that the apostate constructs a detailed personal history with the targeted religious group where there was once only superficial contact (if even there was contact at all). Each of the four other cases that we have mentioned falls into this more extreme camp. Monk (1836b) accounted herself an initiate into the Hotel Dieu Convent of Sister Bourgeoise, although there exists not a shred of "evidence that the author had ever been within the walls of the cloister" (Stone 1836, p. 26). Warnke (1991, and Warnke et al. 1972) claimed for himself high priesthood in the "Satanic Brotherhood," leadership of a 1,500-member satanic coven spanning three cities, and continual involvement in ritualistic sexual activities. Yet according to his college friends and roommates—who consorted with him nearly every day during the time period in question—about the most exciting thing Warnke and his crowd ever did was play croquet or, perhaps, dabble with a Ouija board (Trott and Hertenstein 1992). Laurel Anne Willson (1988) had her fictionalized self—Lauren Stratford—sliding into and then fleeing "Victor's" world of pornography, drug use, and satanic ritual sacrifice, all during years that Willson actually spent in the homes of her separated—but devoutly Christian—parents, in college, in the Rialto First Assembly of God (where she was the choir director) and, occasionally, in psychiatric counseling (Passantino, Passantino, and Trott 1989). Finally, Rivera (Chick 1979, 1981) claimed to have served as a Jesuit priest—specially charged with "destroying Protestant churches" and "bringing the whole world under the pope's control"—when all evidence suggests that he was all the time employed as a fare collector on the Canary Island bus lines and enrolled as a member of an evangelical Protestant church (Metz 1981; Pement 1981; Livesey 1991).

These cases represent something more than the efforts of individuals to rewrite their respective pasts. When social actors deal in apostate narrative, they are dealing in powerful shapers of present and future identities. For it is the stories that these people tell that confirm them in the role of apostate, and this is the role that defines them for who they are—sometimes for the rest of their lives. In this respect, Bromley has done well to remind us of Coser's suggestion that the apostate is one "who, even in his new state of belief, is spiritually living not primarily in the content of that faith . . . but only in the struggle against the old faith and for the sake of its negation" (Coser 1954, p. 250). This insight acquires new meaning when considered in the present context. If the apostate is one who, above all else, defines his or her present self by pitting it against a former self, then what we have in the cases here considered are instances where *absque facto* past identities are contrived to secure for their contrivers *de facto* identities in the present.

We could probably lay the present inquiry to rest right here if apostasy were solely a matter of narrative self-creation. We could simply lump apostates in with a broader class of social actors who strive to define themselves against the backdrop of fully fictionalized pasts—recalcitrant "bullshitters," fraudulent members of twelve-step groups, career confidence artists, and the like. More tellingly, we could catalog apostates alongside some of the other more clearly articulated exemplars of narrated identity—such as Denzin's "alcoholics," "recovering alcoholics," and "children of alcoholics" (1987a, 1987b, 1989b)—exemplars whose primary analytical purpose is to point the way to more mundane processes whereby *all* social actors tell tales of themselves, securing present identities and future careers by (re)constructing past histories. We could thereby content ourselves with explaining the apostate phenomenon with reference to the deep-seated need of some to "find" themselves in a world that offers them few avenues by which to distinguish themselves.

But we see in apostasy a thoroughly social phenomenon, one that is social in origin just as surely as it is social in outgrowth and implication. As such, the specter of the apostate narrative's emerging in the absence of a touchpoint in biographical history leaves us still wanting for a suitable explanation of where in the (social) world it comes from.

Artificial Contextualization

The next natural place to turn in the quest for such an explanation is to the second component of the historical circumstances that presumably shape nonfictional accounts—that is to say, to what I have called "contextual history." Here the prospect of finding a suitable anchor for apostate narrative is perhaps more promising than it was previously. There are genuine religious groups in the social world, groups that believe and profess and act, that grow and evolve and stagnate, that expand and shrink and die. In short, there are groups that maintain a tangible social existence, etching real histories into the fabric of social life. These histories furnish the requisite context for the telling of tales. To the extent that apostate tales are given to denigrating certain aspects of them, the mere presence of the histories may suffice to explain the presence of the tales. Seen in this light, the autobiographical element in the apostate account may be little more than an effective narrative device, and as such it may be grounded in fact or fiction; ultimately, the purpose of the account is to convey a contextual history, and here it must somehow resonate with reality.

Some of the arguments that the participants in apostate cases have made through the years dovetail quite nicely with the basic premise of this hypothesis.

Rebecca Reed's case has been especially singled out for consideration along such lines. In terms of length as well as of substance, there is really little to the story that Reed tells of herself in *Six Months in a Convent*. Each published edition of the original work, however, was prefaced by some "Preliminary Suggestions for Candid Readers"—penned by the "Committee of Publication"—and was anchored by a brief evangelistic (albeit rather insulting) "Letter to Irish Catholics." These texts turned out to be far more vituperative in tone than was the apostate account they bracketed, and they offered far more by way of argument against the "Romish" church, its practices, and its encroachment onto American soil than did anything that Reed had to say. As such, their insertion alongside *Six Months* led to speculation that the spreading of Reed's comparatively punchless personal tale was not the real reason for the publication of the work. Indeed, some of the principal investigators in the case went so far as to publish their suspicions "that the avowed design of the publication of Miss R's narrative was not the true one, but that it was to serve merely as a scaffolding to the introduction, and that the latter is the real book designed to write down Catholicity" (Moffatt 1835, p. iv).

This practice—whereby the specific tales told by an apostate were "fortified" by their placement alongside more general denunciations of the targeted group's beliefs, practices, and history—grew with the publication of each successive edition of works like Reed's and Monk's. Its prominence bears witness to the critical role that the construction of a credible contextual history plays in the reception of the apostate narrative.

It says nothing, however, of a supposed need for the contextual details provided in and for the apostate narrative to accord with historical realities. The "truth" of the apostate's narrative need only be a political (rather than an ontological) truth. All it has to do is resonate with what factional hearers understand to be the reality of contextual history, and this kind of "reality" is a constructed reality in its own right. So here again, given the apostatic urge to portray the targeted religious group in the worst of lights, it is to be expected that most apostate narratives will venture pretty far out into fictional waters when constructing their contextual histories. Once again, the only real question is "How far will the 'non-fiction' be able to stray?"

Here as before, the best answer is probably "farther than one might expect." Monk, for example, had her fellow nuns of the Hotel Dieu giving birth to, baptizing, and suffocating the offspring of their priestly trysts at a rate of two and one-half babies per nun, per year (Monk 1836b, pp. 194–96; Stone 1836, p. 32). Rivera had the Pope secretly supporting the jihads of the prophet Mohammed—in the hopes that he could move the Vatican to Jerusalem once the Jews were eliminated (Chick 1983, 1987)—at a time when the Western church was all but impotent, many years before it was even thought to recognize the Bishop of Rome or a seat called "the Vatican" as the locus of church rule. In each of these instances, the targeted group is itself defined, at least in part, by

the apostate narrative. The beliefs, practices, and history—indeed, the very identity—of the targeted group is reworked in keeping with the dictates of the social
form called apostasy.

Yet all of this only scratches the surface, for here as before we occasionally
meet apostate accounts that "go all the way," casting themselves completely
adrift from the details of a real-world contextual history. The accounts of participation in and escape from satanic circles are the most conspicuous in this
regard. What Warnke et al. (1972), Warnke (1991), and Stratford (1988) provide
as a backdrop for their respective tales is a vision of a vast, organized network
of satanists, united in occultic faith and murderous practice. On this score the
record is clear: There is no empirical evidence that would confirm the existence
of such a group (Richardson, Best, and Bromley 1991; Victor 1993; Nathan and
Snedeker 1995). There is no tangible evidence that makes a real-world presence
of the kind of satanic religious order that is needed in order for a real-world
apostate to apostatize. There is, to be sure, a popular history of satanism (i.e.,
a narrated history of satanism) and some of the points of that history probably
have some grounding in factual events. In its modern American manifestations,
however, the "Satanic Brotherhood" is not a tangible social movement. It has
no actual historical substance by which it can reach out and touch people.

What this means is that Warnke's and Stratford's apostate accounts, in addition to contriving autobiographical former selves against which present and
future selves can be defined, must build from the ground up the very religious
groups that they are supposed to be tearing down. The task facing them and
their fellow "satanism sellers" is nothing less than the conjuring of a contemporary social movement out of empty sociohistorical space. That their conjuring
acts meet with such success in some storytelling circles bears witness to the
power of narrative to generate the very realities of which it speaks.

At this point, both the specific biographical histories of individuals and the
more general contextual histories of religious groups have been effectually removed from consideration as generic sources of apostate narrative. What we are
left with is this: that something so flimsy and contingent as a story should be
responsible for the creation of complete selves—identities past, present, and
future—and whole sociohistorical entities. This is truly the stuff from which
post-modernist dreams are made.

There we may well be tempted to let matters lie, consigning ourselves to the
ideographic analysis of wholly contingent developments in a ubiquitous field of
power relations. Abandoning all hope of formulating general understandings of
the social structures surrounding the disjointed episodes of apostatizing, we
could let our analyses of the politics of religious apostasy devolve into analyses
of the micropolitics of religious apostasy. There we might be tempted to let
matters lie . . . if only the various apostate narratives exhibited anything like pure
contingency.

RECOGNIZING NARRATIVE COMMONALITY

Despite the apparent freedom enjoyed by apostate accounts in their dealings with the facts of social histories, we would be hard-pressed to characterize these accounts as being completely free to range where they will. Even within the class of apostates who never were, we find enough common threads running through their accounts to continue to speak of the apostate narrative as a distinctive literary genre. Indeed, it may be precisely in this special class of apostates that these common threads are the most conspicuous. Given the fact that the noise and static associated with historical groundedness have been filtered out of them, we can treat the signals that remain behind as ideal-typical manifestations of the commonalities of style and substance that the political structure of religious apostasy induces. That is to say, we can see in them evidences of deeper, structural congruities that suffuse the political contexts in which apostasy is generated.

As far as purely substantive commonalities are concerned, we have little to add to the analysis of apostate narrative that Ebersole provides (1988). The apostate accounts here considered accord with the other representatives of the genre in that they all follow the basic outlines of the "captivity narrative." The protagonists—acting in accordance with their own desires and without any foreknowledge of potential danger—follow the representatives of the religious groups in question into "captivity." There they are subjected to increasingly manipulative techniques designed to make them true followers, and for a time these techniques hold. Eventually, however, they "wake up" to find themselves isolated from all aid and subjugated to the perverse demands of religious leaders who have revealed themselves for who they truly are. Somehow, the protagonists are rescued or manage to escape. Finally, under the dramaturgical supposition that the real captivity in question is as much mental, emotional, or spiritual as anything else, the stories culminate with the protagonists' dramatic renunciations of their former beliefs, practices, and adherences.

The characterization of apostate accounts as forms of captivity narrative is familiar enough to students of apostasy that we have little to gain by detailing how our five accounts conform to the basic outlines of the form. Moreover, Bromley and Wright (Chapters 2 and 5) in this volume have already detailed how the political structure of religious apostasy helps to impose this form over the tales that apostates tell of themselves. In this context, the captivity narrative is seen as a structural provision by which apostates are relieved of responsibility for initially affiliating with subversive religious groups, shielded from any censure that may arise as a consequence of their decisions to leave those groups, and enabled to work their ways back into the ranks of conventional society.

This leaves us considering commonalities of style, and here too we may have little to add to the observations deftly recorded by someone who has come before. There may be nothing that we can say here that would provide as thorough an education in the stylistic distinctives of apostate narrative as would a close reading of *Six Months in a House of Correction, or, the Narrative of Dorah Mahony, who was under the Influence of the Protestants about a Year, and an Inmate of the House of Correction, in Leberett St., Boston, Massachusetts, nearly Six Months, in the Year 18___. With Some Preliminary Suggestions by the Committee of Publication*, the anonymously penned satirical rejoinder to Reed's work. Given the unfeasibility of inserting the full text of that parody here, however, we will have to be content with a few summary descriptions of the more conspicuous commonalities of style that mark the narratives of apostates who never were.

Defensive Posturing

From the start, the apostate narrative betrays a sensitivity to the possibility of its being contradicted. Both in the accounts themselves and in the materials that accompany them in publication, apostate narratives are marked by a singular concern with pre-empting any questions that may be raised regarding the facticity of the claims made. It is apparently assumed (and not without reason) that questions of this sort will arise as a matter of course, and the resultant effort to defuse them before they ever come up lends these works a distinctive defensiveness of tone.

The argumentative devices employed in this effort are quite diverse. In some cases, readers meet with forthright pleas for them to believe the accounts given. As Monk entreats her audience, "The narrative through which the reader has now passed, he must not close and lay aside as if it were a work of fiction; neither would I wish him to forget the subject of it as one worthy only to excite surprise and wonder for a moment" (1836b, p. 323). Such sentiments are most prominent in the cases that are focused on satanism, for the very task of exposing "Satan's underground" leads writers to adopt a relentless tone of urgency. In a more circumspect vein, there are often all sorts of simple attestations concerning the truth of the tales to be told (often complemented by references to the corroborative testimony of others). Here the "you just have to believe me" seen above is replaced by a simpler "trust me, what I say is true," as when Monk prefaced her disclosures with these words: "I have given the world the truth, so far as I have gone, on subjects of which I am told they are generally ignorant; and I feel perfect confidence, that any facts which may yet be discovered, will confirm my words, whenever they can be obtained" (1836a, p. 1). These sorts of importunate or plain-spoken protests of truthfulness suffuse the narratives here considered.

They are not nearly so prominent, however, as are the challenges that are continually set before the narrative's readers to go ahead and test the truth of the apostate's claims. Again, we turn to the example set by Monk: "I have appealed to the existence of things in the Hotel Dieu Nunnery, as the great criterion of the truth of my story. . . . I have offered, in case I should be proved an impostor, to submit to any punishment which may be proposed'' (1835b, p. 5). Repeatedly throughout the Monk affair, this same challenge was set forth: go into the Hotel Dieu, and you will see! It did not matter that distance effectively closed this option to the vast majority of the readers. The very fact that Monk, and others like her, were so insistent in challenging readers to scrutinize their tales in such ways was apparently enough to set some would-be questioners at bay.

Nor did the tellers of these tales need to concern themselves overmuch with the prospect of someone's actually testing the facts in the manners prescribed. In Monk's case, for example, it did not seem to matter that the testimony of those who actually took up her challenge to explore the interior of the convent had thoroughly discredited her on this very score. This is because the defensive posturing that characterizes these works is bolstered by a closely knit and continuously tended fabric of deductive reasoning, whereby concerns with the tales' *reliability* are allowed to supplant concerns with their *validity*. The elements of the more general contextual histories that accompany the apostates' tales constitute the bulk of this fabric. In effect, they enable the willing reader to assume the truth of the narrator's specific allegations, since they mesh so well with the myriad ''facts'' documented by others throughout the targeted group's history. The receptive audience can thus absolve itself of all responsibility to go out and test the allegations on its own, reading the apostate's willingness to have others test her allegations as nothing more than a proof of her sincerity.

Even when others do endeavor to discount the apostate's allegations, the fruits of their efforts can be readily dismissed. After all, is it not to be expected that the allies of the targeted group would act precisely that way, and all the more so if the allegations are in fact true (which, by virtue of what others have documented, appears to be a reliable assumption)? Given everything else that is ''known'' about the group, how much can the reader be expected to trust them or their ''allies'' to tell the truth in this case?

The actions of one of Monk's strong ministerial supporters—Dr. W. C. Brownlee—bear witness to the inescapability of this circle of deductively defensive reasoning. At one point, Brownlee was challenged to visit the convent himself by William Stone, who had, in fact, inspected the Hotel Dieu at length and was prepared to expose Monk and her compatriot Frances Partridge as frauds. Brownlee refused. Meanwhile, he remained entirely unmoved by Stone's testimony. Said Brownlee, ''I have as much right to call you a liar, as you have them. . . . In the same sense in which you say they lie, I may say you lie. You say they have not been in the Nunnery. I have a right to say you have not been there'' (Stone 1836, p. 45). So long as the narrative audience is allowed to keep questions respecting the validity of the apostate's tale on the level of competing truth claims, they are free to follow whichever version of the truth they will. The apostate narrative's repetition of challenges to test the truthfulness of specific claims, coupled with the general framework it provides for a wholly deductive mode of truth-testing, gives the audience just such a ''right.''

Reveling in Irrelevancy

Substantively speaking, the portions of the apostate narrative that demand and receive the most attention are those that somehow derogate the religious group with which the author was formerly involved. And yet reports of abomination and atrocity actually constitute but a small portion of the typical apostate narrative. Far more words are spent in these works reporting on minor details than on laying out and repeating the specific charges to be filed against the targeted group.

One factor that can help to explain their prominence is that apostate narratives are meant to be just that—narratives. They are not formal essays or expository compositions designed to lay out in systematic terms their authors' principal objections to the groups or practices under scrutiny. They are stories, and as stories they are to do more than simply berate and condemn; they are to entertain. As such, a fair portion of what is included in them is there simply for purposes of plot development or character development, or even for its pure entertainment value.

Even bearing this in mind, however, one cannot help but be struck by the welter of completely irrelevant details that get worked into these apostate narratives. On one occasion, for example, Reed enlightened her readers with the following account: "On one of the holy days the Bishop came in, and after playing upon his flute, addressed the Superior, styling her Mademoiselle, and wished to know if Mary Magdalene wanted to go to her long home" (1835a, p. 127). Neither the prelate's flute playing nor the evident playfulness of his relationship with the Mother Superior were ever cause for consideration anywhere else in Reed's work. And while not every example would be so striking, all of these narratives are marked by peculiar passages such as this, passages that are set off by the fact that they do nothing to advance either the plot or the plot's pejorative subtext.

They may do some things, however, to advance the cause of the narrative. For one thing, the shock value of the atrocity stories that do get told is clearly enhanced by juxtaposing them against accounts of the routine and frivolous. Treachery, debauchery, and murder appear all the more atrocious when they spring forth unheralded out of the utterly mundane. Beyond this, the attention paid to superfluous details may add to the illusion of the apostate's intense personal involvement with the religious group in question. Someone who recalls such trivialities, it may be reasoned, is someone who must have really been there. Clearly, this is an important affirming leap for the narrative audience to be able to make. So important is it, in fact, that the tellers of these tales are not always content to let their audience make the leap on their own. Instead, their readiness to recount trivialities is often bound up with the defensive challenges that they lay down for their readers. With each fleeting detail, the deductively defensive posture is implicitly (if not explicitly) reassumed: "See how definitely she mentions places, names, and events, and how fearlessly she opens the widest door to denial and refutation. She does not talk like the maker of a myth, but with the plain straight-forwardness of one telling a true tale'' (Watson 1927, p. 22).

I would suggest that it is in this latter effort to secure an audience that we find the great relevance of this characteristic reveling in irrelevancy. Indeed, I would go so far as to suggest that it is there that we find its very source, that we find where it first comes from. The exact sense in which I mean this, however, will not become completely clear until we begin to consider the roles played by various strategically placed actors in the construction of apostate tales. For now, we simply note the presence of this stylistic commonality and let it serve as another indication that there are perhaps deeper commonalities in the political structures that are responsible for generating apostate narrative.

Realization of Risk/Realization of Duty

To hear the apostates tell it, the acts of leaving their respective religious groups and exposing those groups' true natures were acts fraught with danger. At the time they undertook them, the apostates realized that they were inherently perilous—even life-threatening—undertakings. Nonetheless, they were things that the apostates simply had to do. As far as the actual acts of leavingtaking go, they found it impossible to endure their previous situations any longer. As for their decisions to tell of the atrocities committed in their former groups, they were occasioned by the growing conviction that they were duty-bound to say something. These twin realizations—of risk and of duty—represent the final stylistic commonality that distinguishes the apostate narrative.

The realization of risk is a critical component of apostate accounts in that it furnishes the requisite backdrop for the climax of the captivity narrative. Quite often, the "risks" discussed involve straightforward threats of bodily harm. Monk, for example, made her own physical endangerment the leitmotif for the sequel that she wrote to *Awful Disclosures* (1836b). Likewise, the second installment of Rivera's story was premised on his need to flee for his life: "After his salvation, Alberto is a hunted man. No Jesuit can leave his order alive!" (Chick 1981, cover). The risks described by those who left their satanic "pasts" behind them were similar.

Yet apostate narrative makes frequent mention of risks that are far less corporeal as well. One that surfaces occasionally is the risk to one's reputation, such as when Reed reports that a priestly acquaintance counseled her not "to break my vows to God and expose myself to the world; because, if I did, I should be ridiculed and laughed at" (1835a, p. 179). Another concerns the apostate's belief that certain courses of action may put him or her in spiritual peril: "I was occasionally troubled with a desire of escaping from the nunnery, and was much distressed whenever I felt so evil an imagination rise in my mind. I believed that it was a sin, a great sin, and did not fail to confess at every opportunity" (Monk 1836b, p. 197). Non-corporeal risks such as these are no less daunting to the apostates who report them. They are more than enough for the purposes of the narrative, which is to say that they are more than enough to make for credible moments of crisis.

Of course, moments of crisis cannot just emerge all of a sudden if they are to be credible. The narrative must build up to them. One of the most prominent stylistic conventions by which this requirement is met involves a studied selectivity in the revelation of secrets. Much of the selling power of apostate narrative is related to the promises it makes to reveal things that were formerly kept secret. And yet apostate accounts are never simple tell-alls. Even in those cases where the apostate "never was," and thus does not really have anything to tell, she must go beyond the simple fabrication and telling of secret things and must effect a disposition that there is much more that she could tell. Every related secret then helps to confirm the readers' suspicions that there were, in fact, "mysterious goings on in that group." Meanwhile, the repeated insinuations that there is more to tell whet their appetites for mystery even more. The net effect is a growing sense of foreboding, a sense of peril that builds as the realm of the (still) unknown is repeatedly pressed upon the reader's consciousness.

There are a number of stylistic conventions that are generally used to effect this growing sense of foreboding. For one thing, the apostate's desire to leave the group is generally introduced well in advance of his actually doing so. The interim between the first thinking of the act and its eventual commission is then laced with subtle reminders of the festering thought. Whether the reasons for the apostate's failing to act immediately on the thought are explicitly recounted again or not, the effect is to give the impression of a deepening urge to escape that is continually thwarted by a similarly burgeoning sense of fear. This impression is often further enhanced by the narrator's introduction of a parallel character—such as Reed's "Miss Mary Francis"—whose own soul-searching about whether or not to risk an attempted escape becomes the subject of secretive conversations. Finally, the very manner in which the escape sequence is laid out scribes a heightening sense of tension back upon all that precedes it. The successful escape is never something that is planned in advance. Rather, circumstances just arise that afford the apostate character a chance to escape. On the spur of the moment, he seizes the opportunity and, after a few feats of the sort readers expect of those who are fleeing for their lives, finds himself on the outside of a former life looking in. All of these narrative devices help to convey the idea that the apostate character was possessed of a mounting sense of danger that kept him from doing what he desperately desired to do, until something finally just "snapped."

The narrative potential of this growing realization of risk is not fully realized, however, until it gives birth to an attendant realization of duty, to a sense that the apostate character is duty-bound to reveal what she knows to the world. Again, the testimony of Monk: "the recollection of the dreadful crimes I had witnessed in the nunnery would come upon me very powerfully, and I would think it a solemn duty to disclose them before I died. To have a knowledge of those things, and leave the world without making them known, appeared to me like a great sin'' (1836b, p. 290). A moment such as this is an especially poignant one for the apostate narrative, for there several matters of grave concern to the narrator are intensified and made to intersect—to wit, the past, present, and future tribulations faced by the apostate, the gravity of the claims to be lodged against the targeted religion, and the motivations that might lead the apostate to lodge those claims. Thus are attestations to the effect that, despite all risk, the apostate has found it necessary to fulfill a duty to conscience regularly trumpeted in the apostate narrative.

Taken together, the realizations of risk and of duty seem to serve certain of the apostate narrative's more basic functions as well. Simply put, they serve to enhance the credibility of the apostate (and of the tale that she tells) while at the same time minimizing her responsibility for the mess in which she supposedly found herself.

RECOGNIZING THE POLITICAL STRUCTURE OF APOSTASY

The stylistic traits that we have identified—the defensive posturing, the reveling in irrelevancy, and the joint realization of risk and duty—are familiar enough to anyone who has spent much time sifting through apostate narrative. Indeed, they are so famliar that we may well overlook the question that their very familiarity poses: namely, where do they come from in the first place? What is there in the originary political structure of apostasy that makes the presence of these stylistic commonalities in apostate narrative so natural to us?

In answering these questions, it is not enough for us to point out the many ways that these common stylistic devices serve narrative purposes, as we have already done. While we might try to trace their origins to the conscious efforts of narrators to fabricate stories and effect a style of telling them that will be as believable as possible, two observations serve to undermine this kind of argument. First, the creation of a life history is always a collective endeavor, one that invariably involves joint action (Plummer 1990). This is one tenet of narrative theory that we would be hard-pressed to rebut. Second, it is exceedingly difficult for loosely bound coalitions to be deliberate in collaborating to deceive others. As the work of J.A. Barnes (1994) suggests, it is highly unlikely that a formerly unformed group will be able to get together and immediately set out to concoct the shrewdest fiction possible; there must be some mechanism by which the group allows itself to deceive itself first. And yet out of this, the stylistic commonalities of apostate narrative still emerge. So again we are left with the question: What is there in the political structure of apostasy that shapes apostate narrative so determinatively?

One part of the answer that social scientists have grown accustomed to providing themselves comes quickly to our lips: Apostate accounts must always secure for themselves an audience, and it is the audience—the dynamics involved with securing it and the feedback that it provides—that does so much to shape the accounts themselves. I am ready to accept this explanation in the present context, but in order to do so we must be prepared to undergo a profound shift in the basic mode of explanatory reasoning that we employ.

The argument presented by Bromley in his introductory chapter to this volume faithfully reflects what has been installed over the years as the conventional mode by which references to social structure are introduced into explanations of apostasy. It suggests that the mechanism by which sociostructural elements shape various aspects of apostate phenomena involves the simple insertion or removal of various structural facilitators or inhibitors. In this it is assumed that the basic precipitates of apostasy are always present in social life; all it takes is the right political constellation and apostasy will emerge as a matter of course. In Bromley's own words, all organizations are marked by "ongoing internal practices that would be contested if externally visible, disputes that could be the basis for revealing discrediting information, repressive responses, and resistance to control that create a pool of potential opponents, some rate of organizational exiting that creates a pool of former members potentially available for oppositional roles, and ambivalence about exit transition that potentially can serve as a motivation for opposition to a former organization" (Bromley, this volume.) Note all the potential in the scenario that Bromley describes as the routine condition of social and organizational life. Note also what it takes for all of this potential to be realized as instances of apostasy: "social conditions of high tension in which both exiting individuals and external groups have strong interest in mobilizing opposition to the targeted movement(s)" (Bromley, this volume). What it takes is a specific constellation of structure.

The problem that the cases of apostates who never were pose for this mode of reasoning has to do with the nature of the social constants that are supposed to generate this universal potential for apostasy. Here, in a nutshell, are the critical constants: real people—with real biographical histories—in real organizations—with real contextual histories. Yet these are precisely the things that are removed from consideration by the instances of apostasy here considered.

What this means is that we must be willing to argue a little more for structural variables than just that they either inhibit or release the ever-present potential for apostasy. We must be willing to say that certain political structures can do more than simply transform potential states into realized ones. We must be willing to say what the apostates who never were tell us: that social structures are actually generative rather than transformative, that certain political constellations can actually create apostasy out of situations where Bromley's apostatic precipitates are nowhere to be found. And then (here comes the tricky part) we need to be able to describe how it all happens.

Let us begin at a point that has already been suggested, by considering the role of audience in the construction of apostate narrative. Or to put it more precisely, let us begin by considering the role of a particular type of audience in the construction of apostate narrative. For our quest demands that we observe a crucial distinction between two very different apostate audiences.

On the one hand, there is the audience that is responsible for sponsoring the narrative account: Reed had her "Committee of Publication;" Monk had Theodore Dwight, W. C. Brownlee, John J. Slocum, Andrew Bruce, and William K. Hoyte; Rivera had Jack T. Chick; Warnke had "the Hotline" and David W. Balsiger; and Stratford had Johanna Michaelson and Hal Lindsey. In the public arena, the sponsorship of these individuals and groups means precisely what we generally associate with the term: standing behind the apostate and the tale that he tells. In this capacity, sponsors encourage the apostate to go public and furnish the means for him to do so—serving as ghostwriters, securing publishers, financing fact-finding trips or speaking engagements, staging the rituals that typically accompany the apostate's going public, adding extra-narrative materials that situate the story in a broader contextual history, etc. Needless to say, such services can be critical when it comes time for the candidate for apostasy to step into that role.

Even after the apostate's tale is made public, the sponsoring audience continues to offer support—vouching for the apostate's character, performing "damage control," soliciting corroborative testimony, and so forth. In fact, once the apostate's account is ready for distribution to the public, the sponsoring audience generally assumes effective copyright control over it. Their public backing of the account involves a substantial investment on their part, and they are understandably concerned with seeing that they receive returns on that investment. Accordingly, they go to great lengths to preserve the account that was made public. If a prominent member of the coalition should renounce the account, or if it should be discredited in some other way, the sponsors make every effort to rehabilitate it. In extreme cases, there is yet a more striking display of the sponsors' commitment to the story as originally told: Even if the apostate herself decides to distance herself from the tale, her sponsors may strive to keep the story alive. Their ownership of the copyrights extends so far that they can effectively deny the apostate her ability to recant.

The control that the sponsoring audience secures over the apostate's published works is no mean usurpation of narrative property that does not rightly belong to it. Long before the public sponsorship of the apostate's account there was private sponsorship, and in this connection it can be seen that the sponsoring audience actually co-authors the narrative, not as literal co-authors, but as an audience in the truest sense of the word. Here their sponsorship is not of a polished narrative ready to secure for itself a listening public, but of a developing narrative, one that they, as hearers, help secure in the first place. At its most basic level, this involves providing a contextual framework toward which the would-be apostate can orient his stories, as well as inducing him to do just that. Beyond this, it means listening intently as he weaves his tale, assuring him of its believability, offering feedback that notifies him when certain parts do not work, asking leading questions that help him fill in the gaps, and so forth. In all of this, the sponsoring audience plays a role that some in the circles of narrative theory have identified as that of the "coaxer" (Plummer 1990).

These sorts of efforts are the most critical tasks in the development of apostate narrative, yet all of them, I have argued, can proceed without open collusion between the would-be apostate and the audience that sponsors the developing tale. It all occurs without there being an explicit understanding that narrator and audience are conspiring to (re)construct the narrator's past. Unfortunately, it also occurs almost entirely behind the scenes, a fact that clearly makes it difficult for social scientists to analyze any of it. Nonetheless, were we to conduct an in-depth analysis of the dynamics inhering between apostate and sponsoring audience, I suspect that we would find explanations for most of the stylistic commonalities by which we have characterized apostate narrative.

For example, it is likely that the so-called "reveling in irrelevancy" that we observed is a residue of the occasions wherein the sponsoring audience listens to and affirms the apostate's developing account. It is during such times of informal self-presentation that the telling of trivialities and tangential details is most natural . . . and most important. These are the sorts of small stories that arise in the course of casual conversation—"I remember one time when"—and the ability of the would-be apostate to work them smoothly into conversations with would-be sponsors may do much to ensure the eventual acceptance of the whole of the account. Once they are firmly established as part of the apostate's repertoire, it is easy to see how they might work their ways into the public narrative, regardless of how awkward they may appear in that more formal context.

The twin "realizations of risk and duty" that figure so prominently in apostate narrative may have their origins here as well. In this context, they may emerge not so much in a deliberate effort to valorize the apostate or excuse his affiliation with the targeted group as in response to a concern that gradually presses itself upon the coalition as the apostate's tale begins to congeal: "Given the horrors revealed in this story, how can we explain our failure to tell people sooner?" Out of the ongoing, collective quest for narrative coherence, a suitable answer slowly works its way into the narrator's mouth: "Out of fear for myself and others, I simply could not 'go public' for some time; it is only because I have since come to grips with the duty that is incumbent upon me that I am able to do so now."

In these and perhaps many other ways, we can expect to find the apostate and his sponsoring audience unwittingly conspiring to construct a story that has all the stylistic trappings of apostate narrative. Contrast this with the comparatively minor role that the receiving audience has to play in the actual development of the apostate narrative. Put simply, these "readers," as Plummer (1990) calls them, need do no more than "hear and believe."

So much for considerations of audience. The final pertinent station in the structural spaces surrounding apostasy is occupied by individuals or groups whom we might label "truth-tellers." As the name implies, this class of social actors consists of those who take it upon themselves to investigate and separate what is "factual" from what is "fictional" in the accounts that apostates offer the public. For the most part, a social science oriented toward more typical cases of apostatizing has been given to conflating this group with the targeted religious group itself. One glance at the cases here considered is enough to show why such conflation will never do: There are no representatives of the "Satanic Brotherhood" stepping out to contradict Warnke, and to date, no one has ventured forth from "Victor's" haunts to expose the errors in Stratford's account. As it turns out, the truth-tellers who spoke out against these accounts were drawn from the ranks of those who were generally expected to occupy seats in the accounts' receiving audiences.

This is not as rare a development as it may seem at first glance. Even when we come to cases that do target a real-world religious group that can "stick up for itself," the role of the truth-teller as a separate participant in the political dynamics swirling about apostasy is still a prominent one. For as much effort as targeted religious groups sometimes put into the defense of their reputations, they reserve a special place for evidences put forth by those who are not on "their side," by those who, indeed, are actually part of the apostate tales' intended audiences.

This is seen most clearly in the "Catholics versus Protestants" cases from the eighteenth century. The defenders of the Ursuline Convent on Mt. Benedict took great solace in the fact that the Boston Committee—who had investigated the happenings there and produced a report that exonerated the convent completely—consisted of many of the most respectable citizens of Boston, Protestants all. "Fortunately in the case of Miss Reed," they commented, "we do not depend on Catholic testimony alone" (Moffatt 1835, p. xxxv). Similarly, in defending the Catholic church against Monk's charges, the first place to which the *Dublin Review* turned was to the "universal testimony of the Protestant press at Montreal." The *Review* commented that the denials printed in the Protestant papers were "of the most unqualified character; and as the parties from whom they emanated are, for the most part, politically opposed to the section of the population to which the priests belong, they are . . . the more valuable the evidence" (Catholic Truth Society 1898, pp. 18–19). Finally, the most prized bit of testimony that the Catholic press held up (and repeatedly so) in Monk's case was *Maria Monk and the Nunnery of the Hotel Dieu: Being an Account of a Visit to the Convents of Montreal and Refutation of the "Awful Disclosures"* (1836), written by one William L. Stone, Esquire (and staunchly partisan Protestant).

Needless to say, the motives of those who play this kind of truth-teller role are often called into question by the sponsors of apostate accounts. The most prominent charge laid against them should be familiar enough: "He who is not with Me is against Me." "It has been kindly hinted that I have become 'semi-papist,' and that in putting down the wretched imposture of Maria Monk . . . I have written a panegyric upon the life of the nuns," wrote Stone. *Cornerstone Magazine*, in the wake of the Stratford affair, reported that it had received numerous letters suggesting that since "Satanists and secular humanists want to disprove [Stratford's] story, the article must be a product of some sort of collusion between *Cornerstone* and 'the other side.' In fact, some even hinted that we were part of 'the other side' " (Passantino and Passantino 1990, p. 14). Charges such as these are immanent in the politically charged atmosphere of apostasy, so much so that truth-tellers tend to adopt their own distinctively defensive mode of argumentation when presenting their findings. It is a mode marked by repeated statements concerning the truth-teller's true religious loyalties and continual attestations to the truth-teller's commitment to remain dispassionate and objective.

Truth-tellers may have less cause to fear the explanations offered by social scientific observers who are less personally involved with these cases, but we too might be led to trace their behavior to something other than a pure desire to "get to the bottom of things." The extreme stories that apostates offer are potentially destabilizing. Where they receive a wide hearing, they promise to upset the tenuous "peace accords" that are sometimes achieved in the religious realm. While there may be genuine controversy and conflict between coalitions on either side of a given creedal divide, the dominant authorities within those coalitions generally have a great deal more to lose by failing to maintain some semblance of peace than they have to gain by allowing religiously inspired conflict to reign unchecked. As such, denunciations of an apostate's questionable tales are at least as likely to issue from what would be the tales' receiving audience as from the group that those tales target. Viewed from this structural perspective, it would seem as though the truth-teller is moved as much by a concern with preserving the prevailing order of things (even if it means "sticking up for" the targeted group) as by a concern with learning and speaking the "truth."

Yet, regardless of what motives we link with the truth-teller's actions, there is one thing that we can say for certain: The truth-teller's appearance on the apostatic political stage surprises no one. Far from being a latecomer to the social dynamics that generate apostasy, the truth-teller makes his presence felt from the very outset of the production process. Indeed, the very tone of apostate narrative—the very defensive posturing that so marks it—presupposes the truth-teller's existence.

The apostate's defensiveness of tone clearly represents a pre-emptive strike of sorts against the truth-teller, but it is also something much more than that. It is also an attempt to co-opt the truth-telling function. The logic of apostate narrative is such that truth-tellers come to be placed in a special, positive niche that gets carved into the apostatic order of things. Far from being simply the negaters of the apostate's truth claims, they come to represent the fulfillment, the perfection, the proof of those very claims. The reason for this relates back to what we observed concerning the distinctive mode of deductively defensive reasoning that apostate narrative installs for its willing hearers. Again, this mode of reasoning is such that the very act of denying the apostate's account is almost immediately transformed into a confirmation of those claims.

Seen in this light, the defensive posturing that marks apostate narrative appears as a series of moves geared toward provoking the requisite response from the targeted group's designated truth-teller and toward channeling that response in certain predictable ways. In a sense, then, the ends that apostates and sponsoring audiences associate with the publication of their tales are left unfulfilled in those cases where social actors are slow to step into the truth-teller's shoes. Where truth-tellers do speak out, by contrast, apostate narrative is made whole. With every voiced denial, the apostate's claims are repeated and reaffirmed for all who have ears to hear. With every counterclaim advanced, the presumptions of the apostate's sympathetic audience are confirmed anew.

Apostate narrative acquires an additional alarmist edge in cases where the truth-teller hales from the coalition from which the narrative was to have drawn its receiving audience. Such instances serve notice to willing hearers that they confront a danger that is perhaps far more insidious than anything found in the targeted religious group. That danger involves the prospect that advocates for the targeted group have infiltrated the circles occupied by the receiving audience. If such sympathizers are not secretly in league with the damnable group, then they are at the least prepared to defend it in any way they can (and this is just as bad).

And here we see most clearly what may well be the most important lesson that apostate narrative presses on its hearers. It is a lesson that the apostate, sponsoring audience, receiving audience, and truth-teller all conspire to convey: Beware, for the worst of evils lurk amidst the sacred.

CONCLUSION

I have suggested that any attempt to analyze the social construction of religious apostasy must make room for an analysis of the social construction of apostate narrative. For it is the stories that apostates tell—stories of captive involvement with targeted religious groups in the past and of rescue and redemption in the present—that confirm them in the apostate role. Moreover, I have suggested that those stories are not self-given, that they are, rather, socially constructed. Now at one level, this is an understanding that most every social scientist would surely allow. The tales that apostates tell do not consist of straight recitations of real-world happenings and experiences, they would argue, but are socially constructed insofar as those happenings and experiences are recast along the lines dictated by an established literary form called apostate narrative. But I have suggested that social scientists will need to take this understanding to a deeper level if we are ever to grasp more fully the social dynamics that make apostate narrative what it is. I have suggested that we will need to entertain the possibility that substantial portions of apostate accounts—

indeed, perhaps even entire accounts—have nothing to do with "real-world happenings or experiences."

Even if we are unprepared to accept this point on purely philosophical grounds, the empirical specter of "apostates who never were" leads us to recognize that there are cases where the political structure of religious apostasy has been responsible for generating stories out of mere "tissue." These are stories that are fully recognizable as apostate narrative, both stylistically and substantively, but that have no discernible "real-world happenings or experiences" standing behind them. Out of a void marked by the absence of any ties binding them to personal experience (biographical history) or to the real-world development of specific religious groups and practices (contextual histories), the tales of the apostates who never were spring forth, challenging us to rethink the role of the social in the construction of apostasy.

In rethinking that role, I have suggested that we would do well to consider questions of *how* it is that apostates are led to construct the accounts that they do. This chapter has made a first pass at such questions, exploring some of the sociostructural features that led certain individuals with little or no direct involvement with targeted religious groups to construct self-histories that fit the form of apostate narrative. In addition to the apostates themselves, it has identified three prominent elements in "apostatic" political structure—sponsoring audiences, receiving audiences, and truth-tellers. It has further identified some of the key variables that link these elements one to another, as well as to the narratives that they are responsible for generating. And while it has done all of this in connection with a truly unique class of apostates, it holds out the hope that there is much to gain by taking a similar approach to the analysis of more conventional cases of apostasy. For without a forthright appraisal of how much political structures do to generate apostasy, even where apostasy's "real-world" precipitates are present, we cannot hope for a full understanding of the politics of religious apostasy.

REFERENCES

Adams, Timothy. 1990. *Telling Lies in Modern American Autobiography*. Chapel Hill: University of North Carolina Press.

Anonymous. 1835. *Six Months in a House of Correction, or, the Narrative of Dorah Mahony, who was under the Influence of the Protestants about a Year, and an Inmate of the House of Correction, in Leberett St., Boston, Massachusetts, nearly Six Months, in the Year 18___ . With Some Preliminary Suggestions by the Committee of Publication*. Boston: Benjamin B. Mussey.

Barnes, J.A. 1994. *A Pack of Lies*. New York: Cambridge University Press.

Booth, Wayne. 1988. *The Company We Keep: An Ethics of Fiction*. Berkeley: University of California Press.

Bruner, Jerome. 1987. "Life as Narrative." *Social Research* 54:11–32.

The Catholic Truth Society. 1898. *The Awful Disclosures of Maria Monk, a True History*. San Francisco: The Catholic Truth Society.

Chick, Jack. 1987. *The Prophet: Alberto, part 6.* Chino, CA: Chick Publications.

———. 1983. *The Godfathers: Alberto, part 3.* Chino, CA: Chick Publications.

———. 1981. *Double-Cross: Alberto, part 2.* Chino, CA: Chick Publications.

———. 1979. *Alberto* (Comic Book). Chino, CA: Chick Publications.

Coser, Lewis. 1954. "The Age of the Informer." *Dissent* 1:249–54.

Denzin, Norman. 1989a. *Interpretive Biography.* Newbury Park, CA: Sage.

———. 1989b. "The Sociological Imagination Revisited." *The Sociological Quarterly* 31:1–22.

———. 1987a. *The Alcoholic Self.* Newbury Park, CA: Sage.

———. 1987b. *The Recovering Alcoholic.* Newbury Park, CA: Sage.

Livesey, Roy. 1991. "Alberto Rivera Update." *New Age Bulletin* 3(3).

Metz, Gary. 1981. *The Alberto Story.* Chicago: Cornerstone Publications.

Moffatt, Mary Anne Ursula. 1835. *An Answer to Six Months in a Convent, Exposing Its Falsehoods and Manifold Absurdities. By the Lady Superior. With Some Preliminary Remarks.* Boston: J. H. Eastburn.

Monk, Maria. 1836a. *Awful Disclosures of Maria Monk, as Exhibited in a Narrative of Her Sufferings during a Residence of Five Years as a Novice, and Two Years as a Black Nun, in the Hotel Dieu Nunnery at Montreal.* New York: Howe & Bates.

———. 1836b. *Awful Disclosures, by Maria Monk, of the Hotel Dieu Nunnery of Montreal, Revised, with an Appendix, Containing, Part I: Reception of the First Editions, Part II: Sequel of Her Narrative, Part III: Review of the Case. Also, a Supplement, Giving More Particulars of the Nunnery and Grounds, Illustrated by a Plan of the Nunnery, &tc.* New York: Maria Monk.

Nathan, Debbie, and Michael Snedeker. 1995. *Satan's Silence: Ritual Abuse and the Making of a Modern American Witch Hunt.* New York: Basic Books.

Passantino, Robert, and Gretchen Passantino. 1990. "Fabrications Unlimited, or Where's the Evidence?" *Cornerstone Magazine* 19(92):14, 16.

Passantino, Robert, Gretchen Passantino, and Jon Trott. 1989. "Satan's Sideshow." *Cornerstone Magazine* 18(90):23–28.

Pement, Eric. 1981. "The Alberto Chronicles, Part III." *Cornerstone Magazine* 10(55).

Plummer, Ken. 1990. "Herbert Blumer and the Life History Tradition." *Symbolic Interaction* 13:125–44.

Reed, Rebecca. 1835a. *Six Months in a Convent, or, The Narrative of Rebecca Theresa Reed, who was under the Influence of the Roman Catholics about Two Years, and an Inmate of the Ursuline Convent on Mount Benedict, Charlestown, Mass., nearly Six Months, in the Years 1831–2. With Some Preliminary Suggestions by the Committee of Publication.* Boston: Russell, Odiorne & Metcalf.

———. 1835b. *Supplement to "Six Months in a Convent," Confirming the Narrative of Rebecca Theresa Reed, by the Testimony of More than One Hundred Witnesses, whose Statements have been Given to the Committee. Containing a Minute Account of the Elopement of Miss Harrison, with Some Further Explanations of the Narrative, by Miss Reed, and an Exposition of the System of Cloister Education, by the Committee of Publications. With an Appendix.* Boston: Russell, Odiorne, & Co.

Richardson, James, Joel Best, and David Bromley. 1991. *The Satanism Scare.* New York: Aldine de Gruyter.

Shaw, George. 1969. *Shaw: An Autobiography, Selected from His Writings by Stanley Weintraub.* New York: Weybright and Talley.

Stone, William. 1836. *Maria Monk and the Nunnery of the Hotel Dieu: Being an Account of a Visit to the Convents of Montreal and Refutation of the "Awful Disclosures."* New York: Howe & Bates.

Stratford, Lauren. 1988. *Satan's Underground.* Eugene, OR: Harvest House.

———. 1993. *Stripped Naked.* Gretna, LA: Pelican Publishing Company.

Trott, Jon, and Michael Hertenstein. 1992. "Selling Satan: The Tragic History of Michael Warnke." *Cornerstone Magazine* 21(98):7–9, 11–14, 16–17, 19, 30, 38.

Victor, Jeffrey. 1993. *Satanic Panic.* Chicago: Open Court.

Warnke, Michael. 1991. *Schemes of Satan.* Tulsa, OK: Victory House.

Warnke, Michael, David Balsiger, and Les Jones. 1972. *The Satan Seller.* Plainfield, NJ: Logos International.

Watson, Thomas E. 1927. *Maria Monk and Her Revelations of Convent Crimes.* 2d ed. Thomson, GA: The Tom Watson Book Company.

Zablocki, Benjamin. 1996. "Reliability and Validity of Apostate Accounts in the Study of Religious Communities." Paper presented at the annual meetings of the Association for the Sociology of Religion, New York.

Part IV

The Organizational
Context of Apostasy

Apostasy, Apocalypse, and Religious Violence: An Exploratory Comparison of Peoples Temple, the Branch Davidians, and the Solar Temple

_____ *John R. Hall and Philip Schuyler*

In the past two decades, countercultural religious movements have become increasingly associated with violence. Many individuals have died in acts of terror, murder, and mass suicide. Others have been critically injured. In addition to the physical violence (and leaving aside the controversial issue of coerced participation), countless individuals have faced true personal crises of choice in confrontations between their families and friends and the religious groups they have joined, and some of these individuals have become unwitting pawns or willing protagonists in episodes that fed back into the violence. But religious violence is not solely a matter of conflicted family, social, and religious commitments. Countercultural religious movements have the capacity to challenge the symbolic construction of an established social order in ways that may expose previously hidden fragilities. And when such symbolic violence occurs, it does not go unnoticed. As we write today, the sense of inviolability of the established social order in various nation-states—most notably Japan, Germany, and France—has been undermined by persistent concerns about the threats posed by religious movements such as Aum Shinrikyo and Scientology. The perceived danger of so-called cults thus belies the ridicule often heaped upon them. Indeed, however marginal and bizarre countercultural religious movements may appear, they must embody a rare transformative potential of social and cultural power, for they are not just ridiculed; they are also sometimes subjected to state efforts at repression and social control.

A general framework for understanding contestations between an established social order and countercultural movements has been available for some time. More than a half century ago, at the time when the Nazi movement was gaining ground in Germany, Karl Mannheim (1936) considered the dialectic of ideology and utopia. In Mannheim's account, the ideological task of maintaining an established social order requires that any alternative ordering of society be treated as "utopian," which is to say fantastic and unworkable. He emphasized that whatever the intrinsic potential or problems of utopias in their own terms, they are implausible precisely insofar as they challenge a society's bedrock assumptions, such as institutions of family or private property. Yet this does not mean that utopias can't work; indeed, the histories of certain utopian countercultural movements suggest quite the contrary. Religious movements such as Mother Ann Lee's Shakers and the Amish are testaments to the alternative possibilities of social order at a given level of technological development, and the Mormons' tremendous growth over the past 150 years shows that religious social movements have the potential to transform themselves from seemingly marginal cultural curiosities to vehicles of world-historical change. Explicit recognition of this potential can be found in the pitched opposition to religious movements in many times and places (Knox 1956; Cohn 1970).

The present chapter takes as its thesis the proposition that the most extreme cases of collective religious violence do *not* emerge from an intrinsic property of the groups themselves. Rather, our sociohistorical model theorizes the genesis of such violence in social conflicts *between* utopian religious movements on the one hand, and on the other, ideological proponents of an established social order, who seek to control "cults" through loosely institutionalized, emergent oppositional alliances. These alliances are typically crystallized by (1) cultural opponents of deviant groups, especially apostates and distraught relatives of members, but their consequences for violence depend on the degree to which they mobilize; (2) news reporters who frame cult stories in terms of moral deviance; and (3) modern governments that have incorporated the "religious" interest in enforcing cultural legitimacy into a state interest in monopolizing political legitimacy. In short, extreme religious violence is a result of the interaction between a complex of factors typically set in motion through apostasy and anti-subversion campaigns.

This interpretive sociohistorical model of *apocalyptic religious conflict* centers on contestations over whether countercultural religious movements have the cultural legitimacy to pursue their collective visions. Although these contestations bear comparison to other kinds of violence that mix politics and religion, the relations are complex, and we do not deal here with cases where political violence is carried out in the name of religion, as is the case in Bosnia, Palestine, and Northern Ireland. For utopian religious conflict with an established order, the argument, in brief, is as follows. A religious movement's structural location "outside" the existing social fabric frequently combines with its typical character as a "greedy institution," often demanding a member's complete commitment of time and energy; this, in turn, creates a gulf between group members and their families and previously established social networks, and it can promote both external militancy and the internal violence employed in social control (cf. Coser 1974).

Among various types of utopian countercultural communities, those that embrace the apocalypse—the end times of a war between good and evil giving way to a new era of heaven brought to earth—have long been associated with high degrees of collective solidarity (Hall 1988a). But these features of utopian communal movements per se are not sufficient to explain outcomes of collective religious violence. Instead, in terms of the typology advanced by David Bromley (Chapter 2 this volume), compared to more "legitimate" organizations such as churches, businesses, and prisons, utopian communal movements are much more likely to be regarded as "subversive," and they are therefore especially likely to produce defectors who will take up the role of oppositional apostates and work to mobilize external opponents. If the opponents succeed in mobilizing agents of established social institutions (in our era, the mass media, politicians, and the state) to frame the movement as a threat to the established order, these agents may take actions intended to discredit the movement in the public eye, or subject it to actions and policies that undermine its capacity to exist as an autonomous organization. The principals of the apocalyptic group, in turn, may perceive these external challenges as threats to their own legitimacy and the power of their prophecy. Under these circumstances, violence toward opponents and collective suicide offer a way for the group's true believers to attempt to salvage their own sense of their legitimacy, albeit at the cost of their own survival, by refusing to submit either to state authority or to external definitions of their identity.

This basic account of apocalyptic mass suicide is not new (Hall 1979; Robbins 1986; Hall 1987), but previous studies have mostly been limited to individual cases. The social dynamics of the process can be further clarified by "deepening analogies" between different cases in ways that examine peoples' individual and shared motives of action, and how these motives are shaped by structural circumstances (Stinchcombe 1978). As Larry Griffin (1993) has shown, such comparisons can bring into view a generic narrative structure that encapsulates the details of multiple cases. In this chapter, we consider the violent unravelling of three religious social movements of the past two decades—"Jonestown," "Waco," and the less widely known Solar Temple. "Jonestown," of course, is the name of the American utopian settlement in Guyana visited in 1978 by California Congressman Leo Ryan, who was murdered along with four other people as they prepared to depart from an airstrip near the community, after which Jim Jones immediately led true believers and coerced other members at Jonestown into committing "mass suicide." The second case is equally well-known. In 1993, near Waco, Texas, a raid by the U.S. Bureau of Alcohol, Tobacco, and Firearms (ATF) on the Branch Davidians, a sect led by a man named David Koresh, resulted in the deaths of both Davidian and ATF sharpshooters. After a siege of more than a month, most Branch Davidians who remained in the compound died in a fire that started during an FBI assault. As for the third case, in October 1994, Luc Jouret, a new-age homeopath, and 52 of his associates in the Temple Solaire, died in Canada and Switzerland in an event that letters left by the deceased described as a "Transit" to the distant star of Sirius; 16 of their colleagues died in a similar incident in France fourteen months later—on the winter solstice of 1995, and five more committed ritual suicide at the time of the spring equinox in March 1997.

The three religious movements are quite different from one another. Peoples Temple was a leftist political religious movement; David Koresh awaited the fulfillment of the Book of Revelation; and the Temple Solaire included many wealthy, mostly former Catholic participants who trafficked in both concerns about imminent ecological apocalypse and reinvocations of medieval Catholic traditions. Presumably, the trajectories of religious violence of these groups were variable and highly contingent, so that analyzing them makes it possible not only to assess the validity and range of applicability of our general model, but also to consider how specific conditions affect the play and outcome of violence.

For a fuller analysis, it would be important to compare these case histories both with cases that did *not* result in extreme violence, and with others, such as the collective suicide of Heaven's Gate in April of 1997, where violence was not directed outward and seems to have lacked any significant apocalyptic basis in external conflict. Further development of this comparison must await a more comprehensive study. However, even sampling on one outcome of the dependent variable (the most extreme cases that involved at least some externally directed violence), certain kinds of generalization may be achieved. As the logic of John Stuart Mill (1843) suggests, if commonalities are found among otherwise diverse cases, these commonalities are likely to be implicated in any explanation of their similar outcomes. Beyond looking for commonalities, we explore the robustness of our findings here through the methodology of what Weber called mental experiments, described more recently by Hawthorne (1991) as the consideration of alternative "plausible worlds," and by Bernstein (1994) as "sideshadowing." That is, we evaluate arguments to the effect that "such-and-such probably would never have happened if . . .". Such arguments are hypothetical, of course, so we limit ourselves to considering only highly plausible yet non-trivial ones. Overall, our methodology, though tentative in its conclusions, makes the best analytic use of a (thankfully) small number of cases, at the same time that it avoids generalizing from single cases.

There has been much shock, outrage, and handwringing about so-called cults, but these reactions do little to help us understand the dynamics of apocalyptic religious conflict. Our analysis, in contrast, will not be directly concerned with the moral issue of whether the acts of opponents, the mass media, the state, or religious social movements are justified or legitimate. The development of a sociological analysis will, however, suggest that all parties to these tragic episodes ought to reconsider their strategies and their objectives in light of the larger social processes to which they are parties.

THE GENEALOGY OF APOCALYPSE

The beginning of the third millennium of the Christian calendar is fast upon us. Much already has been written about the chiliastic expectations that such a rare temporal transition generates, and recent apocalyptic events may seem somehow connected to the shift. It is worth remembering with Norman Cohn (1993), however, that the historical emergence of apocalyptic ideas more than two millennia ago had nothing to do with rationalized time. The powerful ancient images depicted a final battle between good and evil, resolved by the triumph of a god who then presides justly over an eternally blissful world. But neither the time of struggle nor eternity could be contained within mere rational calculation.

In our era, Jonestown and Waco do not calibrate to calendrical expectations about the millennium, and as we will see, the Solar Temple's millennialism of astrological eras does not sit easily with its apocalyptic violence. Instead, the apocalyptic side of the Solar Temple is part of a *genealogy* of apocalypse—a historical thread that connects the three groups. Specifically, in the wake of Jonestown, the cultural opponents of the Branch Davidians used the trope of "mass suicide" drawn from Jonestown as a basis to raise the alarm against Davidian leader David Koresh, and their invocation of this trope became interwoven with the legal rationales and strategic plans of U.S. federal authorities, with disastrous results (Hall 1995). In a less consequential way, what happened at Waco clearly figured in the Solar Temple leaders' sense of their own destiny and their belief that their own group was the object of "systematic persecution" (Hall and Schuyler 1997).

As these brief allusions suggest, local dynamics of apocalypticism may weave genealogical threads into a fabric that connects distinctive episodes to other episodes, thereby yielding a substructure of apocalyptic history that undergoes a sort of public phase amplification, to become experienced at least temporarily as a mood or *zeitgeist*, a culture of generalized apocalyptic expectations. Given the possibility of cultural mediations, the dynamics of any given case of apocalyptic religious violence cannot be assumed to occur in a vacuum, isolated from prior events. Yet neither can the weight of past events be assumed to work like some contagious cultural virus, replicating itself in its passage from one group to another. For the genealogies, to the extent that they are significant, come into play for religious social movements within specific conjunctures that must be examined in their own terms.

THE MASS SUICIDE AT JONESTOWN

The tendency to treat Peoples Temple as the *cultus classicus* headed by Jim Jones, psychotic megalomaniac par excellence is still with us, like most myths, because it has a grain of truth to it. But the myth is both completely inadequate for explaining the mass suicide and, at the same time, psychologically necessary for maintaining peace of mind in the public at large. That is, the myth has a long half-life because it serves a vital cultural need *not* to understand the murders and mass suicide at Jonestown. Jonestown was both utopia and anti-utopia. In its utopian aspects, it challenged race and class inequality in the United States, and in its anti-utopian aspects, it borrowed its most dubious practices of manipulation, social control, and political aggrandizement directly from parallel institutional worlds in American society-at-large. In other words, to understand Peoples Temple too well would be to deconstruct the dominant social construction of reality (Hall 1987; Chidester 1988).

Even Jim Jones's strongest countercultural images—of an impending American apocalypse of race and class warfare—simply borrowed old Protestant ideas about the Church of Rome as the whore of Babylon, and these ideas themselves come from deeper apocalyptic wellsprings of Western thought (Cohn 1993). True, Jones evoked apocalyptic imagery in ways that amplified latent resentment among those drawn to his cause, and he exploited a posture of radicalism to attract true believers, and to widen the gulf between Peoples Temple and the rest of the world. Yet reductionist analyses of the demented manipulations by Jim Jones and the apocalyptic mentality that took hold within Peoples Temple are not sufficient to explain the path Peoples Temple followed into murder and mass suicide. The stark fact is that the Jonestown leadership unleashed the murders and mass suicide in November 1978, in response to a two-year struggle against Peoples Temple mounted by its cultural opponents, a group that called themselves the Concerned Relatives. It was the initiative of this group that led Leo Ryan, the U.S. Congressman from San Mateo, California, to visit the jungle community, accompanied by a delegation of four Concerned Relatives and a pool of television and newspaper reporters. On the departure of this entourage with 16 defectors, Jonestown sharpshooters followed the group to a nearby airstrip and murdered the congressman, a reporter, a newspaper photographer, a television cameraman, and a young defector. As the airstrip attack was underway, back in Jonestown, Jim Jones led his followers in a ritualized mass suicide.

Initial media and popular accounts of Jonestown suppressed the question of whether the Concerned Relatives' actions contributed to the grisly outcome for a simple reason: the interpretive frame adopted in most accounts of the movement was that of its cultural opponents. Beginning late in 1976, some two years before the mass suicide, a group of apostates from Peoples Temple coalesced into an organized group of opponents. In 1977 this group became allied with one journalist sympathetic to the apostates and other journalists hostile to Peoples Temple for reasons having to do with the local politics of San Francisco. (Jones had been appointed housing commissioner by George Moscone, a liberal mayor being subjected to a recall movement by conservatives.) Together, they succeeded in generating a flood of negative news accounts. These reports overwhelmingly depicted Peoples Temple through an anti-cult lens that raised questions about supposed financial ripoffs, extravagant living, and hair-raising strategies of social control that depended on practices of self-humiliation and brainwashing. The Concerned Relatives initially found their place in these journalistic narratives as apostates and relatives courageous enough to expose the group, despite their fear of reprisals (Hall 1987, pp. 175–90). As the conflict between the apostates and relatives and the Temple unfolded on multiple fronts, the opponents solidified exposé as the frame though which most journalistic coverage viewed Peoples Temple. Later, after the murders and mass suicide, the Concerned Relatives became the most knowledgeable outsiders about a group that had carried out an appalling act of mass suicide. Indeed, because the Concerned Relatives had consistently sought to raise the alarm against Peoples Temple, they could take the mass suicide as sad validation of their concerns.

Notably lacking from this frame, however, is what sociologists call *reflexivity*—the capacity to describe how the actions of the Concerned Relatives and the media affected an unfolding set of events in which they were not only observers, but also participants. Indeed, the cultural opponents had a vital interest in denying reflexivity, which probably helps account for their consistent promotion of a doctrine of *cult essentialism*, that treats religious movements as subject to internal dynamics unaffected by interaction with the wider social world. Such an analysis would free the cultural opponents and the media from any responsibility for incidents of religious-movement violence. But precisely because the proponents of cult essentialism are themselves participants in unfolding events, sociological analysis must consider whether and how their actions can help explain those events.

The task in analyzing Jonestown is to identify preconditions and precipitating factors that adequately explain the murders and mass suicide. A list of necessary preconditions probably would include the existence of (1) a charismatic religious social movement with (2) an apocalyptic ideology, (3) an internal organization adequate to maintain solidarity, with (4) legitimacy enough among followers to exercise collective social control over the affairs of the community, and (5) sufficient economic and political viability to (6) live within strong social boundaries in cognitive isolation from society-at-large. Without these circumstances, minor incidents of violence might occur within or against countercultural communal movements, but it is difficult to imagine that they would trigger violence on a large scale.

Yet if these characteristics are particularly conducive to violence, they are hardly sufficient. Numerous apocalyptic and quasi-apocalyptic religious communities, from Mother Ann Lee's Shakers to contemporary ''heavens on earth,'' like Seattle's Love Family and the Krishna farm in West Virginia (Hall 1978), have all these characteristics without experiencing major incidents of collective religious violence. Thus, apocalyptic religious movements may be especially prone to violence, but that tendency is only realized under specific additional conditions. Our general model identifies these conditions in contemporary circumstances as involving (1) the mobilization of a solidary group of cultural opponents, (2) the shaping of news media coverage through the cultural opponents' frame of interpretation about ''cults,'' and (3) the exercise of state authority. By some combination of these factors or their functional equivalents, we argue, the capacity of a group to persist as an authentically apocalyptic movement is undermined, and under these conditions, violence becomes both a vehicle of aggression against detractors and affirmation of a principle of self-determination within the apocalyptic community.

How well does this schematic account capture the circumstances that led up to the murders and mass suicide at Jonestown? Certainly, from the early days of Peoples Temple in Indianapolis, Indiana in the 1950s, to California in the 1960s and the establishment of a communal settlement in Guyana beginning in 1974, Jim Jones effectively used the apocalyptic trope of "persecution" to enhance his charisma, demonstrate the legitimacy of his movement's ideals, and strengthen the boundaries between followers and the outside world. His maneuvers ranged from such simple devices as posting guards at Temple facilities or interviewing newcomers to Temple services, to the establishment of Jonestown, an isolated community that was to offer a post-apocalyptic sanctuary—a "Promised Land"—to which Jones and his followers could depart at the "first sounds of outright persecution from press or government" (Hall 1987, p. 133).

It is widely but incorrectly assumed that the collective religious migration of Peoples Temple to Jonestown in the summer of 1977 was precipitated by the flood of bad press about the Temple published as a consequence of the alliance between the Concerned Relatives and various journalists. But close archival research shows that these events simply compounded a rationale for migration that had already crystallized at the end of 1976, when Temple principals became concerned that they might be the target of a U.S. Internal Revenue Service investigation into their financial practices and political involvements. It was these concerns that led to the first concrete steps toward collective migration, steps that gained greater urgency when Temple operatives learned that the increasingly organized defectors had been talking with a "Treasury agent" (Hall 1987, pp. 178–84, 197–99).

When the collective migration of some 1,000 people finally took place during the summer of 1977, the concurrent flood of negative press stories heightened the anxieties about separations between family members and stirred concerns among relatives of Temple members who might otherwise have been less involved. Most notorious was the strange case of the "child god" John Victor Stoen. The boy was claimed by Jim Jones as his own biological son, though legally he was the son of his mother, Grace Stoen, and her husband, Timothy Stoen. The Stoens had left their child in the legal custody of Temple members when they had departed, separately, from the folds of Temple membership. John Victor Stoen was raised socially within Peoples Temple as the son of Jim Jones, and Tim Stoen brought the boy to Jonestown before defecting himself. But these countercultural constructions of John Victor Stoen's identity made no sense from the standpoint of basic social mores within society-at-large, and after Grace, and later, Tim defected, they went to court to try to regain custody of John Victor, and they waged a publicity campaign in Congress about the custody battle.

The controversy over John Victor Stoen, however, was not the only custody struggle, nor were custody struggles the only frontiers of conflict between the cultural opponents and Peoples Temple. The Concerned Relatives engaged in protracted efforts to alert government authorities—from the San Francisco Police Department to the Customs Bureau and the Federal Communications Commission—about "nefarious acts" on the part of Peoples Temple. They also initiated "welfare and whereabouts" requests to the U.S. State Department. One father embarked on a desperate and inconsequential scheme to kidnap his adult daughter from Jonestown.

The Concerned Relatives' efforts on the various fronts were largely unsuccessful. The Stoen custody case became bogged down in legal issues in the Guyana courts, the governmental investigations failed to come up with significant prosecutable offenses, and the "welfare-and-whereabouts" efforts of the U.S. embassy in Guyana found that people at Jonestown were living an austere, third-world lifestyle but nevertheless "expressed satisfaction with their lives," as an embassy consul reported after one visit to the jungle community (Hall 1987, p. 217). The lack of success led the frustrated opponents to amplify and generalize their charges against Peoples Temple, which reinforced a siege mentality within the Jonestown community. Thus, even though the opponents' efforts failed in their direct goals, the Jonestown leadership took the campaign of opposition as inspiration for an increasingly apocalyptic posture. Years earlier, Jones had borrowed the concept of "revolutionary suicide" from Black Panther leader Huey Newton, who argued that the slow suicide of life in the ghetto ought to be displaced by revolutionary suicide that would end only in victory or death (Hall 1987, p. 136). At Jonestown, this radical rhetoric came to signify that "it is better even to die than to be constantly harassed from one continent to the next." As time wore on, in response to the Jonestown posture, the Concerned Relatives mounted a publicity campaign that portrayed Peoples Temple as "employing physical intimidation and psychological coercion as part of a mind-programming campaign" in violation of their human rights specified in the United Nations declaration of 1948 (Hall 1987, p. 229). By small steps, their campaign became refocused into an effort to "dismantle" what they portrayed as a "concentration camp" (Hall 1987, pp. 232–33).

Although the expedition of California Congressman Leo Ryan to Jonestown was publicly billed as a "fact-finding effort," Ryan had previously informed Jones of his sympathy with the Concerned Relatives, and he was accompanied unofficially by a delegation of Concerned Relatives and allied journalists. The motives that animated Ryan, the Concerned Relatives, and journalists were varied and complex, but the outcome was intended to be favorable to all their interests. On November 18, 1978, the expedition brought 16 people, mostly whites, out of Jonestown under the auspices of a U.S. congressman whom the Jonestown leadership regarded as allied with their opponents. The apostates were departing for the nearby Port Kaituma airstrip under the glare of mass media coverage, talking about how Jonestown was nothing but "a Communist prison camp." From Jones's viewpoint, these circumstances insured further accusations by the Temple's opponents, more media scrutiny, and increased intervention in the affairs of the Jonestown community by external legal authorities. These were the circumstances under which the Jonestown leadership translated revolutionary suicide from a self-styled struggle against injustice in this world into a final decisive act against their opponents, sending sharpshooters to the airstrip, where they killed Leo Ryan, three journalists, and a defector.

Clearly, by directing the airstrip attack on Leo Ryan and his entourage, Jones and his principals constructed a situation of such overriding stigma that followers understood their collective life to be at an end. Back at Jonestown, Jones correctly perceived that his enemies would surely prevail against the community's claim to a countercultural legitimacy of collective self-determination. Refusing to submit to this outcome of his own making, Jones then exhorted his followers, "if we can't live in peace, then let's die in peace." Nine hundred thirteen members of the community became caught up in an orchestrated ritual mass suicide and murders. At the end, invoking Huey Newton's words, Jones preached to the believers and the doubters assembled in the Jonestown pavilion: "This is a revolutionary suicide. This is not a self-destructive suicide." Whatever their individual sentiments, the people of Jonestown departed to their own promised land through death (Hall 1987, ch. 11).

Absent the airstrip attack on Ryan and the others, the mass suicide would have lacked a credible rationale; in the context of the attack, Jones presented it as the only honorable choice of the collective in the face of certain subjugation to external authority. In the construction of the Jonestown leadership, then, the murders and mass suicide formed a unity, but that unity was predicated upon the airstrip attack. The attack itself was hardly an act of random violence; other than the perhaps accidental killing of a young girl defector, the gunfire seems to have been carefully targeted toward individuals whom Jonestown principals regarded as their opponents in the ongoing struggle. It was, as it were, a preemptive strike that snatched victory from opponents, albeit by fulfilling their most nightmarish prophecies. Given the targets, the attack itself has to be understood as an extreme escalation of an intense conflict between the Concerned Relatives and Peoples Temple, a conflict that unfolded for more than a year in the press, the courts, and the U.S. State Department, in the conduct of espionage on both sides, and in strategic actions that had previously come close to direct confrontation. Indeed, it seems incontrovertible that the expedition of Congressman Ryan, the Concerned Relatives, and journalists, and especially their departure with 16 Jonestown residents, was the precipitating occasion of the murderous attack. As an event, the mass suicide must thus be seen in its specific outcome as a consequence of the expedition.

It is not easy to answer the question of what would have happened had the expedition not taken place at all, or not turned out as it did, since there are so many alternative scenarios. Conducting "mental experiments" that project "what would happen if . . ." is a delicate matter. Yet as Hawthorne (1991) has argued, the consideration of alternative scenarios can be analytically useful if the counterfactual hypotheses are neither so distant from the course of events as to be irrelevant nor so unstable in their dynamics as to make prediction unreliable. With these guidelines in mind, it is possible to push toward a deeper, though necessarily tentative understanding of the murders and mass suicide.

On the one hand, had the Concerned Relatives not formed as an organized group, or had they not succeeded in bringing a critical mass of journalistic coverage and a U.S. congressman to their side, it seems unlikely that the mass suicide would have occurred. Indeed, the Concerned Relatives initially understood the powerlessness of their position, and sought out news reporters precisely as patrons who would help them. After Jones's followers migrated to Jonestown, the opponents turned to the media and the political intervention of a congressman's "fact-finding" expedition precisely because their legal and state administrative actions had failed to advance their cause.

Clearly then, the actions of the apostates and relatives were crucial to catalyzing the dynamic of conflict between Peoples Temple and the outside, and this conflict is a necessary component of any explanation of the mass suicide that actually occurred. It is impossible, though, to say with certainty whether a mass suicide would have occurred without the Ryan expedition. Possibly, the opponents might have won some legal battles, gained better access to visitation with relatives, and won other concessions without confronting the Temple with complete subordination to external authority. Even more likely, given time, the entire enterprise at Jonestown would have collapsed from internal dissension, as the vast majority of other communal groups do. In light of these possibilities, the murders and mass suicide were in no way inevitable.

It is also apparent, however, that even without the Ryan trip, the conflict between the Concerned Relatives and the Temple was intense, and the Concerned Relatives might have gained other victories to which the leadership at Jonestown would likely have responded with violence. For example, had Grace Stoen and Timothy Stoen won legal custody over John Victor Stoen, a different violent confrontation—and even mass suicide—might have ensued. In other words, within the broad channels of contestation between Peoples Temple and the Concerned Relatives, the potential for violence could have been unleashed in more than one current of events.

Here, the question of John Victor Stoen's biological paternity is the remaining major mystery of the tragedy. If Jones was the biological father, as some individuals outside Peoples Temple think, then a central claim of the Concerned Relatives—that Jones amounted to a kidnapper of a child—would lose considerable of its moral if not legal force. Resolving this question might sharpen our opinions about the moral highground held by either side. At the time, however, it would not have resolved the cultural conflict between communalism and familial individualism that animated the two sides to the struggle. And it probably would not have altered the commitments of the true believers at Jonestown to extreme violence, should their opponents prevail in subordinating them to external social and legal authority.

THE BRANCH DAVIDIANS, THE CULT BUSTERS, THE MEDIA, AND THE STATE

After November 1978, Peoples Temple became the negative cult par excellence, and mass suicide the ultimate trope signifying the tragic danger of cults in general. That the genesis of the murders and mass suicide lay in an ongoing religious conflict is still not widely understood, but jokes, songs, cartoons, and public statements by politicians came to invoke the word "Jonestown" to represent the ultimate debacle. Even less widely understood is how the symbol of Jonestown influenced the trajectory of the second major case in the United States of violence involving an apocalyptic religious movement—the Branch Davidians who lived at a communal settlement they called Mount Carmel, near Waco, Texas. As with Jonestown, an explanation of the tragic confrontation at Mount Carmel requires an understanding of how the intertwining of agendas between the cultural opponents, the media, and the political/state domain affected the outcome.

The basic events of "Waco" are still strongly etched in many peoples' minds. On the morning of Sunday, February 28, 1993, about 80 heavily armed agents of ATF engaged in a shootout with members of the Branch Davidians, a Seventh-Day Adventist splinter sect led by a young charismatic who called himself David Koresh. Six or more sect members and four ATF agents died in the firefight. After an uneasy truce was established, a new phase of confrontation began: The Federal Bureau of Investigation (FBI) began a siege of the compound, but in the weeks that followed, their attempts to unnerve the Davidians with floodlights and sound blasts of Tibetan chants and an old Nancy Sinatra record seem to have pushed the Davidians only to more intense Bible study, and the FBI concluded that their negotiations with the Davidians were unlikely to bring the besieged Davidians out anytime soon. Then, in the early morning hours of April 19, the FBI, frustrated at the lack of progress at negotiating a surrender of the holdouts, rolled tanks up to the front of the woodframe compound, started injecting tear gas, and in the course of the morning, began destroying walls of the building itself. Shortly before noon, a fire broke out, quickly engulfing the structure. Seventy-four Branch Davidians died in the inferno, either in presumed "mercy killings" by gunshot, or through the action of the blaze itself.

This sad saga, which unfolded in slow motion under intense media scrutiny, has been the subject of numerous governmental, journalistic, and scholarly investigations. It is widely agreed that the ATF badly handled both its investigation and its raid—ostensibly conducted to serve a warrant. The performance of the FBI during the siege and its decision to roll the tanks against the compound have been more hotly debated, in part because some government officials, including Attorney General Janet Reno, and President Bill Clinton, defended the FBI's performance and held that ultimate responsibility must rest with David Koresh. This claim fits well with a rhetoric of cult essentialism, but it is contradicted both by the report of the U.S. Treasury Department about the ATF raid and by any careful effort at sociological explanation.

There are substantial differences between Waco and Jonestown. True, both cases involve a refusal on the part of apocalyptic religious movement leaders to submit to the power of external authority, and in each case, sect members killed external "opponents." But the final deaths of the Branch Davidians were not the highly ritualized mass suicide that Jones and his leadership group orchestrated. In Jonestown, the leaders launched their well-prepared plan immediately after the murders of Congressman Ryan and the others, whereas the Branch Davidians did not choose death over submission to external authority until 50 days after the ATF raid, and then, only in response to the FBI tank tear gas assault. Certain details about what happened on April 19 remain in dispute, but no matter how the fire started, few of the Davidians made any attempt to leave the burning building. Compared to Jonestown, the external threat was far more immediate, and the refusal to yield to tear gas–injecting tanks can be plausibly viewed as an affirmation of martyrdom. Whether this martyrdom amounted to "mass suicide" is more ambiguous, but the incidents at Jonestown and Waco share two outstanding features: the killing of outsiders by members of the sect followed by the group's own collective death as a community. The sociological question then is whether the outcome at Waco is best explained by factors parallel to those that we have shown at work at Jonestown, components of what we have termed apocalyptic religious conflict.

David Koresh, the leader of the Branch Davidians at the time of the confrontation, was still a teenager in Texas at the time of the mass suicides at Jonestown, and there is no reason to think that he took particular note of those events. Compared to Jones's left-wing political apocalyptic vision, Koresh's prophecies about the end times were more directly keyed to the New Testament's Book of Revelation, for the Branch Davidian movement was firmly rooted in the fervent expectationism of Seventh-Day Adventist offshoot sects (Pitts 1995; Bromley and Silver 1995). Indeed, Koresh's emphasis on revelation suggests a young man whose sense of the big Apocalypse was open-ended, and closely keyed to prophetic interpretation of events as they unfolded.

David Koresh himself did not originate the invocation of "mass suicide," even though the image came to figure significantly in how the Waco affair developed. Rather, it was cult opponents who raised the specter of mass suicide in a way that led directly to the ATF raid and its tragic consequences: the deaths of the ATF agents and Davidians during the shootout, the ensuing siege, the FBI tank attack, and, finally, the fire and collective death of the Davidians remaining in the compound on April 19, 1993. Like the Jonestown drama, these events were complex, but it seems incontrovertible that the efforts of Davidian apostates against David Koresh were the animating process and the sine qua non, without which the ATF raid would not have taken place in the way that it did, and perhaps, not at all.

The apostates (dubbed "cult busters" by their leader, a young man named

Marc Breault) initially put forward the trope of "mass suicide" as a liturgical invocation of the cult danger that the Branch Davidians posed, and they gradually took to using the trope to alert others to the seriousness of their concerns. Over the course of the Waco events, the idea of "mass suicide" spread from Breault and his network of opponents to law enforcement circles. When the ATF began to investigate the Branch Davidians (very probably through a chain of events initiated by the cultural opponents), the alleged threat of mass suicide, and inferences about group organization deriving from it, became subject to interpretation in a different context—that of strategic law enforcement. Reacting to these heavily charged meanings, the ATF made serious miscalculations about how to proceed in dealing with David Koresh. These miscalculations affected the planning and execution of the initial ATF raid. They were causally central to the ATF's decision to follow the dubious scenario dubbed "dynamic entry" in seeking to serve a warrant on Koresh, and they very likely affected the ATF's otherwise inexplicable decision not to call off their raid, once they knew that they had lost the element of surprise. In short, the foreshadowing of mass suicide by organized opponents became a perversely self-fulfilling prophecy (Hall 1995).

There is thus a *genetic* connection between Jonestown and Waco, but the connection comes not through the apocalyptic groups themselves, but via a bridge created by the capacity of the Davidians' opponents to affect the exercise of state authority by raising the specter of mass suicide. The construction of this bridge was facilitated in part by national operatives of what has come to be called the "anti-cult movement" (ACM) (Wright 1995a, pp. 88–90; Lewis 1995; Hall 1995, pp. 218–25). The process and outcome differ substantially from Jonestown, but adequate explanation of Waco involves exactly the same factors, namely, a group of cultural opponents who were able to focus mass media attention on the Branch Davidians, and more importantly, to mobilize overwhelming state power affected by their frame of interpretation.

The cultural opponents drawn together by Breault were mostly apostates from Koresh's group, appalled that Koresh was teaching falsely from the Bible and engaging in a polygamous practice of fathering children with teenaged brides—sometimes with the girls' parents' consent—for a new dynasty, the "House of David." To mobilize against this cultural deviance, the apostates followed what amounted to a generic ACM strategy. They recruited relatives concerned about their family members in the group, and they took their cause to a wide range of mass media outlets, governmental agencies, and politicians. As with Peoples Temple, the opponents had a hard time getting the media and authorities even to take notice, much less action. And as with Peoples Temple, where the opponents succeeded in mobilizing external sources of legitimacy, the ways in which they did so were consequential for the play of events.

On the governmental and political front, the opponents went to local police authorities in California and Texas, to an official of the Texas state Department of Public Safety, to the Texas district attorney, and the assistant U.S. attorney.

They also contacted the IRS and the U.S. Immigration and Naturalization Service, as well as a U.S. congressman, who contacted another congressman, who forwarded concerns to the FBI, prompting an investigation that ended up going nowhere. Like the Concerned Relatives who opposed Peoples Temple, the Davidian "cult-busters" met with frustration in pursuing law enforcement remedies, partly because they lacked prima facie evidence of legal offenses, and partly because of the substantial gap between the enormous threat that opponents believed Koresh posed and their specific charges concerning such matters as the legality of immigration marriages.

As with the Concerned Relatives, Breault and his associates managed to mobilize journalistic coverage hostile to their opponents—in the case of the Davidians, the television program *A Current Affair*, known for its "in-your-face" investigative journalism—that portrayed the Branch Davidians as a "dangerous cult" (Wright 1995a, p. 87).

More consequentially, Breault mobilized a non-Davidian father, David Jewell, to seek custody of his daughter, Kiri Jewell, whom Breault warned was headed for sexual membership in the House of David. Unlike Jonestown's child-god John Victor Stoen, the issue of custody was not a matter of great symbolic significance for the Branch Davidians, and before a court case was concluded, David Jewell and his former wife, Sherri, a Davidian, worked out a joint custody arrangement. But this was not the end of the matter, for in early 1992, David Jewell contacted Texas authorities about the possibility that Koresh would take other child brides, and soon thereafter, Joyce Sparks of Texas Child and Protective Services (CPS) undertook an investigation of the treatment of minors at the Mount Carmel compound. This investigation developed no evidence of abuse, and the agency closed the case over the objections of Sparks, who subsequently provided background on Mount Carmel to the FBI and to the ATF, for their investigations of the Branch Davidians.

The ATF itself is said to have initiated its investigations of weapons violations on the basis of evidence that emerged independently of the cultural opponents, when a delivery truck driver discovered empty grenade casings, and reported his discovery to law enforcement authorities. But the ATF's initial investigation failed to develop adequate cause to obtain a search warrant, and they then turned to Breault and his network of opponents. The warrant that the ATF eventually obtained was bolstered by tendentious claims of the opponents.

Of greater causal significance, the cultural opponents offered the ATF their most detailed "inside" information about the operation of the sect, and this information, tinged by the trope of mass suicide, tilted the planning of the ATF raid toward the precise strategic miscalculations that resulted in the shootout and subsequent siege. Most dramatically, the ATF: (1) mistakenly assumed the dictatorial control of an authoritarian "cult" leader who had central control over the weapons that the Branch Davidians possessed; (2) developed the plan to serve the warrant against Koresh by a strategy of "dynamic entry" because of their paramount concerns about the possibility of mass suicide, concerns that came to them from the Davidians' cultural opponents; and (3) probably failed to develop a fallback procedure in case the raid failed because a failed raid would raise the specter of mass suicide by the Branch Davidians that dynamic entry was supposed to avoid (Hall 1995, pp. 220–28).

The failed raid and the deaths of ATF agents on February 28, 1993, set the stage for the protracted siege, and it was the FBI's frustration at its inability to end the siege—under the glare of media attention, poorly oriented to the theological issues, with state legitimacy at stake—that led to the tear gas assault by tanks. This assault precipitated the fire (even if the Davidians set it), and thus led directly to the deaths of the 74 Davidians who remained in the compound (Tabor and Gallagher 1995; Wright 1995b).

Clearly, the events that led up to the final debacle were extremely complex. For one thing, the ATF itself was not simply driven by the anti-cultism of the cultural opponents. It had its own institutionalized tradition as a sort of wild-west outfit defending the state's claim of legitimate monopolization of means of violence, historically directed especially toward *groups* that take up arms and establish a "state within a state" by engaging in or threatening non-legitimate violence within their own domain. In addition, the desire to justify the ATF federal budget allocation may have enhanced the bureaucratic interest in staging a "big bust," and ATF contacts with journalists before the raid may have led indirectly to losing the element of surprise on the day of the raid. Moreover, the dynamics of policy and action within the FBI during the siege (defined as a "hostage situation") were influenced not only by an anti-cult mentality (Wright 1995a; Lewis 1995); they were also affected by the media spotlight (Richardson 1995; Shupe and Hadden 1995) and by issues of child abuse— themselves a recurrent (and sometimes dubious) accusation raised by the anti-cult movement toward "cults" (Ellison and Bartkowski 1995).

Yet these complexities add nothing of necessity or sufficiency to the explanation of Waco. If anything, the implementation of state and media agendas at Waco was simply a more extreme re-enactment of events leading up to the Jonestown tragedy, perversely induced in significant part precisely by the cultural opponents' invocation of "another Jonestown." That is, sociological explanation of the genesis of the Waco debacle involves the complex interaction of the same factors at work at Jonestown: cultural opponents, including apostates and relatives, who mobilize mass media coverage in an anti-cult frame, and draw in sympathetic or institutionally concerned segments of the state—in the case of Waco, state agencies that regarded the group as challenging state legitimacy (and in the case of the FBI, its own authority).

We can evaluate this explanation of Waco by considering the plausibility of counterfactual scenarios. In the first place, the siege mentality and weapons acquisition at Mount Carmel began in earnest in early 1992, when *A Current Affair*'s television exposé, the custody court case, and the CPS inquiry were initiated—all through efforts of Breault and his allies (Hall 1995, pp. 219–20). Without the increased weapons acquisition, it is not clear that evidence would have been produced that would have led the ATF to pursue an investigation. But even assuming that the ATF would have come to the point of investigating the Davidians without the concerted actions of the cultural opponents, the dense web of multiple agency concern in which the ATF acted was clearly the product of the opponents' efforts, and it was only with information provided by the opponents that the ATF was able to obtain a warrant. Most important, without the cultural opponents, and the CPS investigator whom they rallied to their cause, the ATF strategy of dynamic entry would have been evaluated in a much different way, less favorably in comparison to alternative strategies—either placing the compound under siege or serving a warrant on Koresh away from the compound (Hall 1995, pp. 220–28). Finally, without the efforts of the cultural opponents, the element of surprise probably would not have been lost on the day of the ATF raid, because news reporters probably would not have known about the Branch Davidians, since the group did not seek mass publicity, instead recruiting among social networks of Seventh-Day Adventists. True, the ATF might have wanted to stage a big raid for its own publicity purposes, but as we have already seen, the choice of a strategy of dynamic entry that made the raid a big one was itself an outgrowth of cultural opponents' input into ATF strategy, not an action autonomously generated within the ATF. At Jonestown, the overall conflict could have followed alternative routes to disaster, but for the Davidians, the fire was highly contingent on the botched ATF raid, subsequent siege, and tank attack. In the absence of the cult-busters' successful efforts to mobilize journalists, state officials, and politicians, it is thus difficult to generate a plausible scenario in which the deaths would have occurred.

This is not to say that cultural opponents are inherently powerful, or that they conspire to produce cult disasters. Instead, it seems that apostates and their allies in contemporary religious conflicts, following a general modus operandi developed within the anti-cult movement, take actions on multiple fronts with sufficient intensity to spark consequences that involve the dynamic interaction of an apocalyptic group with the opposition of legitimate authority under the spotlight of media coverage. These are conditions conducive to apocalyptic religious violence. Although cultural opposition has little power on its own, it seems *necessary* though *not* sufficient—in the strictly explanatory sense of those terms— as a *catalyst*. In effect, the actions of cultural opponents arrange previously disconnected elements into an affinity of opposition elements that becomes greater than the sum of its parts. In confrontation with strongly apocalyptic movements, at Jonestown and Mount Carmel, the consequences were pitched conflict and, in different ways, collective death under anticipated and increasing subjection to external authority. The interactions among apostates, other cultural opponents, the media, and the state were highly contingent, and precarious in relation to other contingencies. The consequences were hardly necessary, and we cannot rule out other dynamics that might have similar outcomes. Still, the parallels between two substantially different groups suggest a certain robustness to the model describing religious conflict that results in apocalyptic violence.

THE SOLAR TEMPLE'S MYSTICAL APOCALYPSE

A useful way to evaluate the scope and validity of this model is to consider the strange story of the Ordre du Temple Solaire (OTS). This group differed significantly from either Peoples Temple or the Branch Davidians, but it engaged in an apparently similar practice of murder and mass suicide that became visible to the world on the morning of October 5, 1994, when police in Switzerland discovered the bodies of 48 members of the group who had died in ritualized ceremonies in two different Swiss villages. These events were quickly tied to the murders of three people and the suicides of two others connected with the Solar Temple in a resort town near Montreal, Canada. Over a year later, on the winter solstice of 1995, 16 more people associated with the sect died in a similar ceremony in a wooded mountain area in France, near the Swiss border. And five more adepts died in a third Transit, held near Quebec around the spring equinox of 1997.

News analysts were quick to compare the Solar Temple's deathly tableaux to Jonestown and Waco. And much the same connection (from a different point of view) was made by the author of four letters entrusted to a young sect member to mail to journalists, scholars, and government officials the morning after the October 1994 fires. One letter, addressed To Those Who Love Justice, claimed the group had been subjected to "systematic persecution" by authorities on three continents and noted "a particularly troubling coincidence" between the Waco standoff and a 1993 operation by the Sûreté du Quebec that targeted the Temple's charismatic homeopathic doctor, Luc Jouret. At the same time, however, the letter also insistently called the deaths in the fires a "Transit, which is in no way a suicide in the human sense of the term." Later, police authorities of Sûreté du Quebec claimed that Jouret and company had intended to depart for Sirius, the Dog Star. Claiming contact with "Ascended Masters" who live outside of conventional time and space, the adepts of the Solar Temple hedged that they could metaphysically move outside time and space themselves, via their ritualized collective death (Hall and Schuyler, 1997).

In already tragic company, the Order of the Solar Temple seems truly bizarre. Whereas Peoples Temple and the Branch Davidians included mostly ordinary folk and the dispossessed, many Solar Temple participants were quite wealthy and socially established, and most others participated in the New Age culture and economy that flourishes in post-industrial cities, resort areas, and other venues of the relatively educated new middle class. Whereas Peoples Temple and the Branch Davidians had strongly Protestant (and in Jones's case, crude communist) sensibilities, the Order of the Solar Temple appealed almost exclusively to people of francophone Catholic cultural background.

In addition, there were important differences among the groups' valences toward the utopian orientations of apocalyptic struggle with "the beast," apocalyptic escape toward other-worldly sanctuary, and mysticism that would transcend "this" world (Hall 1978). The two American groups advanced strongly apocalyptic ideologies that alternated between escape to a heaven-on-earth versus confrontation with their adversaries, with no other mystical element than the mystical imagery of the Bible's Book of Revelation (especially important to the Davidians, who nevertheless were far from mystics). But in the crypts of the Solar Temple, the valence was reversed: although Luc Jouret often espoused apocalyptic imagery in public lectures, the apocalypse was portrayed as a traumatic but tremendously positive transition to the age of Aquarius, initially keyed to the task of gathering the faithful together on a survival farm, to pave the way for the New Age. Moreover, the apocalyptic elements of Solar theology were encapsulated within mystical ceremonies that ritualized participants' connection with divine eternity. Ritual achievement of mystical union with transcendence, rather than either apocalyptic survival or struggle, was the dominant counter-cultural motif of everyday life.

On the face of it, and for multiple reasons, the Order of the Solar Temple does not seem a likely candidate for apocalyptic violence. It is thus important to consider whether the deaths of people associated with the Solar Temple amounted to murder and mass suicide that resulted from a dynamic similar to the conflicts at Jonestown and Mount Carmel. If not apocalyptic violence, what was it? And if it was apocalyptic violence, how can its occurrence be squared with the generic narrative model that fits the other two cases? We can begin to address these issues by considering relevant elements of the group's history.

The Solar Temple was formed in the early 1980s out of the crucible of neo-Templar and Rosicrucian movements in Switzerland and southern France (Introvigne 1995; Mayer 1996). Its principals, a mystagogic habitué of the meta-physical scene named Jo DiMambro and a young charismatic homeopathic doctor named Luc Jouret, worked assiduously to promote a public image of high cultural legitimacy. As "front man," Jouret projected an integrated, holistic, homeopathic vision of the New Age that opened into a secret Templar- and Rosicrucian-inspired society dominated by DiMambro. Jouret travelled a lecture circuit in France, Belgium, Switzerland, Martinique, and Quebec, making presentations on topics like "Love and Biology" and "Christ, the Sphinx, and the New Man." His seminars were held in major hotels, his lectures given at rented halls in universities. Yet the public facade of high scientistic (counter-)cultural legitimacy protected a secret world of an invented tradition that connected the Temple with the famous medieval Knights Templar and the Rosicrucians—both groups historically reputed to possess gnostic secrets of human divinity. As increasing numbers of apostates left the secret society in the 1990s, behind a public facade that turned out to be a fragile construction highly subject to external destabilization, its theology of mystical apocalypse became increasingly specified as a "Transit."

The trickle of defections that began in the 1990s left the Solar Temple potentially subject to embarrassing revelations by its apostates, and it cut into the financial vitality of the group (Hall and Schuyler 1997; Mayer 1996; cf. Bromley, Chapter 2 this volume). Apparently, however, only one of the apostates became a dogged opponent who succeeded in ways relevant to the explanatory model under consideration here. That person, Rose-Marie Klaus, was the Protestant exception who proves the rule of the group's appeal to a culturally Catholic audience. Yet Mme. Klaus did not work alone. To the contrary, her personal grievances with the Solar Temple became amplified because she acted in relation to a francophone network of anti-cult organizations.

Rose-Marie Klaus had followed her husband, Bruno, from Switzerland to Sainte-Anne-de-la-Pérade, Quebec, where the group was establishing its "arch" (or "ark") of survival into the New Age. Her husband became caught up in alliances with other women in the sect, however, and Rose-Marie Klaus became increasingly alienated from both the group and her husband. Sometime in 1990, she contacted Info-Secte (or Info-Cult, as they call themselves in English), a private anti-cult organization based in Montreal.

When Rose-Marie Klaus came to their offices around 1991, Info-Secte already knew about the Solar Temple from scattered, unsubstantiated complaints. Klaus told Yves Casgrain, research director at Info-Secte, about her separation from her husband and her troubled efforts to recoup her investment in the farm at Ste. Anne. But none of what Klaus said provided enough evidence of wrongdoing to warrant Info-Secte's going public with accusations. Casgrain soon learned more, however, from a group similar to Info-Secte—l'Association pour la Défense des Familles et de l'Individu (ADFI), an anti-cult organization with branches around France and on the Caribbean island of Martinique, but not in Quebec. On September 10, 1991, the president of ADFI in Martinique, Lucién Zécler, sent a circular about the Solar Temple to Info-Secte and other organizations in Quebec. He described the Order's message as one of planetary catastrophe and he quoted a 1991 Temple bulletin announcing, "the countdown is locked in." Wealthy and influential Martiniquans were being encouraged to sell their possessions and depart the island for Quebec. "We have come to the conviction," Zécler's letter concluded, "that the only way to save the relatives of our friends and stop the hemorrhage is to unmask this organization in its noxious practices."

This letter did not get many responses from Quebec, but it got one from Rose-Marie Klaus, on October 20, 1991. "It was Casgrain [of Info-Secte] who said to us that if we got in touch with Madame Klaus, she was ready to give us a lot of information," Zécler recalls. By the end of 1992, Rose-Marie had divorced Bruno, receiving a $150,000 settlement from the Solar Temple, amounting, in the court's reckoning, to half the money that the couple originally had put into the Ste. Anne project. But Rose-Marie still asserted that the Solar Temple owed her money, and the settlement freed her to amplify her denunciations. With ADFI-Martinique paying for the plane ticket, she travelled to the Caribbean island in December of 1992. During a stay of about two weeks, Rose-Marie spoke to the Rotary Club, and stories about her appeared in the island's newspaper, *Frances Antilles*. From what Zécler heard, after Klaus's visit, some

Martiniquans "went to Canada to demand the money that they had invested in the project. Because they realized finally that Jouret had fooled them.''

To this point, the Solar Temple had managed to keep increased internal dissension and apostasy outside the public eye in Europe (Mayer 1996, pp. 55–61). The developments in Martinique revealed what a determined opponent could do to fuel public controversy. And indeed, the apostate career of Rose-Marie Klaus soon became connected to a different chain of events in Canada, already in motion. At Ste. Anne, Luc Jouret had been replaced as Grand Master in 1990, when he began to put what some members found to be too much urgency into his already apocalyptic message. Jouret had responded by founding a new group, called l'Académie de Recherche et Connaissance des Hautes Sciences, ARCHS. In the schism, he took a number of loyalists with him. His key ally, Jean-Pierre Vinet, a vice president at the state-run Hydro-Quebec power company, then helped Jouret establish himself on the lecture circuit as a "management guru.''

Vinet and Jouret drafted a Canadian businessman named Herman Delorme to become president of ARCHS, and in November 1992, Jean-Pierre Vinet asked Delorme to supply a pistol with a silencer. Vinet explained that he needed protection, but he didn't know how to shoot and he wanted to practice without disturbing neighbors. Delorme pursued the request, eventually making contact with a man who turned out to be a police informant.

At about the same time, the Sûreté du Québec (SQ) later reported, someone identifying himself as "André Massé" began calling government offices, threatening to assassinate the Minister of Public Security, Claude Ryan, and several parliamentary deputies. The Sûreté du Québec has never been able to find out anything about "André" or the organization he claimed to represent, "Q-37" (supposedly named for the 37 Quebecers who made up the group). However, SQ asserts that at the time, investigators saw a possible connection between Q-37's threats and Delorme's interest in buying guns. Following this slim lead, they arranged a sting operation. At a rendezvous on Nun's Island in Montreal on the afternoon of March 8, 1993, Delorme bought three pistols. Forty-five minutes later, as he was exiting a freeway on the drive home, police surrounded and arrested him. Within hours, police took Jean-Pierre Vinet into custody and issued a warrant for the arrest of Luc Jouret, who was in Europe at the time.

Three days after the arrests, less than three months after her return from Martinique, Rose-Marie Klaus was on the front page of the tabloid *Journal de Montreal*, scowling and holding up a white robe with a red cross. "I Lost One Million," the headline declared. A week later, Quebec's *Photo Police* had a picture of Rose-Marie in the same pose, the headline promising "What They Haven't Told You About THE HORROR OF THE ORDRE DU TEMPLE SOLAIRE." These stories—and interviews with other newspapers, radio, and television stations—turned out to be repetitions, with some elaboration, of Rose-Marie's allegations to Info-Secte in 1991.

Jouret's attorney, Jean-Claude Hébert, thought he could win acquittal on the weapons charges. Faced with a trial amid intense media interest, however, Jouret didn't want any more publicity. "At that period, they had the wind in their sails," Hébert said later, "and I could understand that the negative publicity put out in Canada might come down in France, in Switzerland, in Martinique, and spoil his whole network of activities." At a brief trial in July 1993, the Crown Prosecutor accepted a plea bargain. The judge reasoned that the weapons had been purchased for defensive purposes and that the defendants had already been abundantly penalized by the media. He sentenced Jouret, Vinet, and Delorme each to one year of unsupervised probation and a fine of $1,000, to be donated to the Red Cross.

In law enforcement circles, however, the gun incident became categorized as illegal arms trafficking, and it triggered a chain reaction of investigations. Within two days after the arrests, SQ publicly announced an inquiry into financial aspects of OTS. Australian police opened a parallel inquiry later in 1993. A bulletin went out from the international police organization, Interpol, alleging that Jo DiMambro and a woman confidant, Odile Dancet, had taken part in two banking transactions in Australia of $93 million each. French authorities initiated a separate investigation in 1994, putting a temporary delay on reissuing the passport belonging to DiMambro's wife, Jocelyne. By March 1994, the Royal Canadian Mounted Police were cooperating with Australian Federal Police inquiries concerning possible money laundering.

Temple principals never fully understood the extent of these investigations, but they had their suspicions. A Transit letter sent to the French interior minister, Charles Pasqua, asserted, "Police intimidation increased and the harassment went beyond what could be endured" (Cohen and Brown 1996). Another letter, To Those Who Love Justice, did not mention the rumors of money laundering that circulated on the Interpol network. But it did claim that the Solar Temple had been the target of a "pseudo-plot" concocted by connecting them with Q-37, the supposed terrorist group that had never been publicly mentioned before the gun arrests.

By 1995, SQ sergeant Robert Poeti would say, "Q-37, as far as we're concerned, never existed. It was a joke, a guy who called. There are people who are deranged, who do this. We are convinced that the one who made the calls had nothing to do with the Ordre du Temple Solaire. Nothing at all." If so, we are left with an irony of history—that a mere coincidence should have drawn together police action, the Temple's most formidable dissident, and exposé coverage of a cult in the mass media.

The initial "Transit" took place in October of 1994, more than a year after the gun incident and the negative press stories centered on the claims of Rose-Marie Klaus. The writers of the Solar Temple's Transit letters clearly assert the belief that the group was the target of a conspiracy, and the beleaguered tone of their writings is unmistakable: "We do not know when they can close the trap on us again . . . what days, what weeks?'' (Mayer 1996, p. 100). And yet, although investigations of the group were continuing at the time of the Transit, they amounted to nothing like the direct state assertion of jurisdiction at Jonestown and Mount Carmel. Indeed, the Solar Temple as a whole never faced any proximate visible threat. Moreover, the Solar Temple had long held to a secret doctrine of soul travel between earthly existence and eternal transcendence (Hall and Schuyler 1997), and even in the absence of persecution, their theology might have been developed toward warranting a "Transit," which would look like mass suicide in earthly terms.

Because of these complexities, no one now is in a position to conduct the experiment with History to reveal what would have happened if the followers of the Ascended Masters had not believed themselves to be the target of a conspiracy. But certain elements can be disentangled. At Jonestown and Mount Carmel, the violence began with murder of opponents, and Solar Temple faithfuls followed this pattern, killing two apostates and their young child, one of them a handyman who knew the secrets of the technology used in the crypts to create fantastic sensations during "visits" from the Ascended Masters. Absent Rose-Marie Klaus and the gun incident, *if* the Temple had attempted a Transit, this family with knowledge of organizational secrets probably still would have died.

The key question, then, is whether the Temple would have attempted its initial Transit in the absence of the negative publicity from Rose-Marie Klaus and the gun incident. The Sûreté du Québec has asserted that they prevented an *earlier* Transit by their arrests, whereas the Transit letters describe the departure as "premature." This very description acknowledges the plan for Transit, independent of external opposition, a plan that can be tied to ideas of a French metaphysician, Jacques Breyer (1959), who calculated the beginning of the third millennium such that "The Grand Monarchy ought to leave this world around 1995–96," that is, around the time of the *second* Transit, at the winter solstice of 1995. Even a fixed prediction for apocalypse is subject to revision, however. (Most famously, the nineteenth-century American Millerites, and other groups expecting the big apocalypse as well, have watched the planned date pass and have then either re-calculated, or lost the critical mass of support for their movement.) In the case of the Solar Temple, Breyer's calculations left considerable room for revisionist flexibility, and other theological resources oriented the group toward post-apocalyptic survival on earth.

On the other hand, if the Solar Temple were to follow some version of Breyer's script, the plan would not be to *wait passively* for an external sign of the Apocalypse, but to *take action* to "leave this world" at a specific point in time in order to feed upon the presumed convergence of harmonic energy force fields. It is thus not completely implausible that the initial Transit could have taken place even without either the specific elements of apocalyptic conflict that *did* occur (i.e., the gun incident, the efforts of Rose-Marie Klaus brokered by

Info-Secte, the resulting media coverage, the trial, and subsequent investigations), or some alternative crisis that might have been precipitated by actions of other apostates in the wings (e.g., Europeans, Martiniquans, the Dutoits).

How, then, would a hypothetical *non*-confrontational Transit be understood within the sociology of religion? This question brings us to core issues about the meaningful structures of mass suicide, apocalypticism, and mysticism. By considering it, we can come to a clearer understanding of the parallels and differences among the episodes of violence associated with Peoples Temple, the Branch Davidians, and the Solar Temple.

On the one hand, a Transit seems contradictory to any ideal typical logic of mysticism, since mysticism does not acknowledge either time in its social construction or a strong dualism between this world and some eternal world (Hall 1978). On the other hand, the model of religious violence presented here characterizes apocalyptic mass suicide as bound up with issues of collective legitimacy in the face of mobilized public opposition. A counterfactual "pure" Transit of the Solar Temple in the absence of perceived external threats (as opposed to the first Transit that occurred) does not approximate this model either. Mysticism has other routes to eternity than physical death, and without a manifest social opposition, mass suicide lacks any apocalyptic *raison d'être*.

These theoretical considerations about ideal typical logics suggest that the specific hybrid character of the Solar Temple has to do with how it combined apocalyptic and mystical elements. The production of religious experience in the Solar Temple depended on a spiritual hierarchy in which a mystagogue, acting as priest, served as an intermediary between divinity (the Ascended Masters) and the audience of religious seekers. Believers did not need to be particularly "musical" in matters of transcendence; instead, they took the role of clients who received a mystical experience produced through participation in ritual.

But here another puzzle arises, for "client mysticism" is a staple of New Age spirituality, found in other templar and more strictly Rosicrucian groups, tarot readings, and ritual practices under diverse other auspices. Yet there is no obvious theological reason to anticipate mass suicide or any other form of collective death among Rosicrucians in contact with Ascended Masters. Thus, even in client mysticism not so dissimilar from the Temple's, physical death as a sine qua non seems odd. Either death is illusory, and transcendence (i.e., the Transit) doesn't depend upon it. Or in the realist Zen Buddhist view, death is the end of life, which closes off the possibility of transcendence. There are indications that the Solar Temple theology finessed these alternatives by the thesis that the trauma that *seemed* like death in the Transit wasn't really death at all, only the wrenching shift from quotidian to eternal reality by Ascended Masters whose existence eclipses life and death in any humanly understood terms. Yet any such claim begs the question of why previous templar and Rosicrucian adepts had not found suicide necessary for union with the eternal.

These are deep puzzles, and ones that are not subject to any tidy answer now that the spiritually most evolved of the Solar templars have orchestrated their own deaths, along with those of certain of their enemies. With the third Transit in 1997, perhaps all their closest followers have now departed. The difficulty in squaring the Transit with either pure mysticism or currently predominant kinds of client mysticism on their own suggests that these cultural structures are not adequate to explain the violence. A much more likely cultural source is the Western religious dualism that equates life with temporality, death with eternity and (potentially) transcendence. After all, the Solar Temple operated as a neo-traditional, quasi-Catholic organization that both mirrored the client mysticism of the church itself and embraced the saga of the medieval Knights Templar, who reputedly died martyrs because they dared to embrace the true teachings of the gnostic Christ. In these aspects, faced with opposition, the Temple drew from the deep well of the Western tradition that mixes the client mysticism of dispensed salvation with quasi-apocalyptic struggles for the true faith—in the death of Jesus, the martyrdom of early Christians, and the burnings at the stake of the Knights Templar who refused to recant their allegiance to the order (Cohn 1993; Williams 1975; Frend 1967; Riddle 1931; Partner 1982). Specifically, Temple theology, which appropriated the idea of Transit from the writings of Jacques Breyer (1959), combined Christian millenarianism with the concept of astrological eras and mystical harmonics of transcendence. In sum, a meaning-fully coherent model of *mystical* mass suicide is difficult to consolidate. When this sociological incoherence is traced in relation to empirical forms of religi-osity, its source is to be found in a mysticism colored both by dualism and by connections with Christian apocalyptic martyrdom.

In the Solar Temple, the theology of ecological apocalypse and survival ini-tially did not depend on apocalyptic opponents for its meaningful coherence within the group. Thus, if the Transit letters had not ranted against the "per-secution" that the group alleged, the insistence in one letter that the collective death was "in no way a suicide in the human sense of the term" would have been perfectly plausible. Absent the sense of persecution, the deaths would not amount to mass suicide of the sort that we have posited as the potential de-nouement of conflict between an apocalyptic group and its detractors. Instead, the deaths would be better understood as the product of an idiosyncratic theology made possible by a form of client mysticism that mapped transcendence within a dualistic matrix of life and death. This complex of mystical ideas may also be the theological locus of the extremely orderly April 1997 collective suicide by 39 members of Heaven's Gate, who claimed to use ritualized death to travel via the Hale-Bopp comet to the Kingdom of Heaven. As Mayer observes, Jo DiMambro was flexible and syncretic in tapping theological sources and prin-ciples as occasion required. From what empirical information is available, it seems that the initial Transit in October 1994 was neither the product of a purely mystical theology nor did it stem from mysticism colored only by an ideology of apocalyptic survivalism. Rather, there was a shift from earthly apocalyptic survivalism to passage beyond the earthly apocalypse in the early 1990s, but this theology only became fully elaborated as "departure" in the context of an increased perception of earthly opposition, from February 1993 onward (Mayer 1996, pp. 70–78).

Whether the deaths would have been orchestrated absent the opposition and ensuing scandals is a counterfactual experiment that cannot be completed. Nor will we ever know whether the second and third Transits would have occurred in the absence of the initial one. The evidence remains ambiguous. What does seem plausible as a conclusion about what *did* happen—especially given the Transit letters' condemnation of the Temple's opponents, and also the murder of the Dutoits—is that opposition was *sufficient* to push believing Adepts already enamored with mystical transcendence to the initial physical enactment of Transit through death under apocalyptically framed circumstances. Although apocalyptic mass suicide is properly associated with external confrontations, the dialectic between the Solar Temple's theology of mystical consocation with eternity and the play of events on the ground shows that apocalyptic developments of confrontation can be quite powerful, even if the apocalyptic element of theology is initially relatively weak and other-worldly.

CONCLUDING REFLECTIONS

The religious violence at Jonestown, Mount Carmel, and within the Solar Temple differ in important ways, but they all can be located theoretically in relation to a set of broadly shared social circumstances. In general terms, the stakes of "cultural legitimacy" for an established social order are typically defined territorially and in relation to "subversive" organizations. Under this regimen, there is a propensity for countercultural movements to become embroiled in conflicts with "cultural" opponents, the "church," and the "state." In modern states where the institutional power of "churches" tends to be in decline, states increasingly act as their surrogates in enforcing the boundaries of cultural legitimacy. It is also the case today that "cultural opponents" tend to become crystallized as loosely institutionalized social networks that emerge when countercultural religious social movements arise. Such networks typically draw together apostates, families of members, anti-cult organizations, and news reporters who frame "cult" stories in terms of moral deviance (Hall 1987; Bromley, Chapter 2 this volume).

Much remains unknown about the Solar Temple, or for that matter, the events at Jonestown and Mount Carmel. We therefore do not want to claim analytic closure prematurely. In lieu of a conclusion, it is nonetheless important to point out three interesting parallels between Jonestown, Waco, and the initial Transit of the Solar Temple that may contribute to a more general understanding of the relationships between apocalyptic movements, their apostates, and extreme violence.

- All three cases ended in some approximation of specifically apocalyptic "mass suicide" in which principals of the religious movement group—and those who willingly followed—engaged in murder of detractors and the more weakly committed among their members, and took their own lives as a way of salvaging their own construction of the collective honor and legitimacy of the group.

- In all three cases, what we have described as a loosely institutionalized "cultural" opposition—involving apostates, one or more anti-cult organizations, and sympathetic news reporters—was central to the production of circumstances in which mass suicide came to be regarded as a viable course of action by the principals of the group.

- In all three cases, the state, or states, came to be seen by the group as allied with the cultural opposition, and committed to active opposition to the group.

By comparison to Jonestown and Waco, *l'affaire Temple Solaire* is distinctive in two central respects. First, there are lingering questions as to whether and how the cultural opposition by apostates and their allies was mediated through networks of the francophone anti-cult movement in ways that go beyond the facilitating role of Info-Secte in Montreal and the entrepreneurial role of ADFI-Martinique that we have identified. Evidently, within the broad sphere of Catholicism, a significant cultural struggle manifests itself today between schismatic traditionalists, the church itself, and what we have called "neo-traditionalist quasi-Catholic" religious social movements. The trajectories of this cultural conflict and its relation to state secular hostility to countercultural religious movements are important in themselves as dynamics of contemporary history. A key agenda for future sociological research thus concerns understanding the social processes of coordination or influence by which religious and state opposition to countercultural religious social movements become, in effect, aligned with apostate-centered cultural opposition.

Second, by comparison to Jonestown, and certainly to Waco, the external pressures on the Solar Temple were considerably less. In a nutshell, so far as we are presently able to determine, the major developments were the following: Rose-Marie Klaus denounced the group in Martinique, the Sûreté Quebec pursued the gun arrests, and there were media and investigatory consequences of these actions. These pressures were all "indirect" in the sense that they did not subject the Solar Temple to a territorial confrontation of the sort entailed in Leo Ryan's fateful visit to Jonestown, nor was there anything like the standoff between the FBI and the Branch Davidians after the ATF's botched raid on Mount Carmel. Yet just as clearly, the external pressure was sufficient to generate a set of circumstances that effectively destabilized the group (see Hall and Schuyler 1997). Thus, the capacity of opponents to destabilize a religious social movement in ways that set the stage for an apocalyptic denouement do not necessarily depend on direct spatial confrontations; apparently, even developments that do not immediately threaten a movement's territory but undermine the potential for its effective future operation can open the door to a quest for a denouement in murder and mass suicide that reaffirms the group's self-definition. The critical issue seems to concern whether the group's principals can legitimate to their followers the claim of persecution by apostates and other external opponents as the basis of their troubles. Here, the avenues of legitimation are channeled by the group's social construction of reality, and they are thus subject to complex and emergent meanings, including broadly religious ones. Whatever we are to make of such meanings, at the end of the second millennium, apocalyptic conflict is mercurial in the pathways of its resolution.

NOTE

This study has benefitted from the comments of participants in conferences and seminars where the analysis was first presented: at the annual meetings of the American Sociological Association in New York in August 1996, and at the Departments of Sociology at the University of Edinburgh, the University of Surrey, and the London School of Economics in the fall of 1996. We are also very grateful to Guenther Roth and David Bromley for their comments on a written draft. As authors, we take final responsibility for the text.

REFERENCES

Bernstein, Michael. 1994. *Foregone Conclusions*. Berkeley: University of California Press.

Breyer, Jacques. 1959. *Arcanes Solaire; ou, Les Secrets du Temple Solaire*. Paris: La Colombe.

Bromley, David, and Edward Silver. 1995. "The Davidian Tradition." Pp. 43–72 in *Armageddon in Waco*, edited by Stuart Wright. Chicago: University of Chicago Press.

Chidester, David. 1988. *Salvation and Suicide*. Bloomington: Indiana University Press.

Cohen, Daniel, and David Carr Brown. 1996. "Death of the Solar Temple." Television program, September 20. London: Asteride/Psychology News/France 2/Channel 4.

Cohn, Norman. 1993. *Cosmos, Chaos and the World to Come*. New Haven: Yale University Press.

———. (1970 [1957]). *Pursuit of the Millennium*. Oxford: Oxford University Press.

Coser, Lewis. 1974. *Greedy Institutions*. New York: Free Press.

Ellison, Christopher, and John Bartkowski. 1995. " 'Babies Were Being Beaten': Exploring Child-abuse Allegations at Ranch Apocalypse." Pp. 111–49 in *Armageddon in Waco*, edited by Stuart Wright. Chicago: University of Chicago Press.

Frend, W. H. C. 1967. *Martyrdom and Persecution in the Early Church*. Garden City, NY: Doubleday.

Griffin, Larry J. 1993. "Narrative, Event-structure Analysis, and Causal Interpretation in Historical Sociology." *American Journal of Sociology* 98:1094–1133.

Hall, John R. 1978. *The Ways Out*. London: Routledge and Kegan Paul.

———. 1979. "The Apocalypse at Jonestown." *Society* 16(6):52–61.

———. 1987. *Gone from the Promised Land*. New Brunswick, NJ: Transaction.

———. 1988a. "Social Organization and Pathways of Commitment: Types of Communal Groups, Rational Choice Theory, and the Kanter Thesis.'' *American Sociological Review* 53:679–92.

———. 1988b. ''Jonestown and Bishop Hill: Continuities and Disjunctures in Religious Conflict.'' *Communal Studies* 8:77–89.

———. 1995. ''Public Narratives and the Apocalyptic Sect: From Jonestown to Mount Carmel.'' Pp. 205–35 in *Armageddon in Waco*, edited by Stuart Wright. Chicago: University of Chicago Press.

Hall, John R., and Philip Schuyler. 1997. ''The Mystical Apocalypse of the Solar Temple.'' In *Millennium, Messiahs and Mayhem*, edited by Thomas Robbins and Susan Palmer. London: Routledge.

Hawthorne, Geoffrey. 1991. *Plausible Worlds*. New York: Cambridge University Press.

Introvigne, Massimo. 1995. ''Ordeal by Fire: The Tragedy of the Solar Temple.'' *Religion* 25:267–83.

Knox, Ronald. 1956. *Enthusiasm, a Chapter in the History of Religion*. Oxford: Oxford University Press.

Lewis, James. 1995. ''Self-fulfilling Stereotypes, the Anti-cult Movement, and the Waco Confrontation.'' Pp. 95–110 in *Armageddon in Waco*, edited by Stuart Wright. Chicago: University of Chicago Press.

Mannheim, Karl. 1936. *Ideology and Utopia*. New York: Harcourt, Brace and World.

Mayer, Jean-François. 1996. *Les Mythes du Temple Solaire*. Geneva, Switzerland: Georg Editeur.

Mill, John Stuart. 1950 [1843]. *John Stuart Mill's Philosophy of Scientific Method*. New York: Hafner.

Partner, Peter. 1982. *The Murdered Magicians*. New York: Oxford University Press.

Pitts, William L., Jr. 1995. ''Davidians and Branch Davidians, 1929–1987.'' Pp. 20–42 in *Armageddon in Waco*, edited by Stuart Wright. Chicago: University of Chicago Press.

Richardson, James. 1995. ''Manufacturing Consent about Koresh.'' Pp. 95–110 in *Armageddon in Waco*, edited by Stuart Wright. Chicago: University of Chicago Press.

Riddle, Donald. 1931. *The Martyrs*. Chicago: University of Chicago Press.

Robbins, Thomas. 1986. ''Religious Mass Suicide before Jonestown: The Russian Old Believers.'' *Sociological Analysis* 47:1–20.

Shupe, Anson, and Jeffrey Hadden. 1995. ''Cops, News Copy and Public Opinion.'' Pp. 177–202 in *Armageddon in Waco*, edited by Stuart Wright. Chicago: University of Chicago Press.

Stinchcombe, Arthur. 1978. *Theoretical Methods in Social History*. New York: Academic.

Tabor, James, and Eugene Gallagher. 1995. *Why Waco? Cults and the Battle for Religious Freedom in America*. Berkeley: University of California Press.

Williams, Sam. 1975. *Jesus' Death as a Saving Event*. Harvard Dissertations in Religion, no. 2. Cambridge: Harvard Theological Review.

Wright, Stuart. 1995a. ''Construction and Escalation of a Cult Threat.'' Pp. 75–94 in *Armageddon in Waco*, edited by Stuart Wright. Chicago: University of Chicago Press.

Wright, Stuart, ed. 1995b. *Armageddon in Waco*. Chicago: University of Chicago Press.

Chapter 8

Apostates, Whistleblowers, Law, and Social Control

James T. Richardson

Large numbers of participants in minority religions cease their participation voluntarily through "voluntary exiting," which is a term referring to the high attrition rates of most of the newer religious groups (Richardson, van der Lans, and Derks 1986). Much smaller numbers of participants are "deprogrammed" out of such groups, a process known as "extraction," while others are "expelled" from the groups by leaders in a process similar to traditional excommunication (Richardson, van der Lans, and Derks 1986). Some of those who leave, whatever the method, become "apostates" and even develop into "whistleblowers," as those terms are defined in the first chapter of this volume.

Which form of leaving might produce more apostates and whistleblowers is not obvious, and the question has not been directly addressed by researchers. However, some suggestions about possible patterns can be derived from the scholarly literature on leaving religious groups. For instance, it seems reasonable to assume that most people who leave voluntarily, whatever the type of group, would not be motivated to adopt the roles of apostate and whistleblower, and could be termed "defectors." They just leave and get on with their lives. But there are examples of the adoption of apostate and whistleblower roles by voluntary exiters, some of which will be discussed herein.

The examples of voluntary exiters becoming apostates and whistleblowers usually involve something dramatic happening that sours the participant on the group and its leaders in a somewhat rapid and dramatic way (see Wright 1987, for example). However, as scholars have noted, what appears dramatic and rapid may actually have been developing over a period of time, with some event then becoming the proverbial "straw that broke the camel's back."

The apostate and whistleblower roles may also develop from circumstances of "extraction"; this is more likely to occur with organizations in high tension with the external environment. Bromley (Chapter 2 this volume) refers to these organizations as "Subversive" in a very specific sense: *they are perceived and labeled "Subversive" by oppositional groups as a tactic for status degradation that legitimates implementation of extraordinary social control measures.* Some research, such as that by Solomon (1981) and Lewis and Bromley (1987), shows that deprogramming is actually a form of radical resocialization that sometimes results in the deprogrammee adopting a quite negative perspective toward the former group of membership. Indeed, deprogrammers might define development of this negative perspective as a successful deprogramming. It is instructive on this point that a number of prominent deprogrammers have themselves been deprogrammed, sometimes quite dramatically. Thus deprogramming has sometimes resulted in a person changing from devoted member to avid apostate and even whistleblower, as he or she acts out a new role of deprogrammer (or "exit-counselor" as some now prefer to be called).

Expulsion of a member by a group, a little-appreciated process (see Richardson, van der Lans, and Derks 1986), can also lead to apostasy and whistleblowing. Some who are expelled might be so angry at their expulsion that they adopt the role of apostate and whistleblower to achieve revenge on the group that asked them to no longer participate. And, of course, sometimes expulsion might itself occur somewhat simultaneously with voluntary exiting, as a part of the development of "accounts" functional to the group and to the former member during a time of stress brought on by the expulsion/exiting (more on this later).[1]

This chapter will examine the role of apostates and whistleblowers in exerting social control over controversial new or minority religious groups, especially examining the role played by apostates and whistleblowers within the legal arena as a part of social control efforts.[2] As the examination proceeds, the issue of the derivation of apostates and whistleblowers will also be addressed, in an effort to better understand how apostasy and whistleblowing develop within the context of the world of newer and smaller faiths.

SOCIAL CONTROL OF DEVIANT RELIGIOUS GROUPS

Social control in the context of minority religious groups refers to attempts to exercise formal or informal authority over these religious groups, including efforts by governmental authorities as well as by private parties. Such efforts often involve legal or regulatory actions, but also may include use of media and other means to assist in constructing certain definitions of minority religious groups that facilitate exertions of social control over the groups.

Former members of controversial religious groups often play a major legitimating role in efforts at social control. They can claim to have been eye witnesses to key events, and can offer interpretations as an insider of the group of former membership. As such, the disaffected former members are apostates, playing the role of whistleblower, with claims to unique knowledge about the inside workings of a given religious group.

These claims can be thought of as "atrocity tales" or unique "accounts" in the technical sense of those terms as used in sociology. Atrocity tale is a concept developed by Bromley, Shupe, and Ventimiglia (1979) which refers to events that flagrantly violate some fundamental cultural value and which evoke moral outrage to the extent that social control actions against the group perpetrating the event are warranted. Apostates acting in the role of whistleblower can claim to have seen or participated in events, while a member, that meet the definition of atrocity tale, and their account of what happened can legitimate social control efforts.

Accounts are functional for those proposing them, and they can have a major self-serving element (Scott and Lyman 1968). Apostates' accounts also may serve the interests of those trying to discredit such groups, and thus such defectors can achieve a position of prominence with organizations opposed to certain religious groups (Richardson, van der Lans, and Derks 1986). This confluence of interests of anti-cult movements and apostates from new religions is often a key feature in legal battles that attempt to exert social control over new and minority religions, and the apostate qua whistleblower often plays a lead role in such battles.

Social control of deviant religious or political groups is dicey business, however, particularly in a society that values free expression. Effective social control requires authorities willing to exert official authority and a populace willing for that to happen (assuming, of course, that the populace is aware of the effort at control). Neither of those elements is automatically present, but must be engineered.

Sometimes that engineering is easy, requiring no special effort, because the activities thought to be practiced by a given group are considered so outrageous as to warrant almost automatic response by official authority, with the response being supported by the institutional structures of society as well as the general public. That is, if a group can be defined as engaging in those kinds of actions, then the authorities have what might be termed a permanent or automatic warrant to intervene. Indeed, if they do not intervene, then they might be considered negligent in accomplishing their duties, and thereby may suffer sanctions themselves for dereliction of duty.

In the present social climate, for instance, accusations of child sex abuse in a religious group, or terrorist activities in a political group will sanction almost any effort at official social control (see scholarly literature on the Waco tragedy, for instance, such as Wright 1995). Also, activities which are perceived to threaten the autonomy of individual adults (such as allegations of "brainwashing") often have furnished legitimation for strong social control activities (Richardson, van Driel, and Kilbourne 1989; Anthony and Robbins 1992).

DEFINITIONS AND REDEFINITIONS

The list of activities involving an automatic warrant for social control varies in terms of content and length in any given society. That is to say that the list of negatively sanctioned activities warranting intervention by authorities is socially constructed and varies over time. Activities are added to the list through efforts by individuals, groups, and official agencies. What might have been considered harmless or even positive action by a group might later become defined as unacceptable, as "moral entrepreneurs," many of whom are apostates acting as whistleblowers, organize new definitions of acceptable and unacceptable behavior and beliefs. There are many such examples from the world of new and minority religions in Western societies (many of which easily fit the definition of "subversive" used in this volume).

For instance, simple acts of evangelizing and recruitment were sometimes defined positively early in the history of contemporary new religions around the late 1960s and early 1970s. Some authorities thought it better for young Americans to be involved in religion than in the anti-war movement, in the drug subculture, or in lifestyles that involved rampant sexual activity. Mass baptisms in the Pacific Ocean were presented on the evening news in sharp contrast to riots and demonstrations occurring sometimes within relatively short distances from the site of the baptisms, and there was sometimes a focus as well on the "clean living" apparently engaged in by some new religions.

Communal living practiced by some new religious movements was sometimes viewed early on in the history of the new religions as a positive alternative to drug addiction, premarital sex, and other activities, including political ones. For instance, some now quite controversial religious groups were treated well for a time by the media and official authorities because of the groups' efforts to fight drug addiction. Reverend Moon was given the keys to many large American cities in ceremonies that focused on this drug rehabilitation aspect of participation in his movement. His strong stance against communism also did not hurt his image with the populace and contributed to an initial positive reaction by many in society, including even fundamentalist Christians, who were also strongly anti-communist.

Both recruitment and communal living of new religions lost their positive sanction, however, and were redefined as "subversive" activities in the minds of the general populace and official authorities within a relatively short time. Proselytizing was redefined as "stealing children," even though those being recruited were usually of legal age. Leaders of some new religions became redefined as evil modern-day "pied pipers," coming through town and leaving with the "best and the brightest," a feat that could have only been possible through the use of some magical and powerful psychotechnology that came to be described using rubrics such as "brainwashing" and "mind control." Communes were defined as the location where this psychotechnology was best applied, and there were also often accusations of rampant sexual activity, drug use, and other unacceptable behaviors such as begging, stealing, and fraudulent methods for financing the groups.

Some would suggest, of course, that these "subversive" groups were doing such evil things all the time, and that it just took a while to find this out, due to group efforts to conceal such actions. This is especially the claim with a few groups which practiced sexual mores at odds with those of the dominant society. But even claims concerning sexual activities by those who were opposed to the groups sometimes were problematic. Even with the other, more ordinary, activities mentioned, a re-definition process sometimes occurred, transforming what had been otherwise acceptable activities into unacceptable ones. This re-definition process was often facilitated by the accounts of apostates acting as whistleblowers. Thus, recruitment became "brainwashing," work to support the groups' communal lifestyles became unacceptable exploitation of members who were "brainwashed," devotion to a new lifestyle became fanaticism and was cited as evidence for loss of individual autonomy, and so on.

Controversial contemporary religions are not the only settings where such re-definition occurs, of course, and it is instructive to examine other instances of this process with older groups which were themselves defined similarly to how new religions are thought of today. A recent example of re-definition of an older and even well-known religious group (which might be defined as "Contestant," using the Bromley scheme), which will be examined in more detail, concerns how the public and governmental officials think of healing methods of Christian Science, which had achieved considerable respectability. A sign of this respectability for Christian Science was that use of "Spiritual Healing" has previously been positively sanctioned, with special exceptions to criminal statutes written into both state and federal laws. This situation has changed remarkably of late (Richardson and DeWitt 1992), with a number of major cases that have developed around the country in which Christian Science parents of children who died after being treated using Spiritual Healing have been charged with child neglect, child endangerment, child abuse, and even negligent homicide or manslaughter, in spite of apparent legal prohibitions against such charges.

In most of the states involved there were exemptions written into the law for Spiritual Healing so that those practicing it would not be prosecuted when the methods did not seem to work. However, these exemptions have often been overpowered by newfound concern about the welfare of children being promoted by a few apostates acting as whistleblowers.

One such Christian Science apostate, a woman named Rita Swan, had voluntarily exited the group when her child died after being treated by use of Spiritual Healing. She has become a major source of information about the use of such methods, and a proponent of limiting the use of Spiritual Healing by law and through the use of legal actions. She and others of similar views have had a dramatic impact on the way that law enforcement officials and others view Spiritual Healing with children. Thus, what was legally sanctioned before is now thought by some prosecutors and juries to violate the law. This concern about welfare of children that has affected Christian Science is related, of course, to the concern about controversial newer religions which are alleged to harm young people who join them, as well as the children of members who are being raised in such groups.

"SELF-HELP" SOCIAL CONTROL OF NEW RELIGIONS

Some social control efforts are private in nature, even if they receive great attention from the general public. That is, they involve private citizens who feel strongly enough about something to spend their time and resources trying to change a situation that allows the activity in question to occur. In the history of controversial religious groups some of the most ardent critics have been former members of some of the groups. When former members adopt such a critical stance and act on their views they easily fit the definitions of apostate-turned-whistleblower that informs this collection. Some of those strong critics have become involved in dramatic activities, including deprogrammings and whistle-blowing-type claims that have provoked official action against the groups. Motivations are not always obvious in such instances, but what is clear is that sometimes former members devote their lives to efforts at social control. They may spend large amounts of time educating media representatives, governmental officials (including those in law enforcement), and others about the alleged evils of a group.

Such self-help social control actions are given impetus when official authorities cannot or will not take action that some detractors think is warranted. The legal context within which new religions develop in the United States offers a set of circumstances that encourages self-help social control efforts when such groups become controversial. First Amendment protections within American society of groups claiming to be religious has been an impediment to official action in response to the growth of interest in new religions among many youth. Direct efforts to get the federal Department of Justice to take actions against some of the new religions failed, with officials citing freedom of religion and other First Amendment protections as precluding their being able to act.

This refusal by governmental officials to take direct action protected some of the new religious experiments, but it also encouraged more self-help remedies by former members and others interested in controlling the growth of new religions. Often the self-help remedies involved apostates acting in a whistle-blower role, helping justify claims that the groups were violating laws or values of society.

The same point about apparent legal protections of new and minority religions contributing to self-help efforts can be made concerning older minority faiths, as well. The inclusion mentioned above of explicit exemptions in the law of many states to allow Spiritual Healing, which precluded punishing parents who use this approach, has served as an impediment to those who would like for authorities to exercise direct control over use of such healing methods. Hesitation by authorities asked to take action against parents whose children died after such healing methods were used has apparently contributed to efforts of detractors, including former members, to get such exemptions deleted from the statutes, and to find other ways of exerting control over the use of such healing methods with children.[3]

APOSTATE SELF-HELP SOCIAL CONTROL AND LEGAL ACTIONS

Self-help efforts at social control have taken a number of forms, as will be shown in brief descriptions of some prominent recent episodes of social control involving former members of new and minority religions, most which are examples of what Bromley calls "Subversive" organizations. First, a discussion of one apostate's impact on the Church Universal and Triumphant will be offered, followed by a discussion of the role of defectors on legal cases involving the Unification Church, the Hare Krishna, and The Family (formerly known as the Children of God). After that, the situation involving Christian Science Spiritual Healing will be described in more detail, to illustrate similarities between the way apostates qua whistleblowers operate with newer and more traditional religious groups in our society.

The Church Universal and Triumphant and "Brainwashing"

The Church Universal and Triumphant (CUT) has become one of the more controversial new religions, especially after it moved over in 1981 from southern California to occupy a large tract of land near Yellowstone Park. Since this move CUT has been in the national news many times, with accusations of stockpiling weapons and fears that a mass suicide was planned. Also, there have been many concerns expressed about the group in terms of environmental impact, concerns developed in large part because of its proximity to the major park. CUT has made efforts to overcome the enmity that developed between itself and its neighbors, and the concern of environmentalists. It has become the subject of scholarly study, as a part of its efforts to prove that it is harmless to its members and to the environment (Lewis and Melton 1994a).

What is less well-known about CUT is that the move to Montana was brought about in part because of a legal action involving an ex-member. A house designer named Geoffrey Mull was recruited by CUT to design some buildings planned for CUT's large headquarters property in southern California. He lived communally with the group at its headquarters for about two years while he designed the buildings requested by CUT leaders. Mr. Mull had been brought into CUT under quite favorable arrangements because of his talents at building design, with CUT agreeing to furnish him some funds to cover expenses incurred when Mull gave up his house designing practice in the San Francisco area. Mull also negotiated some agreements while a participant (such as the loan of some $37,000 from the group to cover personal expenses he had) that are rare in the annals of new religions.

However, after CUT leaders rejected his designs and decided against building them, Mull became upset with the group, withdrew as a communal member, and started attacking CUT in forums around the country. Mull became a regular on the anti-cult circuit for a time, giving speeches in which he accused the group of many unethical and illegal practices. CUT leaders eventually attempted to silence him by threatening to sue him on notes for loans of $37,000 that Mull had signed while a member. They did this on the advice of an attorney with whom they had talked because of the continued attacks by Mull.

The threat to sue Mull was some of the worst advice ever given by an attorney to a religious group. When the threat was delivered, Mull seemed to redouble his efforts at attacking CUT in speeches around the country, and eventually a suit was filed, as CUT made good on its threat. Mull, using an experienced attorney in anti-cult circles, countersued for $253 million, alleging fraud, duress, assault, extortion, intentional affliction of emotional distress, and quantum merit (see Homer 1994). The two actions were joined in what became a major legal action involving so-called "brainwashing"-based claims, which was the popular theory that underlay most of the claims Mull was making in his countersuit.

Mull's countersuit claimed that he had been "brainwashed" into joining the group, and that CUT had exploited his talents while a member, getting him to do things he otherwise would not have done except for the use of "mind control" techniques on him. The suit was unusual in that it involved an older adult (Mull was in his fifties when he joined), thus making it a rare use of such claims with someone not of the younger ages typical of participants in newer religions. Mull also became ill from a neurological disease after he left the group, and made claims that his time in CUT had contributed to developing this disease. Mull, who has since died, could barely walk and was unable to speak without great difficulty. His appearance in court in such a condition made an impact on the judge and jurors, who apparently accepted his claim that his condition derived in some way from his experiences with CUT.

The outcome of the suit was an award of $1.5 million to Mull, including a half-million-dollar award directly against Elizabeth Claire Prophet herself, the spiritual leader of CUT. This award against Prophet, upheld on appeal, was to have major repercussions, as it was eventually paid from church funds, which later helped fuel an action by the IRS that resulted in loss of tax exempt status for CUT (Homer 1994). Also, the outcome of the suit, according to sources within CUT, contributed directly to a decision of the group to withdraw from California and relocate in rural Montana. Thus, it is clear that the case involving Mull had a number of major impacts on CUT, some of which are still being played out.

Unification Church and "Brainwashing" Claims

Former members have also had direct major impact on the Unification Church, easily one of the most controversial of the new religions and one which easily fits the definition of "Subversive" group. UC apostates have been involved in extralegal social control methods such as deprogrammings, as well as in a number of legal actions filed against the UC. A number of ex-members of the UC have become involved in deprogramming, a new quasi-profession peopled in part by former members of groups who have decided to devote their lives to "rescuing" others from the group (Shupe and Bromley 1980; Barker 1984). Few of the new religions have experienced so much attention from deprogrammers, in part because some key deprogrammers were formerly affiliated with the UC (Galanter 1983).

Of special interest are legal cases in which a few former members have used the courts to exert control over the UC, usually through civil suits for damages that claim such torts as intentional affliction of emotional distress and fraud associated with recruitment into the group. Such legal claims are undergirded usually by claims that the group brainwashed people into joining and used mind-control methods to retain them as members, assertions made in cases involving other such groups such as the CUT situation described above.

Such suits have had mixed success, but they had definite impacts on the UC. When such suits are filed they are usually accompanied by large amounts of media attention, thus spreading a negative message about the UC and its activity. Such claims have served as the basis for a number of television movies and have furnished plots for a number of action television series. And the message has been received, as a number of studies have demonstrated, that the UC is one of the most despised groups in the United States, and that many people believe it brainwashes participants (Richardson 1992).

One case in California, brought by former members David Molko and Tracy Leal who were deprogrammed out of the UC, became a national issue involving many different people and groups on both sides. The plaintiffs made claims that, although they had known who the group was when they decided to join, they had not been informed immediately about the nature of the group recruiting them. They further claimed that, by the time they were told that the group was the UC, they were already under the sway of the group's impressive recruitment techniques to the extent that they could not say no to the recruiters.

The case was dismissed at the trial level, with the dismissal upheld at the appeal court level. Some quite strong language was used by the trial and appeal court judges criticizing some of those who might testify against the group in the trial using "brainwashing-based ideas about recruitment." The courts thought such actions untenable, given First Amendment protections for religious freedom in America, and they also thought testimony of alleged "brainwashing" was scientifically unsound and based on bias against the UC.

However, the plaintiffs did not give up after two losses, and filed a motion to appeal with the California Supreme Court. A huge battle erupted at this point, involving major professional social science organizations, as well as a number of groups supportive of or opposed to the action being brought by Molko and Leal. Amicus briefs were filed on both sides by groups and individuals.[4] The result was a decision that ordered the case to be tried, a decision as upsetting to some as it was heralded by others. Some were upset because the decision seemed to breathe life into questionable claims that the UC used "brainwashing" tactics in their recruitment (see Anthony 1990; Anthony and Robbins 1992).

The decision was appealed by the UC to the United States Supreme Court, with more amicus briefs being filed on both sides and more controversy associated with some of those briefs (see Richardson 1996). The U.S. Supreme Court refused to hear the case, thus leaving the decision standing. The case was then settled, with the UC paying damages of an unknown amount to the two plaintiffs.

Repercussions of this case continue to this day. The case had an impact on the group, leading to changes within the UC in terms of recruitment practices and the allocation of resources. The negative publicity associated with the case (and others similar to it) dogs the UC continually. The legal status of brainwashing-based claims is more established, especially in cases where allegations of deception are made. The case impacted a number of individual scholars on both sides of the issue in not always positive ways, and the controversy still reverberates within some of the professional organizations that were involved in the development and filing of amicus briefs (see Richardson 1996).

A Hare Krishna Case Involving an Apostate

Another "Subversive" group, the Hare Krishna, has had considerable attention over the decades of its existence (Rochford 1985). Robin George, a former member, has caused great difficulty for the organization by bringing a legal action against the group. Her case went to the U.S. Supreme Court, and has been written about in law reviews and other scholarly publications (Laycock 1994; Richardson 1991). This is perhaps the best known of a number of legal actions brought against the Hare Krishna, and it shows the broad implications of such actions for all concerned, as well as how apostates turned whistleblowers can impact a group.

George was fourteen when she joined the Krishna, using them in part to flee her parents who were attempting to overcome her interest in the organization, which she had visited with a friend prior to coming into the group. The Krishna made some problematic (even stupid) decisions concerning George, who was underage, and they came to regret having done so. The Krishna decided to assist George in hiding from her parents, and they sent her to other communes outside of California. Her parents made major efforts to locate her, and gained support from some law enforcement personnel and others in their efforts. George returned home on one occasion, only to be imprisoned by her parents in the home to keep her there (they chained her to a toilet off her bedroom, for instance).

Eventually, the Krishna gave up the fight with George's parents, and asked her to return home (a unique form of expulsion). A few months after she did this her father died of heart trouble that, it was later claimed, derived directly from the distress of trying so long to get his daughter back. George also became involved in a fundamentalist religious group that was quite opposed to Eastern religious groups, and she developed contacts with participants in the so-called anti-cult movement.

A suit was then filed against the Krishna organization, with Robin George and her mother listed as plaintiffs. Claims were made concerning emotional distress of both Robin and her mother that were directly derived from brain-washing allegations, and there was an unusual claim of wrongful death as well, filed on behalf of Robin. The case was heard and resulted in an initial verdict of $32 million dollars, most of it in punitive damages. The trial judge reduced the verdict to about $9 million, and then the case was appealed.

When a case is appealed, the one appealing is usually required to post a bond or furnish some legally binding lien on property to the amount of the judgment. To do this the Krishna were forced to attach a lien on all their property in California. In short, the judgment, if paid, would require all the assets of the Krishna in California, and if not paid but appealed, the Krishna still had to sign away control of all their property. Laycock (1994) has discussed the devastating impact of such judgments on smaller religious groups, and indicated how close the Krishna came to losing every asset they had in California.

When the case was appealed a number of scholars and some professional organizations filed an amicus brief on behalf of the Krishna organization.[5] The California Appeal Court overruled the trial court on some issues, such as the intentional affliction of emotional distress claim by Robin, but it allowed the wrongful death award to stand, as well as the emotional distress claim of the mother, apparently because of the distress caused her by the Krishna's concealment of Robin.

The case was then appealed to the U.S. Supreme Court, which agreed to hear the case as one of a number of punitive damage cases that were being appealed on grounds that the punitive damage awards were excessive. The case was never officially heard, however, as it was remanded along with several others for more hearings using new criteria for punitive damages established in a decision rendered shortly after the George case was accepted. The case was eventually settled, with the Georges receiving some money (the amount is secret), although apparently not nearly as much as they had been awarded by the trial court.

This case has had a number of ramifications, including the clear establishment of policies by the Krishna about accepting underage participants. Now the Krishna will not accept an underage member without written approval of the parents. The case also was a vehicle for scholars concerned about brainwashing-based testimony to again come together in an effort to inform the court that such testimony is questionable. It seems reasonable to assume that the amicus brief filed with the California Appeal Court had some impact, as most of the direct claims based on such testimony were thrown out. This effort by scholars in the George case aroused some controversy among some who disagreed with their position, or who were concerned about new religious groups' recruitment practices. But, the effort did not have the same controversial effect as did similar involvement in the Molko Leal case described earlier (see Richardson 1996).

Apostates and Child Abuse Cases in The Family

Perhaps the best known episodes involving whistleblowing apostates and their involvement in legal actions concern The Family, formerly known as the Children of God, possibly the most controversial of the early new religions, and one which also fits the definition of ''Subversive'' in the eyes of many in our society (Lewis and Melton 1994). A small group of former members, some of whom were engaged in custody fights over children born while they and their spouses were participants in the group, have expended considerable effort to spread negative information about The Family. The information often has involved claims of child abuse, including sexual abuse. When such information is given to authorities they often are required by law to take action to investigate. Such claims, particularly if made in the mass media, can force authorities to act, which means that defectors can exert considerable social control against groups of former membership, if they are willing to make such claims (see Richardson 1997). Thus, these instances are rare occurrences when self-help remedies can provoke an almost immediate reaction by official governmental agents.

This negative information has sometimes been acted on, both in the United States and other countries, leading to dramatic interventions in the life of the group. Hundreds of children have been taken away from parents in The Family, and major efforts to make them wards of the state have been launched (Richardson 1997). This has occurred in Australia, France, Spain, and Argentina, with related smaller battles in other countries. It is significant that The Family claims to have averted such a mass raid in the United States by pre-emptive efforts such as requesting official visits and examination when such claims were being made about treatment of children in the group.

All the children were eventually returned to their parents, and all the parents who were jailed because of child abuse charges were eventually released, some after having spent months in foreign jails. The cases against The Family and individual parents have failed because no evidence of child abuse has been found, even after exhaustive testing of the children by authorities and specially assigned experts chosen by the courts. Scholars who have studied The Family support the conclusions that the organization does not sanction child abuse and that its children are healthy and relatively well educated (Lilliston and Shepherd 1994; Shepherd and Lilliston 1994). However, the interventions by governmental officials have had dramatic effects on the lives of all members of The Family.

The Family has had to spend huge amounts of energy, time, and resources in fighting these battles over its children. The raids have also resulted in major media efforts that have painted The Family in a very bad light. Headlines such as "Children Rescued from Sex Cult" have not helped the group's public image, and have been very disturbing to Family members. The raids and related social control efforts have forced some major changes in The Family in terms of relations with former members and relatives of members, methods of educating its children, as well as with the scholarly community and governmental and legal officials. Indeed, the judge in one major United Kingdom case virtually required that major efforts be made to re-establish contact with former members, in an effort to ameliorate their concerns about their experiences while in The Family. Changes that were occurring in The Family in a "natural" way as they became more "domesticated" because of the rapid growth of large families were perhaps speeded up, as The Family sought to demonstrate to authorities that it was not a danger to children in the group.

Spiritual Healing with Children of Christian Scientists

As indicated, Christian Science is not thought of as a typical "new religion" or "cult," in large part because it is much older than most of the controversial religious groups discussed in this volume, and its membership at this stage of its existence is considerably different than that of the controversial new movements. Most people would probably not define Christian Science as a "Subversive" organization, which is the way that this collection would define organizations such as the HK, the UC, or The Family. Christian Science can fruitfully be defined as a "Contestant" organization in that it is at odds with the dominant culture on at least one major element of its beliefs and practices, that being its approach to health and healing (Nobel 1991).

As indicated above, partially as a result of the growing concern about children in our society, Christian Science healing methods have become quite controversial of late, especially when used with children. One woman, Rita Swan, who was a former member of Christian Science has led the battle against the continued acceptance of such Spiritual Healing for treatment of children. The woman had made use of such methods in treating her own son's illness some years ago, when she was a practicing Christian Scientist. The methods did not succeed, however, and her son died, leaving the woman very disillusioned and distraught.

Since that time Ms. Swan has led a crusade against the church and its approach to healing, striking a resonant chord with other disillusioned former members, with some in the medical profession who think use of such methods should not be allowed, and with those who are concerned about the welfare of children in general. Ms. Swan has travelled the country giving speeches attacking the church's approach to healing, using her experience as proof that the church sanctions unproven methods of healing and that the church is willing to see children die rather than modify its approach to illness. She has published a widely circulated newsletter, and she and others who agree with her work with prosecuting attorneys and other officials in jurisdictions in which a Christian Science child has died after use of Spiritual Healing to treat an illness. Ms.

Swan's personal testimony, which she has offered in several cases involving deaths of children, makes a strong statement. She has been able to influence law enforcement authorities that charges should be brought, and she has been effective with juries in such cases, as well. Her efforts have caused considerable media attention to be directed toward Christian Science and its healing methods. The efforts of Ms. Swan and others, which contributed to a negative climate of opinion toward Christian Science healing methods, have apparently led to changes in the church's position on the use of Spiritual Healing with children and toward parents who choose not to use Spiritual Healing (see Richardson and DeWitt 1992).

Thus, this one apostate turned whistleblower has served as a major link among cases around the country, and probably knows more about them than virtually anyone. The efforts appear to have been successful in that a number of the cases have been brought, with some "successes," especially at the trial court level. Her apparent success can also be measured in part by the concern that has developed around the country about the exemptions present in laws of a number of states that preclude prosecution for crimes when Spiritual Healing is used unsuccessfully with children, and recent decisions to not allow payment of Christian Science practitioners under federal Medicare and Medicaid programs. Also, as Richardson and DeWitt (1992) document, the pressure of the many legal cases had apparently led the church to modify its basic approach to use of Spiritual Healing with children.

CONCLUSIONS AND THEORETICAL IMPLICATIONS

This examination of the role played by apostates from new religions on their groups of former membership reveals that such individuals can have a dramatic impact on the groups. Even a small percentage of people who leave through various routes (exiting, expulsion, or extraction) and then adopt the apostate and whistleblower roles can force changes in group life, as well as impact public policy toward the groups. Efforts at social control by authorities may be validated by whistleblowing-type claims made by ex-members, and self-help social control efforts by ex-members can be tacitly sanctioned as well, because of claims some former members are willing to make. Some claims are more obviously factual than others (a claim based on the fact that a child had died has more concreteness than a claim that someone was "brainwashing," for instance), but even if such claims are not borne out after investigation, the claims can still be very disruptive for the groups involved.

Relatively few ex-members make negative claims about their group of former membership (Wright 1987), but if even a few do, then actions may be taken (or sanctioned) against religious groups with impunity. The resulting actions in turn force the group to take defensive actions which may be disruptive of the group and the accomplishment of its goals.

Nowhere is the impact of ex-members demonstrated more dramatically than in legal actions, both criminal and civil. When criminal charges are brought against a leader or member of a religious group, then defenses must be made. Otherwise, the charges will probably be found to be true, with guilty verdicts imposed. As has been shown in a number of cases here and elsewhere, criminal charges have been given impetus by claims made by apostates, causing great disruption in the life of the group and its members. When a group and its leaders are sued in a civil action (as a number have by ex-members) defenses must also be mounted. Otherwise, a default judgment can be entered that could bankrupt the group. Even if defensive actions are taken in civil actions, jury verdicts can and have effected the same result, sometimes coming close to forcing religious groups out of business, as was the case with the George case against Hare Krishna.

Thus, the cases described herein demonstrate the dramatic and potentially thorough-going impact that apostates and whistleblowers can have on small religious organizations. Especially when the claims such ex-members make resonate with growing concern about children and about individual autonomy, the claims will be taken more seriously. Such claims may also mesh well with the interests of governmental bureaucracies which have been established to enforce new laws about protecting children. And such claims seem to fit a society with a growing trend toward litigiousness. The "eyewitness" aspect of apostate whistleblowing claims make them especially powerful within the legal framework, as has been shown with the several cases described herein.

THEORETICAL IMPLICATIONS

Any research should shed light on underlying theories that give the research impetus. Examination of several legal cases involving apostates and whistleblowers from minority religious groups has implications for the theoretical scheme informing this volume. For instance, although the examples are limited in number, it seems clear that apostates and whistleblowers can develop in all types of religious organizations. The Christian Science situation demonstrates this, as do other examples not discussed herein, such as accusation of child sex abuse against a number of priests and other officials in the Catholic Church. It is not the case that apostates and whistleblowers only develop in "Subversive" groups, which is the designation given in this volume to those groups most at odds with the dominant culture.

Another implication of situations described herein is that there seems to be a logical relationship between apostasy and whistleblowing. Although the two roles may develop in some circumstances almost simultaneously, it seems reasonable to assume that apostasy predates whistleblowing in most cases. A person becomes an apostate and then seeks (or has thrust upon him or her) the role of whistleblower, and is rewarded for playing the role in ways that encourage such a path of evolution into whistleblowing.

For instance, a person may, after observing some major breach of ethics by a leader or experiencing some traumatic event not covered adequately by a group's theodicy or practice, become disillusioned, leading to apostasy. This apostasy might come to the attention of other groups in conflict with the original group of membership (such as anti-cult organizations). Such opposing groups could cultivate the apostate, seeking to turn him or her into a whistleblower. This appears to be what happened with the George case against the Hare Krishna, as well as the cases of Molko and Leal against the Unification Church.

Robin George became an apostate, probably as a result of rejection by the HK, when she was asked to return to her parents. Subsequently, she converted to Fundamentalist Christianity and developed ties with the anti-cult movement. Molko and Leal both experienced deprogramming, a traumatic event that they could not absorb easily. Molko held out for several days, defying the deprogrammers with vigor before succumbing. Later, apparently at the urging of parents and others opposed to the UC, Molko and Leal filed their suit against the UC.

This process of "courting of apostates" deserves more attention than it has been given. Plainly, one might predict that such a process would be more prone to develop in situations involving strong oppositional groups. This leads to the prediction that groups more in conflict with the values of the dominant culture ("Subversive" according to Bromley) would be more prone to experience the whistleblowing phenomenon. But, "apostate courting" might also occur with more traditional groups, usually on specific issues.[6] The examples of Christian Science and children's health discussed herein and the briefly mentioned conflict over child sex abuse allegations within the Catholic Church suggest that whistleblowing can be nurtured in less controversial settings.

This discussion, in turn, leads to the idea that whistleblowing may be a phenomenon isolated in a few areas of major concern to the greater society. It may be that, whatever the type of religious organization, apostasy and especially whistleblowing are prone to develop around certain themes in a given society. It is obvious, for example, that accusations of child abuse can give impetus to whistleblowing in different settings (including non-religious ones). It is also clear that the great impetus given the idea that new religions "brainwash" participants derived in large part with concern for the well-being of young adults on the part of their families. Perceived threats against the family, whatever their source, can lead to whistleblowing activity which is rewarded by those opposed to the threat (Kilbourne and Richardson 1981).

NOTES

1. Another variable of import in this process is communal versus non-communal, which may be related to the typology developed by Bromley (Chapter 2 this volume). As Richardson, van der Lans, and Derks (1986) note, the three major types of leaving— voluntary exiting, extraction, and expulsion operate differently, depending on the type

of organization (communal or non-communal) the participant leaves. And the labeling that takes place, both before and after the leaving event, and the accounts of the leaving that are developed by major parties vary in terms of type of organization. The greater the tension with the external environment (i.e., the more "Subversive" a group was perceived), the more leaving such a group would be conducive to the development of contradictory and dramatic labeling and accounts.

2. There is usually a relationship between the apostate role and the whistleblower role, with apostasy coming first, followed by adoption, for a few, of the role of whistleblower. For some, of course, the development of both roles may occur almost simultaneously, as something happens to the person that causes him to withdraw allegiance from the group and become an apostate, while at about the same time the person calls attention to the activities that caused him to become an apostate, thus becoming a whistleblower. Therefore, the relationship between apostasy and whistleblowing is a logical one that is not always easy to differentiate in practice.

3. I am aware of the details of Mull's negotiations because I was an expert witness in the case on behalf of CUT, and thus had access to the documentation of the trial. For another discussion of this case, set in the context of many other legal actions involving CUT, see Homer (1994).

4. This author was involved in drafting an amicus brief submitted by some professional organizations, and was an individual signatory to the brief, which argued in favor of the dismissal of the action mainly on scientific grounds. See Richardson (1996) for a discussion of the case and its ramifications.

5. This author helped write the brief and signed it individually as well.

6. "Apostate courting" could also occur in an opposite fashion, as seemed to be the case with those apostates who became whistleblowers against The Family. Apparently, some members of the apostate group sought out and worked with anti-cult groups, as a part of their efforts to exert influence over The Family.

REFERENCES

Anthony, Dick. 1990. "Religious Movements and Brainwashing Litigation: Evaluating Key Testimony." Pp. 295–344 in *Gods We Trust*, edited by Thomas Robbins and Dick Anthony. New Brunswick, NJ: Transaction.

Anthony, Dick, and Thomas Robbins. 1992. "Law, Social Science, and the 'Brainwashing' Exception to the First Amendment." *Behavioral Sciences & the Law* 10:5–29.

Barker Eileen. 1984. *The Making of a Moonie*. Oxford: Basil Blackwell.

Bromley, David, Anson Shupe, and Joseph Ventimiglia. 1979. "Atrocity Tales, the Unification Church, and the Social Construction of Evil." *Journal of Communication* 29:42–53.

Galanter, Marc. 1983. "Unification Church ('Moonie') Dropouts: Psychological Readjustment after Leaving a Charismatic Religious Group." *American Journal of Psychiatry* 140:984–89.

Homer, Michael. 1994. "Protection of Religion Under the First Amendment: Church Universal and Triumphant." Pp. 119–38 in *Church Universal and Triumphant in Scholarly Perspective*, edited by James Lewis and J. Gordon Melton. Stanford, CA: Center for Academic Publication.

Kilbourne, Brock, and James Richardson. 1981. "Cults versus Families: A Case of Mis-attribution of Cause?" *Marriage and Family Review* 4:81–100.

Laycock, Douglas. 1994. "Free Exercise and the Religious Freedom Restoration Act." *Fordham Law Review* LXII:883–904.

Lewis, James, and David Bromley. 1987. "The Cult Withdrawal Syndrome: A Case of Misattribution of Cause?" *Journal for the Scientific Study of Religion* 26:508–22.

Lewis, James, and J. Gordon Melton, eds. 1994a. *Church Universal and Triumphant in Scholarly Perspective*. Stanford, CA: Center for Academic Publication.

Lewis, James, and J. Gordon Melton, eds. 1994b. *Sex, Slander, and Salvation*. Stanford, CA: Center for Academic Publication.

Lilliston, Lawrence, and Gary Shepherd. 1994. "Psychological Assessment of Children in The Family." Pp. 47–56 in *Sex, Slander, and Salvation*, edited by James Lewis and J. Gordon Melton. Stanford, CA: Center for Academic Publication.

Nobel, Barry. 1991. "Religious Healing and the American Courts in the Twentieth Century." Ph.D. Dissertation, University of California, Santa Barbara.

Richardson, James. Forthcoming. "Social Control of New Religions: From 'Brainwashing' Claims to Child Sex Abuse Accusations." In *Children in New Religions*, edited by Susan Palmer and Charlotte Hardman. New Brunswick, NJ: Rutgers University Press.

Richardson, James. 1996. "Sociology and the New Religions: 'Brainwashing,' the Courts, and Religious Freedom." Pp. 115–34 in *Witnessing for Sociology: Sociologists in Court*, edited by Pamela Jenkins and Steven Kroll-Smith. Westport, CT: Praeger.

———. 1994. "Update on The Family: Organizational Change and Development in a Controversial New Religious Group." Pp. 27–40 in *Sex, Slander, and Salvation*, edited by James Lewis and J. Gordon Melton. Stanford, CA: Center for Academic Publication.

———. 1992. "Public Opinion and the Tax Evasion Trial of Reverend Moon." *Behavioral Sciences & the Law* 10:53–63.

———. 1991. "Cult/Brainwashing Cases and the Freedom of Religion." *Journal of Church and State* 33:55–74.

Richardson, James, and John DeWitt. 1992. "Christian Science Spiritual Healing, the Law, and Public Opinion." *Journal of Church and State* 34:549–61.

Richardson, James, Barend van Driel, and Brock Kilbourne. 1989. "Alternative Religions and Economic Individualism." Pp. 33–56 in *Research in the Social Scientific Study of Religion*, edited by Monty Lynn and David Moberg. Greenwich, CT: JAI Press.

Richardson, James, Jan van der Lans, and Frans Derks. 1986. "Leaving and Labeling: Voluntary and Coerced Disaffiliation from Religious Social Movements." Pp. 97–126 in *Social Movements, Conflict and Change*, edited by Kurt Lang and Gladys Lang. Greenwich, CT: JAI Press.

Rochford, Burke. 1985. *Hare Krishna in America*. New Brunswick, NJ: Rutgers University Press.

Scott, Marvin, and Stanford Lyman. 1968. "Accounts." *American Sociological Review* 33:46–61.

Shepherd, Gary, and Lawrence Lilliston. 1994. "Field Observations of Young People's Experience and Role in The Family." Pp. 57–70 in *Sex, Slander, and Salvation*, edited by James Lewis and J. Gordon Melton. Stanford, CA: Center for Academic Publication.

Shupe, Anson, and David Bromley. 1980. *The New Vigilantes*. Beverly Hills, CA: Sage.

Solomon, Trudy. 1981. ''Integrating the 'Moonie' Experience: A Survey of Ex-Members of the Unification Church.'' Pp. 275–96 in *Gods We Trust*, edited by Thomas Robbins and Dick Anthony. New Brunswick, NJ: Transaction.

Wright, Stuart, ed. 1995. *Armageddon in Waco*. Chicago: University of Chicago Press.

———. 1987. *Leaving the Cults*. Washington, DC: Society for the Scientific Study of Religion.

Chapter 9

Apostates and Their Role in the Construction of Grievance Claims Against the Northeast Kingdom/Messianic Communities

Susan J. Palmer

The Northeast Kingdom Community Church, on first acquaintance, bears a close resemblance to other Christian sects and revitalization movements emerging out of the Jesus People Revolution of the early 1970s. And yet it will stand out in the history of church–state relations as one of the first religions in the United States to be accused of collective child abuse, and to endure a mass raid on its children. Due to extensive media coverage, the main events of the controversial Island Pond raid are well-known.

On June 22, 1984, 90 Vermont state troopers arrived at dawn in their cruisers at the homes of the Northeast Kingdom Community in Island Pond, Vermont, armed with a court order and accompanied by 50 Social Rehabilitation Services workers. They searched the households and took 112 children into protective custody. The parents were allowed to accompany their children, and the families were bussed 20 miles to the courthouse in Newport. District Judge Mahady, after holding 40 individual detention hearings in one day, ruled that the search warrant issued by the state was unconstitutional. All the children were returned to their parents without being searched for signs of abuse, and the legal process ended abruptly. In spite of this auspicious victory, the Northeast Kingdom Community Church (henceforth referred to as the ''Church'' or the ''Community'') is currently beseiged with custody disputes and continues to weather Social Services investigations.

In searching for the forces underlying this dramatic church–state confrontation, the researcher is faced with an apparently innocuous, not atypical communal and millenarian sect; the group adheres to fundamentalist Christian beliefs and has never seriously challenged the laws or norms of society. They do not stockpile weapons, resort to aggressive evangelical strategies, use drugs, nor advocate sexual license. Their founder has made no extravagant claims to be the messiah, nor even a prophet. The group is not large, rapidly expanding, nor wealthy. Nevertheless, a study of their history demonstrates an extremely high level of conflict with society. Aside from a few minor complaints of truancy in the local schools, of practicing medicine without a license, and of neglecting to register births, the major grievance claims have always pointed to the discipline of their children, despite a paucity of evidence that members discipline their children any more frequently or severely than other Christian fundamentalists (Ellison and Sherkat 1993).

In responding to external pressure, the Church has exacerabated tensions with society by refusing to conform to mainstream child rearing methods, but it is important to understand the religious motivation behind its passive resistance. The Church manifests classic sectarian characteristics which serve to protect its budding culture from external assimilation and secular influences. On the one hand, elders encourage members to "render unto Caesar what is Caesar's" and to aim for a peaceful coexistence with society by following the guidelines laid out by American patriot Roger Williams, on the separation of church and state. On the other hand, they regard society as dominated by sin, due to its refusal to be "covered" by "Our Father." Parents in the Community have come out of the wilderness of sin and crossed over into the sacred realm to become the first generation of a New Order. Children play a vital role in their parents' eschatology. They are instrumental to realizing the utopian ideals and millenarian expectations of this fledgling religion. The elders interpret the Bible passage, "the sins of the fathers will be borne until the third or fourth generation" to mean that those living in the "body of the Messiah" (the commune) who avoid sin will be sanctified after three or four generations. Thus, they expect each generation to be less prone to sin than its parents; within the next 70 years they hope to be able to send out 144,000 pure virgin males to preach during the final ingathering of souls before the advent of Yahshua (Bozeman and Palmer forthcoming). In pursuit of their ideal of Restoration, they eat healthy food, wear modest dress, and cultivate selfless and loving relationships. Thus, it is essential to protect their children from secular influences that will necessarily undermine their utopian vision and cause them to "die" through sin. For this reason, when they resist cooperation with authorities, they are resisting demonic forces. When secular authorities seize or seek to control their children, they are attacking the deepest, most fundamental logic whereby this child-centered community defines itself. They are assaulting the Community's very spiritual identity and its most passionate religious aspirations—those invested in their children.

The aim of this study is to analyze the influence of apostates' testimonies on the trajectory of this sect's escalating church-state conflict. There appear to be three phases to the conflict between the Church and the oppositional coalition, which is composed of various interest groups that formed a network in a common mission to rescue the putatively abused children of the "cult." This coalition depended heavily upon ex-members' testimonials to provide the rationale for the moral campaign against the Church. Apostates—both witting and unwitting—exerted a strong influence on the ongoing battle which might be compared to a game of chess. The "moves" of apostates resemble those of the knight in a chess game, who is able to leap over the enemy line in zig-zag fashion and win new territories. There were various types of apostates, however, and their atrocity stories were used strategically during different phases of the "game." The Church's apostates can be classified as follows: (1) Activist Apostates; (2) Passive Apostates; and (3) Resurrected Apostates.

The three phases of conflict will be elaborated below, but first we will look at this new religious movement and its epic confrontation with the state over the custody of children—a confrontation that cast Vermont in the national spotlight.

THE HISTORY OF THE MESSIANIC COMMUNITIES

The Northeast Kingdom Community Church (now known as the Messianic Communities) was founded by Elbert Eugene Spriggs ("Yoneq") in 1972 in Chattanooga, Tennessee. Its roots are in the Jesus People Revival, and its belief system remains very close to Christian fundamentalism. The communities adopt the name of their local town; members are given Hebrew names and identify with the "lost and scattered tribes" of the Jews in diaspora and with the early Christian communities. By renouncing the world and sharing all things in common, members become part of the "body of the Messiah" and hope to avoid a physical death. They believe their church is the "pure and Spotless Bride" awaiting the advent of her Bridegroom, Jesus, whom they call by the name of Yahshua. Through increasing their ranks and "raising up a people"—defined as three generations—they prepare the way for the Jubilee horn that heralds Yahshua's return.

Communities now exist in Londrina, Brazil; Navarrenx, France; Sydney, Australia—but the majority of members live in New England. The Church numbers around 2,000, and roughly half are children. Children are home schooled, and television and fantasy toys are banned. The youth are integrated smoothly into daily chores and are dressed like the adults; girls wear long braids, long skirts, or bloomers, and boys wear jeans, homemade shirts, and headbands.

The Church's guidelines for parental discipline stipulate that children who do not obey upon *first command* must be punished. The millenarian rationale behind this is that children must be alert and ready to respond to Yahshua's call. Chastisements must *not* be performed in anger, and usually consist of a few blows with a flexible reed, such as a balloon stick, on the palm of the hand. It must be the child's *own* parents who decide on and administer the punishment. The notion is that through discipline the child will acheive eternal *life*; otherwise they are "dying" into sin.

Phase One: The Origins of Conflict

In Chattanooga the group's first conflicts occurred at the grassroots level, mainly with worried parents of youthful converts, rival restauranteurs, and ministers of local congregations. These tensions drew the attention of the anti-cult movement to the sect. The first anti-cult organization, FREECOG, was founded by Ted Patrick in 1972 in response to his son's attraction to the Children of God. As FREECOG's bureaucracy expanded and it was superseded by the nationally based Citizen's Freedom Foundation (CFF), the concept of a "cult" and theories of "brainwashing" were developed, and information was collected on other new religious movements (NRMs). The Community in Chattanooga bore a superficial resemblance to the Children of God, since both were millenarian, evangelistic communes and emanated from the Jesus People movement. Both groups recruited middle-class youth from the counterculture who "forsook all for Jesus." Ted Patrick kidnapped eight of the Chattanooga Community's members between 1978 and 1980. Four deprogrammings were "successful," resulting in defections, but four members returned to the group. Three of the defectors assisted in future deprogrammings.

During the Chattanooga phase, the "cult-labeling" process focused on the founder, Elbert Eugene Spriggs. He was condemned as a self-proclaimed "Apostle" who exerted "total control" over his followers and molded them into religious fanatics who held themselves above the law. He was said to employ "mind-control" techniques to enlist his followers in communal and voluntary labor that undercut local businesses (Beverly n.d.). Spriggs has often been described as a former "carnival barker"—a colorful term that conjures up images of the American frontier snake-oil salesman, the charming charlatan with a fast patter. In fact, Spriggs was by profession a high school teacher and fairly successful travel agent/tour guide who worked for one day in a carnival, but not as a barker.

During this phase, the Community's reaction was defensive. They withdrew from the world, ignored the deprogrammers and negative press as much as possible, and relocated to Island Pond in 1979. In Vermont, media stories and grievance claims began to focus more narrowly on their methods of child rearing and discipline. Allegations of abuse first came to the attention of the authorities in 1982 in connection with custody battles involving three families: the Gregoires, the Alexanders, and the Mattatalls. In May 1983 the court awarded custody of the eleven children to the three fathers residing *outside* the community rather than allow the children to be "subjected to frequent and methodical physical abuse by adult members of the community, in the form of hours-long whippings with balloon sticks" (*Gregoire v. Gregoire*). Judge Mahady, who presided over the Gregoire case, expressed his opinion that the children were trapped in "*some sort of holy war*" (*Gregoire v. Gregoire*) between the parents. Out of one, the Mattatall case, the career of a formidable "arch-apostate" was launched.

Juan Mattatall was a Chilean hippie "head" and successful soft "dope dealer" in the 1970s counterculture. According to an elder's account, he had formed a band of hippies called the Lighthouse Family . . . [that] made and sold jewelry at crafts fairs across the country. He met the Community in 1976. His declared motive for joining was to cement his relationship with his 15-year-old girlfriend, Cindy, who lived with her mother and was expecting their second child. The elders approached Cindy, who first visited the Community and then joined. She and Juan reconciled and were married in the Community in 1976.

The elders described Juan as independent and unpredictable, but a valuable asset to Community life ("We loved the guy! He was very talented, charming—a real natural leader"). The trouble started when two little girls complained to their parents that he had made sexual advances toward them as they were sleeping. The elders confronted Mattatal with the allegation; when he denied it, he was ordered to leave. He went to Florida for a few weeks; upon his return he confessed to engaging in adulterous relations with many women. He was sent to live with the Community in Boston. According to an elder, "he was under a discipline and we worked with him, but he never did quite come clean. He confessed, but he always tried to rationalize it." His wife refused to take him back, and he blamed the Community for separating him from his family. He reportedly told Spriggs: "I will destroy the Community!" just before he left.

Mattatall filed for divorce and subsequently sought out Suzanne Cloutier, a nurse working for Social Rehabilitation Services (SRS) in Island Pond. Upon hearing his stories of abused children, Cloutier quickly became a formidable opponent of the Community. Mattatall also contacted Galen Kelly and Priscilla Coates of the CFF. With their support, he won custody of the five children in 1982. His youngest daughter Lydia, however, was overseas in France. Cindy Mattatall, pregnant with her fifth child, had allowed the childless Spriggs to take Lydia to live with them in France. Juan accused Spriggs of kidnapping Lydia, and Cindy appeared before Judge Mahady in a series of hearings. He repeatedly asked her if she could produce Lydia, and she replied in the negative. She skipped the last hearing and made secret arrangements to fly with her children to Europe. The CFF helped Juan track down her passport number, date of departure, and address. According to a Church elder's version of the story, "the New Jersey State Police, Juan, and some people from the anti-cult movement came in and held her at gunpoint in the middle of the night and took the kids away, even the baby who was nursing when they broke in" (Personal Communication).

Lydia was found in 1982 when the Spriggs returned to North America and arranged to meet Cindy in Nova Scotia. Suzanne Cloutier had already appeared in the area and delivered lectures on child-beating in cults. Canadian deprogrammers cooperated with the CFF in "staking out" the house in Cape Sable Island. The Canadian Broadcasting Corporation, which arrived at the scene, followed the Community's cars as they left the house, and alerted the RCMP. Lydia was taken into custody at a roadblock and handed over to her father.

Juan Mattatall moved to Burlington, and a story appeared on the front page of the *Burlington Free Press* showing the triumphant father reunited with his five blonde, mop-haired kids. He hired a nanny and began attending a local church; from the pulpit he described the rescue of his kids from the "cult," and declared that his next step would be to save his wife. He brought the children to Island Pond to visit their mother on two occasions, after he received a court order. However, he arrived in a camper with CFF workers and parked right outside the Island Pond Maples household for the night. He handed out whistles to each of the kids and told them to blow the whistles when the abuse started so that they could be rescued.

Mattatall was soon in trouble again. The nanny he had hired in Burlington became concerned about his sexual activities with the little girl next door. Her complaint to the authorities launched an investigation. Juan then moved to Orlando, Florida and placed his children in the Baptist Christian Home, where they resided from 1982 to 1990. During this time he was reported to the Adam Walch Center in Orlando for sexually abusing a local prepubescent girl, but he arranged a plea bargain to lesser offence and was placed on probation. The director of the Baptist orphanage, who had been warned that the mother was in a "dangerous cult," cooperated with Juan in blocking access to the children. Although Cindy had a court access order granting her permission to see her children, every time she travelled to Orlando she was turned away. She finally gave up visitation attempts and remarried, clinging to a hope that some day she might regain her children. In 1990 she learned that Juan had been shot dead by his own mother. This event was reported in the Clark's Harbour, N.S. *Guardian* (12 June 1990, p. 1).

A well-known defector from the Northeast Kingdom Community Church Juan Mattatall, 47, and his 74-year-old mother, Maria Palmer were found May 7 . . . by his step-father, Bernard Palmer. Juan Mattatall charged that Albert [sic] Spriggs had sexually abused his daughter Lydia while he was her captor, but Juan himself later faced two charges of child sexual assault. . . . Palmer, . . . said . . . his stepson's life had been a non-stop series of problems with children and the law. He speculated that his wife foresaw that Juan's problems would continue and so she shot him to save him from the grief that seemed destined to continue.

Mattatall fits the model of the active, and activist, career apostate. Through his testimonies he defined the deviant aspects of the "cult" for its social audience. He started out as a "whistleblower" (literally handing out whistles to his children) and then sought out and brought together a coalition of disparate interest groups to support his custody case. Initially, he and the other early apostates were the "glue" that bonded the interest groups into one coalition. As the coalition gathered strength, the portrait of a Subversive group was constructed. However, grounds for legal intervention were lacking, a situation opponents attributed to the secretive and self-contained nature of the sect.

Apostates were invaluable, since they had crossed the line between the sect and society; they brought with them vital information that could be fashioned into "evidence" to rally law enforcement agencies against the "cult."

Wright (1995) traces the influence of different interest groups that formed alliances in order to lay grievance claims against David Koresh. A similar process began to take shape during Mattatall's court case when various interest groups responded to his initiative and began to form a network dedicated to the common cause of "saving the cult's children." The most important participants in the network were local businessmen, journalists, and anti-cult organizations. This network gradually constructed a portrait of a dangerous, child-abusing "cult" around the Northeast Kingdom Community Church. For each interest group it was expedient to participate in Mattatall's quest, although their concerns were quite varied. The network began to produce its own moral entrepreneurs, who soon became quite independent of Mattatall's initiative.

Local businessmen found their trade was suffering from competition with a communal organization based on volunteer labor. Countercultists found the elders' doctrinal innovations and Apostle Spriggs' charisma offensive. Social services personnel, who were assigned to protect children, were naturally suspicious of "cults" that made a policy of using corporal punishment to discipline their children. Suzanne Cloutier of Social Rehabiliatation Services embarked on a personal crusade to "save the children." She referred to her home as a "safe house" and sought out defectors and invited them to stay with her. She taped their stories, kept files, and organized and dated everything she heard about the alleged abuse; she even invested around $5,000 of her own money in "fighting the cult" (Harrison 1984).

Journalists, as always, were "in it for the story." During Mattatall's custody suit, journalists from the CBC and UPI had appeared in Island Pond and interviewed him in their camper. Some went on to recruit more defectors, taping angry testimonials and exchanging data with Suzanne Cloutier. The *Cult Observer* was frequently quoted in news reports warning worried relatives of "some 200 pages of affadavits [that] tell us of systematic, frequent, and lengthy beatings of children by parents and church elders with wooden and iron rods and paddles, often drawing blood . . . stripped naked and beaten for several hours" (Braithwaite 1984, p. 3).

In one of the most lurid portraits, "The Children and the Cult," journalist Barbara Grizutti Harrison (1984, p. 58) claimed "the cult is robbing children of their childhood," and compared the youth of Island Pond to the telekinetic, extraterrestrial children of the sci-fi film *Village of the Damned*. Invited by the Community to "come and stay for three days," Harrison was immediately on guard as "Three days is the standard period for what is variously known as 'brainwashing,' persuasive coercion or mind control" (1984, p. 62).[1]

Several Vermont journalists assumed activist roles and were instrumental in bringing about the raid (Bilodeau 1994, p. 36). Sam Hemingway of *Burlington Free Press* admitted he "advocated for action in his columns and hoped the coverage would bring results.'' Mike Donoghue of the *Burlington Free Press* claimed he had covered stories where he had ''up to 18 subpoenas from lawyers for his notes.'' The most intrepid activist was Chris Braithwaite, editor of the Vermont *Chronicle*. He was approached by the Orleans County State's Attorney, Phil White, to look at Cloutier's files, and resolved to ''get involved as a citizen.'' He covered the Mattatall custody case, interviewed defectors and outside relatives, and admits he ''contributed information that aided in getting a warrant to seize the children.'' Even while the raid was in progress, Braithwaite (1983, p. 1) felt he was ''objective enough to do the news analysis.'' He wrote an editorial on the aftermath of the raid entitled ''Have We Lost Our Children?'' In an interview he admits ''on the emotional level I got very involved . . . I only know if I was in the same situation again, I would do the same damn thing!'' (Braithwaite 1994, pp. 36–38).

The least visible but most influential organization in this network was the Citizen's Freedom Foundation, whose officials first visited Burlington in response to Mattatall's invitation. The CFF established a chapter in Orleans in November 1982; they collected funds, contacted the media, and appointed Galen Kelly, a deprogrammer, to aid members to ''escape from the cult.'' Posters appeared on the streets of Island Pond warning residents: ''The Northeast Kingdom Community Church Abducts Children.'' CFF meetings were held in Barton where townspeople were urged to stop buying the Community's bread, and store owners were pressured to stop stocking Community products. The night of the first meeting someone drove through Island Pond and shot bullets through the windows of the Common Sense Restaurant, the Maples household, and a gas station owned by the Community. This event was not reported in the newspapers nor investigated by the police.

Each of these agencies worked to protect the public's interest and operated within the logic of their calling. Once united, they were frustrated by the Church elders' refusal to cooperate and by the inaccessibility of the children. Influenced by the widespread concern about child abuse in our era, they accepted the likelihood of child abuse occurring in a ''cult setting.''

Phase Two: Escalating Conflict

The second phase of this church-state conflict is marked by an escalation in the conflict that culminated in the open confrontation of the raid. This was brought about through a moral campaign in which often passive or unwitting apostates were recruited and stage-managed. The deviance amplification process began to operate as Church elders began to suspect a conspiracy; their refusal to cooperate or compromise in some instances reinforced the public authorities' perception of them as deviant, evoking increased punitive action.

The coalition was highly organized and independent of Mattatall's leadership, and its leaders were waging their own moral campaigns. They began actively recruiting ex-members and tailoring their stories to win public support for their common mission: to rescue the children. New defectors were encouraged to emulate Mattatall's model and reiterate the areas of deviance and discontent he had originally laid out. Some defectors, who were not particularly disgruntled, were coaxed and stage-managed to appear on the scene as ad hoc career apostates. Examples of these "stage-managed" apostates were Michael Taylor and Roland Church.

Michael Taylor had left the Community and lived for several months outside Island Pond before meeting Cloutier. She introduced him to deprogrammer Galen Kelly, who set up a meeting with SRS official Conrad Grimms and a police detective, who recorded his testimony. Taylor was a single, childless member, unmotivated by custody concerns; he later complained to the press that he was cued to exaggerate the few chastisements he had witnessed. His tale appeared in a Vermont newspaper, but when he went to the news office and confessed that he had lied, the paper was not interested in printing his retraction. In 1988 he returned to live in the Community, but later defected once again.

Roland Church's grievance claim resulted in a court case that provided a strong rationale for the raid. Church was an Amish farrier from Maine who joined the Community with his wife and two daughters. However, because he was on the road much of the time plying his trade, the elders were dissatisfied with his community participation. In 1983 his twelve-year-old daughter, Darlynn, got into trouble for encouraging younger children to play sexual games and the elders called Church to a seven-hour meeting urging him to discipline his daughter. According to a Community member, Church responded he was "so mad he was afraid he'd beat her like a horse." He therefore asked Elder Wiseman to do it for him. A week later Church left the Community and met Suzanne Cloutier on May 21. They contacted the Citizen's Freedom Foundation in Orleans, which recorded his complaint. Church charged Wiseman with simple assault of his daughter.[2]

On August 5, 1984, Roland Church recanted. He claimed to have been pressured to lie to the "news media" by Suzanne Cloutier (Harrison 1984, p. 6). "She called everyone in Vermont, I guess," he complained. "She's the instigator of it all." Cloutier, in turn, retorted: "I feel betrayed by Roland Church. It bugs me out. God forgive me, I almost pray a child dies. Nothing will happen until then—and they're all dying a slow death!" The case against Wiseman was held up in court and eventually dismissed in 1984.

The network then launched a search for more corroborating evidence. Priscilla Coates of CFF met with the Vermont attorney general's staff and provided names of defectors. SRS official Conrad Grimms and Vermont State Police official Peter Johnson travelled around the country between 1982 and 1983, tracking down ex-members in seven different states to interview them for child abuse information. These interviews were used in the 18 affidavits that became the basis for the raid. One of these, the *Moran Affidavit*, featured the stories of fourteen defectors. Six of these individuals, all of whom had been deprogrammed by Galen Kelly, recounted stories that were remarkably similar. This collection of atrocity tales was used to convince authorities that the group was subversive and a legitimate target for repressive action by the state.

Besides recruiting more apostates, the network directed its well-coordinated stigmatizing efforts toward several families inside the Community. Minor legal infractions blew up into major legal cases and personal tragedies were suspected of involving criminal intent; the Church soon again became embroiled in controversy. As the cases involving the Chambers and the Campbells demonstrate, the process of deviance amplification appeared to be operating in these escalating conflicts.

The first child of the Chambers couple was stillborn, and the local coroner agreed to issue the death certificate. However, when the coroner called the state attorney with a routine question, the latter immediately arrived at the scene and told the Chambers there would have to be an autopsy. According to one of the elders, Robert Chambers replied, "I refuse to have my daughter taken to Burlington to be mutilated." The sheriff was summoned, but Chambers refused to cooperate. While the sheriff was conferring privately with the coroner, Chambers picked up his dead child and drove to a field, dug a grave, and buried her. The state police sent two squad cars through the town in noisy, but unsuccessful pursuit. When Chambers returned home, he refused to reveal where he had buried the body. He was thereupon arrested and charged with transporting a body without a death certificate.

This conflict became a major media event. The "cult" was portrayed as a fly-by-night secret society that refused to register births or deaths and buried the bones of children in unmarked graves. In fact, members did apply for and receive death certificates on the rare occasions of a death. Nevertheless, this gothic legend soon took on a life of its own, as in Barbara Grizutti Harrison's article, "The Children and the Cult" (1984, p. 6):

They do not send their children to school, nor do they register births and deaths. Island Ponders feed off the persistent rumour that the cult has its own graveyard in which bones of children were found. Bodies of children were found; one baby was stillborn, another died, apparently, of spinal meningitis.

In 1983 another Island Pond couple, the Campbells, took their ten-month-old baby to a doctor who found hairline fractures in his wrists and ankles. Worried about rumors of abuse, he called the SRS and diagnosed the limbs as "broken by force." The parents then consulted a specialist in Newport who diagnosed a rare form of rickets and prescribed Vitamin B. The doctor's letter was sent to the SRS, but two weeks later the judge in St. Johnsbury District Court granted the state temporary custody. Troopers arrived at the Campbells' door and seized the baby on grounds of medical neglect. The baby was then examined by four doctors in a Burlington hospital who again diagnosed rickets ("Officials Tell Why..." *The Caledonian Report*, 22 June 1985, p. 12).

These cases offer clear examples of the deviance amplification process. It is important to understand that their response was conditioned by the vulnerablity of their religion, still in its chrysalis phase, and by the role of children in their eschatology. When Chambers, moved by the authority of his "lay conscience," resisted a perceived injustice, his action was interpreted as further proof of his innate deviance as a "cult member." While it appears the Community was clearly a victim of stigmatizing efforts, it is also clear that they met these challenges with a certain intransigence, and their refusal to compromise on matters of child rearing has tended to reinforce the deviance amplification processes.

The Island Pond Raid and Its Aftermath

By 1984 the network led by Cloutier, Braithwaite et al. created a portrait of a nefarious cult habitually cruel to children, but they were repeatedly frustrated in their intervention efforts. On four occasions they managed to obtain court approval to initiate temporary custody proceedings; but only once (in the Campbell case) was an order executed, and again no evidence was discovered. From their perspective the impediments lay in the inaccessibility of the commune, its "cultic secrecy," and in the *collective* nature of the alleged abuse. Laws on child abuse were designed to apply to *individual* criminal behavior, so as to avoid both the claim that abuse resulted from a child's environment and discrimination against working class families (Richardson 1993). Moreover, current laws are based on the assumption that claims can be readily investigated by interviewing the child's teacher, friends, family doctor, or neighbors—a situation not applicable to religious communes. As Harrison complained (1984, p. 61):

They've taken away all our normal ways to detect child abuse. There are no teachers to report scars, no doctors to report anything funny. . . . The children are moved from communal home to communal home. . . . What this amounts to is that nobody knows who is who, and it is this facelessness and anonymity that led to the Raid of June 22.

Met with passive resistance, the network was unable to gather evidence that would justify using force in its social control efforts on behalf of the children. This is where the grievance claims of apostates proved indispensible. Their atrocity tales provided ammunition to justify a legal intervention.

Three days before the raid, Attorney General John Easton summoned seven Community elders into court, took them before the judge one at a time without a lawyer, and asked them to name the children they lived with. Each man replied that his conscience would not allow him to reveal this information and was then jailed for contempt of court. Hours later, Judge Keyser, an 86-year-old retired Supreme Court Justice released the men, asserting that the court lacked authority to act unless the state produced specific names of people and specific evidence.

Frustrated by the failure of court actions and thwarted by Church elders' unwillingness to cooperate, a network that included the state's attorney general, a social services commissioner, and a local newspaper editor took action. They met with Governor Richard A. Snelling and Attorney General John Easton in Montpelier and convinced them to approve their plan to take all the children of the sect into custody simultaneously so that they could be examined for signs of bruises. Cloutier's files and the police investigators' reports were turned over to Phil White, Orleans' County state attorney, who was sworn in as special assistant attorney general. Judge Wolchik issued a search warrant that was brought to Governor Snelling.

The input of the anti-cult movement was later revealed when Judge Mahady asked whether the acting prosecutor had authority in Essex County. The court was informed the attorney general's staff had met with ''cult experts'' Galen Kelly and Priscilla Coates of the CFF, who cited two cases of child-beating fatalities that had occurred in two other ''cults,'' to justify emergency measures (Malcarne and Burchard 1992, p. 82).[3] According to John O'Donnell, deputy human service secretary at the time, a pediatrician and social worker involved in the Michigan raid were called in for consultation. They compared that situation to the one in Island Pond, concluding that there was a significant potential danger to children at Island Pond.

The raid proved a baffling disappointment for the network intent on rescue, who blamed the decisions of Thomas L. Hayes, chief administrative judge for the Vermont courts, for its failure. On the evening before the raid, Hayes pulled Wolchik off the case and assigned Judge Frank Mahady to preside over the emergency hearings with himself and another judge as backup. Once the search warrant was served, state officials had to return to the court to show they had acted within their authority and to request permission to detain the children for another 72 hours. Deputy Attorney General Bristow and others complained that it was ''unprecedented'' to prevent Wolchik from reviewing the search warrant after it had been executed. Orleans' County attorney White also argued that Hayes wanted a judge who would reject the state's action, and deliberately chose Mahady who had a reputation for being a strong civil libertarian. The next day in court, Mahady reprimanded Judge Wolchik for signing the search warrant, and Wolchik later admitted at a 1986 confirmation hearing that he now regarded the information on which he had relied on granting the search warrant as unreliable and possibly false.

In his written report, Judge Mahady pronounced the raid ''a grossly unlawful scheme'' and commented that the state's motive was not the issue, for ''even when the state acts in a noble cause, it must act lawfully.'' He criticized the language of the original search warrant as ''more general in scope than any this court can find after careful research in the recorded literature. It may, indeed, set a modern record for generality.'' He accused state officials of rounding up children to find evidence they lacked; ''What the state really sought was investigative detention.''

Phase Three: Decentralization and Deescalation

Phase three is marked by a sudden decentralization and deescalation of conflict. Events subsequent to the Island Pond raid follow a pattern described by Richardson (Chapter 8 this volume) in cases of other NRMs brought to court on slender evidence. Once the case is heard in public legal proceedings, third parties are brought in, and members of the group (previously ignored by the media) are given a forum in court; a more realistic, rounded picture of the NRM emerges. All these factors bring some "checks and balances" to the situation and undermine the plausibility of the portrait of the group as Subversive. Moreover, the relative independence of the judiciary impedes future efforts of government agencies or the anti-cult movement to bring sanctions against a new religion (Chapter 8 this volume).

Within the Community, the Church elders abandoned their sectarian huddle and sought to deescalate the confict through legitimate channels. Having experienced intimidating demonstrations of the power and hostility of the state in the raid and Dawson's FBI arrest—not to mention the tragedy in Waco in 1993—they began to reach out. They gained friends and supporters among members' parents and local officials, won concessions from the Vermont school board, and were interviewed by sympathetic journalists. The Island Pond Community organized a voluntary diaspora, sold most of their houses, and established small communal households across the New England states. The Church strove to maintain a more open and conciliatory stance toward the outside world.

For the oppositional coalition the abortive raid proved a major crisis, causing a rift between the law enforcement agencies and the social services personnel. To persevere in their mission, it was necessary to adopt a new oppositional strategy. Since the complexities of the case were too well-known in Island Pond, the battle arena was broadened and decentralized. Small-scale skirmishes are currently fought around the new households that begin to receive negative publicity in the local press once the local social services or (Canadian) Youth Protection agencies receive anti-cult literature, prompting fresh investigations and fueling custody disputes.

Tension remains, as in the 1994 investigation into the Community in Hyannis, Massachusetts that resulted in a hearing at the Barnstable County Courthouse on June 20, 1994. Ironically, among the young parents asked to identify their own babies were a couple who had themselves, as children, been taken into custody by SRS workers in the Island Pond raid of 1984. All cases were dismissed on November 4, 1994. During the same year, the Community in Rutland, Vermont was implicated in a custody dispute over four daughters, who were awarded to the father living *outside* the Community (even though it is quite unusual for the courts to award custody to fathers).

Apostates' testimonies still provide powerful artillery for these battles, although the tales are ten years old, heavily edited, and "resurrected." A close scrutiny of the affidavits submitted in recent court cases reveals how the raw material of ex-members is often padded, tailored, and recycled in order to bolster grievance claims. One recent defector, whose statements were used as evidence against the Community in Hyannis, later complained in an affidavit of the "underhanded operations" of the Department of Social Services. She claimed that the SRS sought her out in 1994, assured her they had substantial files on the Hyannis families, and promised that everything she said would be held in the strictest confidence, not to be used without her prior knowledge and permission. Later, she was upset to find her own name and her daughter's mentioned in an affidavit submitted in evidence; no other sources on the Hyannis Community were cited; and her statements were highly exaggerated. The Community's attorney quoted her as stating that "[The DSS] stated I had seen bruises and marks on the children but I had *never* seen them! I feel like I have been dragged on a fishing expedition!"

According to the Community's lawyer, Jean Swantko, the same affidavits that were used in the early 1980s (the Moran, Mattatall, Church, and Taylor affidavits) keep reappearing in affidavits of the mid-1990s. From a Community perspective (Johnson 1994, pp. 1–2) "repeatedly, law enforcement personnel fail to respect court rulings or documents in passing stale information on to other agencies." Further, the Community's attorney alleges that there is a recurring pattern whereby lawyers, who have been influenced by such information, study previous dismissed cases and decide they had been "handled wrong," and that they could "do it right this time."

As in all communal NRMs, custody disputes arise when one parent leaves the group. Recently, two fathers living in the Community chose to disappear with their children rather than trust the judicial system that has always awarded custody to the outside parent. Stories about the cult that abducts children have appeared in the news, largely due to the activism of apostate Laurie Johnson, who was briefly involved with the Community in Island Pond and has been searching for her two missing boys, Seth and Nathan, since they disappeared with their father, Steven Wooten, in 1989. Seth and Nathan's faces have appeared on *Child Find* and *Childseekers* posters distributed by the National Center for Missing and Exploited Children with the caption: "It is believed that the cult is assisting in the concealment of these and other children sought by custodial parents and authorities" (*Vermont Times*, November 19, 1991). Johnson also hired two private investigators from CRIB, an agency operating out of Philadelphia that specializes in ferreting out missing children. Community members complain that two scary men wearing cowboy gear (including guns) constantly invade their public dance celebrations by circling around on motorbikes peering at the children, and handing out cards to visitors bearing an insignia that closely resembles the FBI's. A search warrant was served on the Community in Winnipeg, Manitoba, in February 1996, and Laurie Johnson accompanied the police and social workers and scrutinized the children—to no avail. As of May 1997, however, Steven Wooten was arrested in Florida by the FBI, and the two boys were given to their mother, who hired deprogrammer Rick Ross as an "exit counselor."[4]

The second alleged "abduction" occurred in Canada in the 1987 *Seymour v. Dawson* custody case. Edward Dawson joined the Community in 1986, leaving their 3-year-old son, Michael, with his mother, Judy Seymour. After several months, she signed a paper awarding custody to Dawson, who took Michael to live in the Myrtle Tree Farm Community in Nova Scotia. In August 1987, a police car and social workers drew up to the farm unannounced, and Michael was placed in his father's custody for 44 days. Social Services officials appealed the court's decision, and Dawson went to the Supreme Court in Nova Scotia while his case was ongoing in the local Family Court. According to Dawson's testimony, the Social Services agency placed an ad in the Montreal *Gazette* in October 1987 to locate the boy's mother. She was shown alarming testimonies of former members, which prompted her to sue for the custody of her son.

During the family court proceedings, Dawson made his son unavailable to the court. He was held in contempt of court and put in jail. After a presentation of belief in February 1988, the Supreme Court ordered his release and deemed him a fit father.

The case did not end with this decision, however. In 1992 Seymour and her lawyer arranged an ex parte hearing with the judge in Nova Scotia. The judge was receptive to a local deprogrammer's argument that the Community qualified as a "cult," granted Seymour interim liberal access for the weekend, and ordered Dawson to appear in court the following week. Dawson refused to allow Michael out of his sight, took him across the border, and lived for a year in a Church household in California.

Mattatall's old tales resurfaced when a Vermont state trooper sent a "Search for Lydia" news clip to California authorities, and RCMP officer Wendell Murchison (who had starred in a television documentary, *Missing Treasures*, dramatizing the search for Lydia Mattatall) wrote a letter recommending that abduction charges be laid against Dawson. Dawson was apprehended by the FBI in the spring of 1994, led out of the commune wearing chains, placed in a maximum security prison for three months, and charged with abduction and contempt of court. The abduction charge was dismissed in the 1995 trial, since custodial parents cannot abduct their own children, but Dawson is still waiting to appear for a retrial in the Supreme Court concerning the "contempt" charge. Michael is currently living with his mother who has de facto custody.

The child abduction theme was echoed in unfounded but persistent rumors surrounding the unsolved disappearance of Lyndon Fuller. The 24-year-old son of the wealthy Fuller Brush manufacturer escaped from a psychiatric ward in Berowick, Nova Scotia in 1991. Rumors circulated through the area that Fuller had joined the Myrtle Tree Farm Community, despite the fact that he had never shown any interest in its religion nor had contact with any of its members. The farm was searched and placed under surveillance for months; helicopters hovered overhead and the Community's double-decker bus was searched on the highway. The case remains open and rumors still abound in Nova Scotia.[5]

CONCLUSION

In analyzing the effect of apostates' grievance claims on the Community, one can observe their use in three phases of the Church's conflict with the oppositional coalition. The first phase was actively launched by Mattatall, who brought the different agencies together and cemented their allegiance with abuse stories to further his custody suit. Defectors during the second phase played a more passive role. Sought out by CFF counselors, their anecdotes were solicited, selected, even distorted to accomodate the anti-cult theoretical framework and to produce a packet on the "cult" replete with shocking stories. Once these packets were delivered to SRS officials, a kind of circular logic ensued. New investigations would be launched; journalists would then interview CFF "cult experts," who would air their views on the "cult" as if they had just descended from their ivory tower where they "monitor such groups." The media would feed their corroborating stories back to police, judges, ministers, and doctors, creating the impression that the information was issuing from several different, independent, and mutually corroborating sources, thereby enhancing their credibility. Today these stories are widely dispersed, untraceable, and unverifiable; they have taken on a ghostly life of their own. While it is highly unlikely they will be used to construct another major church–state confrontation, their stigmatizing power has been directed into the narrow eddies of local newspapers, computer networks, anti-cult literature, and court records.

The Messianic Communities movement is now beginning its third generation; it continues to win allies and found new communes and it still evokes controversy. The raid represented a resounding victory for the Messsianic Communities in a legal sense, and it won sympathy among civil libertarians for whom the Church became a test case. Paradoxically, however, it brought the Church an even greater notoriety, setting it back in its larger struggle for legitimacy. From the members' point of view, justice is not forthcoming. Mattatall is dead, his pederastic pursuits widely reported in the news; Church and Taylor have retracted; and deprogrammer Galen Kelly, who had conducted the interviews for the Moran Affidavit, is in jail. Moreover, the testimonies of the children themselves contradict these grievance claims. Of the eleven children awarded to their defector fathers in the early custody battles involving the Gregoires, Mattatalls, and Alexanders, ten rejoined the Communities when they came of age. Nevertheless, these early, unreliable, and stigmatizing testimonies continue to be packaged, recycled, and widely dispersed. Several members have placed the Church in a vulnerable position by choosing to hide their children rather than submit to a judiciary that has consistently refused to award custody to parents *inside* the commune.

The earlier tales of the apostate who has ventured across the boundary of a "cult" to rescue his/her abused children is now supplanted by a new suspenseful narrative, quite as frustrating for both sides as the rumors of collective child abuse, for the claim cannot be proven, disproven, nor resolved. This is the tale of children who disappear into the mysterious center of a communal society. While in both cases the fathers were the legal guardians at the time of the alleged custodial interference, they were sought out and arrested by the FBI and must now attempt to extricate themselves from the tenacious web of willful inaccuracies spun in the wake of Juan Mattatall.

NOTES

1. Harrison has since produced "Bad Faith" (1993), an article on the children of David Koresh.

2. While the severity of the discipline has never been established, it appears to have been grossly exaggerated in the court affidavit. The seven-hour meeting was reported as seven hours of actual whipping, and the testimony of "eight or nine" welts on her skin, read out by the judge with a heavy Maine accent, was transcribed as "eighty-nine" welts.

3. The two cases were the Stonegate Community in West Virginia and the House of Judah in Michigan. Neither group is connected historically, geographically, or ideologically to the Island Pond Community or to each other.

4. As of May 1997, Steven Wooten was arrested in Florida and the two boys, now 13 and 17, were given to their mother. She hired deprogrammer Rick Ross to counsel the boys for ten days, despite their expressed wish to the social worker to remain with their father. While Johnson has appeared on many talk shows, Wooten remains in jail for lack of the $750,000 bail and faces a custodial interference charge.

5. In April 1997 a police investigation of the Community in Sus, France at "Tabitha's Place" was launched after the death of an infant with a congenital heart defect. The parents are facing charges of medical neglect leading to death, punishable by 30 years in prison. The media were quick to exploit the current fear of "les sectes" in the wake of the Solar Temple's mass suicides. Relying on the countercult organization (ADFI) for their information, the media have printed highly erroneous descriptions of this "secte dangereuse," which may influence the nine-person jury if the case is not tried as a "delit" or misdemeanor.

REFERENCES

Beverly, James. n.d. "Kingdom Concerns: A Critique of the Northeast Kingdom Community Church" (flyer).

Bilodeau, Katherine. 1994. "The Media's Role in the Island Pond Church Story." *The Chronicle*, 22 June, pp. 36–37.

Blades, Kent. 1990. "Cult Defector Killed by Mother." *Guardian*, 12 June, p. 1.

Bozeman, John, and Susan Palmer. Forthcoming. "The Northeast Kingdom Community Church of Island Pond, Vermont: Raising Up a People for Yahshua's Return." *Journal of Contemporary Religion*.

Braithwaite, Chris. 1984. "Cultism and Child Abuse: Cases of Convergence." *The Cult Observer* (September): 3–6.

———. 1983. "Island Pond Cult Loses Custody Fight, Business." *The* (Orleans County, Vermont) *Chronicle*, 25 May, p. 1.

Ellison, Christopher, and Darren Sherkat. 1993. "Conservative Protestantism and Support for Corporal Punishment." *American Sociological Review* 58:131–44.

Ewald, Richard. 1991. "Building Bridges at Island Pond." *Vermont Magazine* (March/April):44–51.

Gregoire v. Gregoire. 1983. Family Abuse Hearing, District Court of Vermont, Chittenden Circuit Unit 2, Burlington, May.

Harrison, Barbara Grizutti. 1993. "Bad Faith." *Mirabella* (August):28–30.

———. 1984. "The Children and the Cult." *New England Monthly* (December):56–69.

Hughes, Robert. 1992. "The Fraying of America." *Time*, 3 February, pp. 44–49.

Johnson, Sally. 1994. "A Former Feminist Lawyer, She Chose Island Pond Life." *Times Argus*, 20 June, pp. 1–2.

Kinsolving, Lester. 1983. "State Should Watch Childbeating Cults," *Sacramento Union*, 8 January, p. A-7.

Kokoszka, Larry. 1994. "Time Mellows Communities Caught in Raid." *Caledonian Record*, 22 June, pp. 1–8.

Malcarne, Vanessa, and John Burchard. 1992. "Investigations of Child Abuse/Neglect Allegations in Religious Cults: A Case Study in Vermont." *Behavioral Sciences & the Law* 10:77–88.

"Officials Tell Why They Pulled Island Pond Raid." 1985. *Caledonian Record*, 22 June, p. 12.

"Open Letters from the Church in Island Pond." n.d. Island Pond, VT: Parchment Press.

Poteet, Lewis. 1989. "The 'Cult' Meets the Cultures of Nova Scotia's South Shore." *Nova Scotia: New Maritimes* VII:10–13.

Richardson, James. 1993. "Social Control of New Religions: From Brainwashing Claims to Child Sex Abuse Accusations." Paper presented at the Australian Sociological Association, Macquarie University, Sydney.

Stokes, Keith. 1993. "Plane Searchers Seek More Help." *Newport Daily Express*, 6 August, p. 3.

Wright, Stuart, ed. 1995. *Armageddon in Waco*. Chicago: University of Chicago Press.

Young, Leontine. 1983. "Private Violence." *Time*, 5 September, pp. 18–22.

Yowceph. 1984. "Kingdom Concerns: A Response from the Northeast Kingdom Community Church to James Beverly." Island Pond, VT: Parchment Press, pp. 1–12.

Chapter 10

The Role of Apostates in the North American Anticult Movement

Anson Shupe

"Apostate" is now a term used frequently when social scientists analyze defectors from new religious movements. The apostate role is understood to be one in which a person exits, either voluntarily or involuntarily, an unconventional or "new" religious group or movement (hereafter NRM) and then becomes an outspoken, visible critic of the latter. Moreover, such persons are understood to represent important resources for any countercult, anti-cult, or oppositional movement seeking to soil the identity of specific religious groups. For example, Shupe (1981, p. 214) states:

> While opponents may suspect the worst of a group, they can only relate what they at best know secondhand. Apostates, however, can claim to have seen firsthand and often personally participated in various horrors. Their testimony is that of the insider and as such provides an apparently irrefutable confirmation for the propaganda [about] a group's opponents.

This chapter has two goals: to present a brief analysis of the development and re-interpretation of the concept of apostasy by modern social scientists; and to consider the evolution of the sociological role of apostates in the North American anti-cult movement (1971–1995) and their exposure by the mass media.

EVOLUTION OF THE CONCEPT OF APOSTASY

Chapter 2 of this volume approaches the entire cult–anti-cult struggle as one in which contested organizations (a category into which many new religious movements fit) possess relatively little power vis-à-vis social control agencies. This minority status lends defectors from such (largely) unpopular movements a degree of leverage with interest groups representing the family, the polity, the media, and established religious denominations. Specifically, such defectors obtain their credibility and legitimacy, not necessarily because their negative accounts of life within given groups are "true" as portrayed (though they may be), but because they serve the propaganda/discrediting needs of countergroups (Bromley, et al. 1979). This is the primary social role of the apostate: he or she literally constitutes a countermovement resource.

Christian tradition defines apostasy as a loss or willful abandonment of faith. According to the *Oxford American Dictionary*, apostasy is a "renunciation of one's religion." Current sociological usage of the term apostasy is somewhat different. Beginning with Coser (1954), and two decades later Bromley, Shupe, and Ventimiglia (1979), the term took on a more specific social movement orientation. In the latter source the authors analyzed a sample of several hundred newspaper articles from the mid- to late 1970s containing unflattering-to-hostile descriptions of the Reverend Sun Myung Moon's Unification Church and its activities in the United States. Of particular interest were the testimonies of angry and disillusioned ex-believers from that group, many of whom had involuntarily left (e.g., been abducted, coercively confined, and "deprogrammed") and who wished to speak publicly about what they perceived as abusive experiences and allegedly horrendous living conditions while Unificationist members. Many such persons coming before the media were also ballyhooed by agents active in the loosely organized countermovement now commonly referred to as the anti-cult movement, or ACM (Shupe and Bromley 1994, 1980). Bromley, Shupe, and Ventimiglia (1979), and later Shupe and Bromley (1981, 1980), termed such ex-members-turned-activist opponents "apostates" and their descriptions of their NRM experiences "atrocity stories" (similar to deliberately crafted wartime propaganda accounts of enemy depredations by combatant governments to shock, arouse, and mobilize citizens against that enemy).

At about the same time, a number of other scholars in sociology and history were independently discovering a nineteenth-century religious hate literature that described persons claiming, entrepreneurially or authentically, to have been members of such religious groups as Mormonism and various Roman Catholic orders (e.g., Shupe, Bromley, and Oliver 1984; Billington 1974, 1952; Davis 1960). These actors seemed to be performing a similar apostate role, condemning groups to which they claimed to have once belonged but from which they later escaped and condemned. In 1812, for example, Anthony Gavin published *A Master Key to Popery, Giving a Full Account of All the Customs of the Priests and Friars and the Rites and Ceremonies of the Popish Religion*. In 1821, Jeremiah Odd published a book entitled *Popery Unveiled*. Samuel Smith, a self-proclaimed ex-Catholic priest, published, in 1834, *The Downfall of Babylon, or the Triumph of Truth Over Popery*. Pseudo-ex-nun Rebecca Reed published one of the all-time best-selling potboilers, [the ghostwritten] *Six Months in a Convent* in 1835, and the next year another pseudo-ex-nun, Maria Monk, published her *Awful Disclosures of the Hotel Dieu Convent of Montreal, or the Secrets of*

Black Nunnery Revealed. Chapter 6 in this volume analyzes some key texts in this literary genre.

Meanwhile, a parallel anti-Mormon literature was discovered: *Female Life Among the Mormons: A Narrative of Many Years' Personal Experience, By the Wife of a Mormon Elder Recently Returned from Utah* (1857), *Fifteen Years Among the Mormons: Being the Narrative of Mrs. Mary Ettie Smith* (1857), and *Wife No. 19: or the Story of a Life in Bondage, Being a Complete Expose of Mormonism* (1875) (see Shupe, Bromley, and Oliver 1984, pp. 25–36) represent only a few examples.

In short, by the 1980s the social functions performed by apostates for countermovements, nativistic or otherwise, were conceptually recognized by researchers (e.g., Bromley 1988; Robbins 1988; Shinn 1987, pp. 144–69). As Shupe (1981, p. 214) observes, such apostates are predictable in times of intersocial movement conflict:

In sociological terms apostasy is a particular status, and one who assumes it—or can make others believe that one is an actual apostate—gains a great deal of credibility. The appearance of persons claiming to have been members of some unpopular group and now willing to expose it is well-nigh inevitable in such conflicts over social movements, for just as the movement or group in question . . . tries to refute opponents' allegations, so the latter "anti's" feel under greater pressure to come up with the better "proof" for their claims. Who can provide better proof of misdeeds than a confessed former perpetrator of them?

It is worth noting that at least in the original formulations of the terms "apostates" and "atrocity tales" the sincerity of the apostates was not questioned. According to Bromley, Shupe, and Ventimiglia (1979), apostates' tales of abuse were simply regarded as accounts (in the social psychological meaning of that term), unexamined corroboratively for their "real" content. The main issue was not such stories' veracity or accuracy but rather the functions they served for countermovements to render other social movements problematic in the public arena.

EVOLUTION OF THE APOSTATE ROLE IN THE ACM

The utility of apostates to the modern ACM can be conceptualized as occurring in three waves, or periods, paralleling the structural development of the ACM itself.

Wave I

The earliest wave of apostate "literature" and apostate activities, in the broadest sense, emerged largely out of print journalism at a time when ACM groups were the most decentralized and, as grassroots efforts, precarious. Parents of offspring, deprogrammed from such groups as the Hare Krishnas, the Children of God (now The Family), the Unification Church, and the Divine Light Mission, often called impromptu press conferences or contacted local newspaper reporters who then interviewed the apostates, the latter eager to tell their dramatic stories of captivity and rescue while they reconciled with their families. Wire services helped disseminate these atrocity tales, which in turn had the latent function of alerting disparate local aggrieved families and groups that similar apostates and ACM groups existed elsewhere. In this way, the ACM as a national movement, with identity and common goals, began to coalesce out of local movement cells (Shupe and Bromley 1994, 1980). Susan Palmer (Chapter 10 this volume) discusses the role of such apostate accounts in energizing the opposition to the Northeast Kingdom Community Church.

One additional tangible result of the apostates' testimonies was to help mobilize at least some (if limited) symbolic response by government officials, such as the 1976 hearings held in Washington, DC, by Senator Robert Dole (Shupe and Bromley 1980, pp. 96–97). Yet while such testimonies created a general cultural climate of suspicion toward the broad coterie of groups labeled "cults," little substance as far as successful repression of NRMs came of apostate accounts during this first wave. The cases discussed by Hall and Richardson (Chapters 7 and 8 this volume) are the exceptions that prove the rule.

However, these accounts became of inestimable value for vindicating the efforts and concerns of the family members of NRM members, the former constituting the backbone of the earliest states (early to late 1970s) of the ACM. The public presence of apostates was cultivated at the grassroots level as one presumed panacea for the superior resources of the "cults."

Wave II

A second popular wave of apostate literature and activities emerged during the late 1970s—indeed, within a very narrow window of publishing time. A number of autobiographical "exposés," imitating (however unknowingly) nineteenth-century testimonies written in "life-within-the-cult" format, appeared, some released by prestigious publishing houses. The latter apparently hoped to capitalize on the sales potential of the sensational drama involving strange, possibly subversive religious cults beguiling and captivating this country's best and brightest young persons. They emphasized the high drama of families torn apart and sometimes reunited. Among these potboilers were *Hostage to Heaven: Four Years in the Unification Church, by an Ex-Moonie and the Mother Who Fought to Free Her* (Underwood and Underwood 1979), *Moonstruck: A Memoir of My Life in a Cult* (Wood 1979), *Crazy for God: The Nightmare of Cult Life* (Edwards 1979), *Moonwebs: Journey into the Mind of a Cult* (Freed, 1980), and *The Children of God: The Inside Story* (Davis 1984).

Structurally, however, the ACM had not advanced since the early 1970s. Local and regional groups sought national centralization without success (Shupe and Bromley 1994, 1980). Meanwhile, the faith in apostates' atrocity stories held out the elusive hope that some "god from the machine" via governmental agencies, outside of the poorly funded and sometimes poorly managed ACM groups, would somehow intervene on the basis of horrific testimonies.

Ironically, at about this time the public value of apostate testimonies was declining. The ACM's various social movement organizations were steadily professionalizing at the leadership levels, high-educational backgrounds pushing out lower-educational ones (Shupe and Bromley 1994). Groups such as the American Family Foundation found less direct use for apostate testimonies in their publications, even if such accounts were still important internally to reinforce movement legitimacy.

Wave III

The third wave of "cult" apostasy witnessed a decline in media interest in apostates and reliance on their accounts by ACM organizations, along with these persons' gradual withdrawal from the limelight of public attention. This curtailed exposure suggests a diminished utility of apostates to the ACM, brought on by several factors:

1. *Transitory media focus.* Issues and problems that do not affect seminal interests of a broad segment of the population have fleeting exposure in the media, regardless of their dramatic or sensational nature. Despite ACM claims, relatively few persons were ever involved in NRMs. The media moved on.

2. *Declining shock value and repetitiveness of apostates.* Originally, tales of intelligent young persons brainwashed or mentally enslaved to raise funds for ruthless prophets and gurus while simultaneously living in slave-like conditions made meaty reading. After a while, however, the similarity of the apostate accounts from a broad variety of groups made them too clichéd to attract further attention except from immediately affected families.

3. *General public disinterest.* Despite ACM warnings throughout the late 1970s and early 1980s that soon everyone would know someone entrapped in a NRM, and inflated figures claiming thousands of dangerous cuts abroad and in the United States along with millions of individuals currently in active "cult" membership, the public was generally unimpressed with this purportedly newest public health menace. Of course, there never were thousands of cults rampaging in North America nor millions of mentally enslaved devotees. Most U.S. citizens during the late 1970s and 1980s were preoccupied with more pressing and tangible issues, such as the Iranian hostage situation, the Carter administration's economic problems, a major presidential election in 1980 and the nation's shift to the political right, assassination attempts on both President Ronald Reagan and Pope John Paul II, and the growing presence of televangelism. In fact, national disinterest in the so-called "cult explosion" continued in spite of the 1979 Peoples Temple massacre at Jonestown, Guyana which seemed to confirm the worst atrocity tales that apostates had been producing for years (Shupe and Bromley 1982).

4. *General ACM disinterest.* Apostates, whose gripping first-person testimonies had so motivated early anti-cultists, moved from frontstage to backstage in ACM publications and at their conferences. Such accounts still surfaced as "data" for ACM-sympathetic behavioral scientists to support their claims of religious abuse (e.g., Singer 1995; Enroth 1979), but they largely ceased to be the primary stuff of why "cults" should be monitored and opposed. In other words, in Wave I apostates by default were the primary spokespersons and legitimators of the ACM. By Wave III they had faded in significance, apart from those who went on to professionalize their ex-member roles in entrepreneurial fashions (e.g., Hassan 1990), replaced by persons who had never been members of the groups they criticized.

But there were more fundamental reasons why apostates' recurring testimonies had lost much of their value for the ACM, and these flowed from the structural development of the maturing ACM.

WHY THE EVOLUTION OF THE APOSTATE ROLE?

It is easy to conclude that apostates as a class of testifiers and newsmakers lost their newsworthiness and notoriety, fading into obscurity and simply going on with their lives as they began to make repetitive charges. However, structural changes in the ACM underlay the changing value of apostates to the countermovement. These changes involved two interrelated processes: (1) the *institutionalization* of the ACM as a somewhat permanent part of the religious scene in late-twentieth-century North America, and (2) the *professionalization* of much of the ACM's leadership.

In the early, decentralized days of the ACM, when groups such as the Citizens Freedom Foundation, Love Our Children, Inc., Free Minds, Inc., and Citizens Engaged in Freeing Minds were spread across the continent, one expectation all activists shared was that as citizens they were not in the "cult controversy" for the long haul. They fully and confidently expected that when they finally "got the word out" to the public and the proper officials in law enforcement and government, steps would be taken to shut down a number of "pernicious pseudo-religions." The original "generation" (i.e., during the 1970s and early 1980s) of anti-cultists were volunteers, and they operated their organizations on an ad hoc "mom-and-pop" storefront basis (Shupe, Spielmann, and Stigall 1977).

However, by the mid-1980s (some 15 years into its existence) it was obvious to anti-cultists that all levels of government basically had adopted a hands-off policy toward most religious groups (which makes the Branch Davidians all the more the exception demonstrating the rule). "Cults" were not going to be legislated away, the ACM was left to develop its own resources as yet another interest group, and the conflict between the latter and NRMs was becoming a permanent fixture in North American religion (as well as elsewhere around the globe; see Shupe and Bromley 1994).

Much of this entrenched existence, or institutionalization, was due to the professionalization of the ACM's leadership. Despite some hold-outs that retained on occasion the earlier vigilante tactics of coercive deprogramming, such as the Cult Awareness Network, non-professionals were increasingly being replaced by degreed, highly educated persons from a variety of backgrounds. According to Shupe (1992, p. 38):

While many of the families and early activists of the ACM in the early 1970s were professional persons (physicians, lawyers, clergymen, and educators) the actual permanent coopting of the countermovement by full-time medical, psychiatric, and psychological professionals who were not personally affected relatives did not occur until the mid-to-late 1980s. For example, the largest and most established ACM group is unquestionably the American Family Foundation. It holds annual conventions and publishes, among other things, a credible academic journal, newsletters, and various monographs. A glance at its 1994 letterhead stationary reveals five directors (its attorney-president, two Ph.d's and two medical doctors). Its Research Advisory Committee is composed of one lawyer; three Ph.d's in religion, education, and psychology; and one psychiatrist. The AFF's professional committee chairs (in areas such as psychology, psychiatry, social work, nursing, medicine, clergy, and interreligious affairs) include five Ph.d's, three medical degrees, one Master's of Social Work, one registered nurse, two ministerial degrees, and one Master's degree.

Shupe (1992, p. 38) concludes of such a trend toward higher education:

Such professionals [often] allied with the mental health professions have coopted the ACM and transformed it into a "growth industry" for therapists. . . . The redefinition of religious innovation and deviance as psychological pathology in a religiously pluralistic society continuously generating such religions makes such professional imperialism almost a certainty.

Thus, the dual processes of institutionalization and professionalization, which created career opportunities for a number of types of degreed persons, and the collapse of naive expectations that government intervention on a massive scale would occur anytime soon, left less of a place at the table for the enthusiastic, if shrill, voices of apostates. They had helped mobilize movement activists in the early days of the ACM, but they increasingly were serving no important function to sustain the countermovement. (Moreover, their atrocity stories were continually being undermined by mainline social scientists who reported field research results on a variety of groups and found few of the egregious atrocities claimed.) Apostates' horrific accounts originally stimulated the most desperate of remedies, coercive deprogramming, but as deprogramming as an ersatz therapy became discredited by both civil liberties advocates and mainline behavioral scientists, their accounts ceased to be so valuable.

More in line with conventional therapeutic counseling modes, "exit-counseling," or voluntary deprogramming, became the norm and subsequently produced fewer angry apostates for the ACM to parade before the media. A few apostates went on to capitalize on their ex-member/victim statuses and develop careers as apostates. One example is ex-Unificationist Steve Hassan. Hassan earned a master's degree in counseling psychology and became a licensed mental health counselor in Massachusetts. He went on to write *Combatting Cult Mind Control: The #1 Best-Selling Guide to Protection, Rescue, and Recovery from Destructive Cults* (Hassan 1990) and became active as a lecturer, consultant, and exit-counselor.

Finally, it must be remembered that the NRMs themselves evolved, providing less fodder for the ACM and fewer angry apostates, deprogrammed or otherwise. NRMs' members aged, married, became parents, and ceased to live communally or fundraise in the old, objectionable ways (Shupe 1992). NRM lifestyles, in the terms Shupe, Busching, and Bromley (1989) used to analyze NRM-ACM conflict, shifted from the covenantal end of the continuum more toward the contractual end, which eased the tension between the movements and countermovement. NRMs were regressing toward the mean of the American middle class. In sum, the apostate role by the end of the twentieth century, *for this particular countermovement*, had either become largely irrelevant or had evolved to accommodate to the ACM's own established structural status.

REFERENCES

Billington, Ray. 1974. *The Origins of Nativism in the United States, 1800–1844*. New York: Arno Press.

———. 1952. *The Protestant Crusade, 1800–1860: A Study of the Origins of American Nativism*. Gloucester, MA: Peter Smith.

Bromley, David G., ed. 1988. *Falling from the Faith*. Newbury Park, CA: Sage.

Bromley, David, and Anson Shupe. 1981. *Strange Gods*. Boston: Beacon Press.

Bromley, David, Anson Shupe, and Joseph Ventimiglia. 1979. "Atrocity Tales, the Unification Church, and the Social Construction of Evil." *Journal of Communication* 29:42–53.

Coser, Lewis. 1954. "The Age of the Informer." *Dissent* 1:249–54.

Davis, David Brion. 1960. "Some Themes of Counter-subversion." *Mississippi Valley Historical Review* 47:205–24.

Davis, Deborah. 1984. *The Children of God*. Grand Rapids, MI: Zondervan Books.

Durham, Deanna. 1981. *Life Among the Moonies*. Plainfield, NJ: Logos International.

Edwards, Christopher. 1979. *Crazy for God*. Englewood Cliffs, NJ: Prentice-Hall.

Enroth, Ronald, 1979. *The Love of The Cults*. Chappaqua, NY: Christian Herald.

Freed, Josh. 1980. *Moonwebs: Journey into the Mind of a Cult*. Toronto: Dorset.

Hassan, Steven. 1990. *Combatting Cult Mind Control*. Rochester, VT: Park Street Press.

Robbins, Thomas. 1988. *Cults, Converts and Charisma*. Newbury Park, CA: Sage.

Shinn, Larry D. 1987. *The Dark Lord: Cult Images and the Hare Krishnas in America*. Philadelphia: The Westminster Press.

Shupe, Anson. 1992. "The Accommodation and Deradicalization of Innovative Religious Movements." Pp. 28–39 in *Religion and Politics in Comparative Perspective*, edited by Bronislaw Misztal and Anson Shupe. Westport, CT: Praeger.

———. 1981. *Six Perspectives on New Religions*. New Yo

Shupe, Anson, and David G. Bromley, eds. 1994. *Anti-Cult*
Perspective. New York: Garland Publishing.

———. 1982. "Shaping the Public Response to Jonestown
and Religious Commitment, edited by Ken Levi. Un
State University Press.

———. 1981. "Apostates and Atrocity Stories: Some Param
Deprogramming." Pp. 179–215 in *The Social Impac*
ments, edited by Bryan Wilson. New York: Rose of Sh

———. 1980. *The New Vigilantes*. Beverly Hills, CA: Sage.

Shupe, Anson, David G. Bromley, and Donna L. Oliver. 1984.
in America. New York: Garland Publishing.

Shupe, Anson, Bruce Busching, and David G. Bromley. 1989.
ligious Conflict." Pp. 127–50 in *The Annual Review of*
Conflict Resolution, edited by Joseph B. Gittler. New Yo

Shupe, Anson, Roger Spielmann, and Sam Stigall. 1977. "Dep
Exorcism." *American Behavioral Scientist* 20:941–56.

Singer, Margaret Thaler. 1995. *Cults in Our Midst*. San Francisc

Underwood, Barbara, and Betty Underwood. 1979. *Hostage to*
Clarkson N. Potter.

Wood, Allen Tate. 1979. *Moonstruck: A Memoir of My Life in*
William Morrow & Co.

Part V

Methodological Issues in the Study of Apostasy

Carriers of Tales: On Assessing Credibility of Apostate and Other Outsider Accounts of Religious Practices

Lewis F. Carter

Practitioners of many religions are periodically challenged to respond to "outside" reports, allegations, claims, and constructions of their practices and ancillary behavior attributed to their members, leaders, and organizations. Several mainstream Christian traditions have recently had to deal with legal and other inquiries into clergy malfeasance (Shupe 1996), and many sects as well as "new religious movements" come under frequent scrutiny triggered by claims of exotic and/or other practices which may run counter to external societal laws or norms.

Although some claims of inappropriate behavior, sometimes even potentially criminal behavior, are dealt with by external authorities, it is often difficult for potential converts, civil authorities, and researchers of religious movements to assess these claims. Part of the difficulty lies in the sources of such claims, usually outside observers (sometimes hostile or defensive ones), dissatisfied prior members (or near-recruits), or representatives of civil authority. On the other side, defenders of specific religious groups (participating members, leaders) will usually contest any potentially damaging claims.

This chapter discusses the dilemma posed for researchers in assessing conflicting claims made by more or less hostile "outsiders" (concerned relatives of recruits, critical members of traditional religions, affiliates of the anti-cult movement, and sometimes law enforcement and regulatory officials), as well as claims made by prior members (apostates or leavetakers from a group), "partial members" who may have become disaffected during group socialization, and recruits who will have had somewhat limited contact with groups. The chapter explores the importance of triangulation, especially of genuinely independent corroboration, and internal (rhetorical and other) evidence which should be brought to bear in examining claims. A case study is developed to illuminate these issues. The case involves the social construction of voter manipulation at Rajneeshpuram in Oregon in 1984, as developed through apostate accounts, accounts of recruits, accounts of "victims," and documentary evidence (including some internal analysis of the rhetoric of claims and counterclaims).

It is important for us to distinguish between the *content of the claims* about the characteristics and practices of a group, the *relationships of our sources* for those claims to the group, and *negotiations or reformulations of claims* which may occur when our sources work with other organizations. Zablocki (1996) distinguishes sources of information about religious groups into "believer," "apostate," and "ethnographer" accounts. Focusing on comparisons of believer and apostate accounts, he demonstrates that, in the aggregate, there is very little difference between the *reliability* (that is, stability across time) of accounts from believers and ex-believers (or apostates). The *validity* picture is a bit more complex. Believers (current practitioners) were found to be more likely to minimize or ignore negative traits in a community. Not surprisingly, apostates (ex-believers or ex-practitioners) were more likely to identify negative traits which the group did not in fact exhibit. Zablocki contends that ethnographer accounts, written from the perspective of an outsider, usually augment direct observation with considerable reliance on both believer and apostate accounts, and he argues that triangulation—using a number of data sources with differing perspectives—is essential for offsetting the inherent biases in reports from the different frames of reference. In addition to these, researchers also sometimes gain insights from documentary evidence of various kinds, as well as narratives and evidence compiled by "opponents" of religious groups and by officials of various kinds. While the negative motivational bias of opponents of religious groups may be taken as a given and some of their narratives amount to little more than unverified atrocity tales (Chapter 9 in this volume), nevertheless, information assembled by opponents is sometimes quite specific and subsequently verifiable; this is especially true of financial records, incorporation papers, court cases, and other kinds of documentary evidence which some opponent groups will collect in dossiers that sometimes reflect considerable technical skill.

KNOWLEDGE, MOTIVE, NEGOTIATION, AND CREDIBILITY

The researcher's dilemma is that each source of information—of believers, apostates, ethnographers, and opponents—has different strengths and weaknesses. Active members are especially well positioned in terms of firsthand knowledge of the practices of a group, while at the same time being most motivated by both perception and by group pressure to emphasize positive aspects of those practices and to censor damaging perceptions. Apostates, or those ex-members who have taken leave from a group, may be as well positioned as current members in terms of knowledge, but their perceptions are more likely to be equivocal or negative. We shall contend later that both members of and apostates from hierarchical groups well may vary considerably in terms of knowledge about the group, and for this reason it is crucial to know the respondents' location in the group and the degree of access which they have had to inner circles. A skillful and committed opponent may know more about some limited aspects of a hierarchical group than will a lower-echelon member. Professional ethnographers will supplement their direct observations with information from all of these sources, and we will develop an argument suggesting that ethnographers may be seen in some ways as "serial apostates," in that their frames of reference will vary through time—with an emphasis on *emic* (or internal) definitions when in the field setting, and more emphasis on comparative and *etic* (or external) definitions when back in the academy. Given these obvious strengths and weakness associated with the credibility of accounts from these sources, researchers (cf. Richardson, Balch, and Melton 1993; Zablocki 1996) conclude that some form of triangulation employing both believer and apostate accounts (as well as direct observation, opponent data, and documentary evidence) may be essential for valid reconstruction of the practices and actions of religious groups. In the Rajneesh case study developed later, we will illustrate the utility of documents—legal identities, medical or educational records, and financial records—in independent assessment of claims, and show specific ways in which triangulation among *insider* and *outsider* claims, logs, letters, official records, and personal experience can assist in establishing credibility of the claims of ex-insiders.

I have intentionally switched language here from believer-apostate-ethnographer accounts to the two older terms, "insider and outsider." The reason for this is that the underlying dilemmas of credibility seem to depend on matters of knowledge, motive, relationships, and the social or interactional circumstances under which narratives are produced. Although convenient as shorthand, the categories "believers," "apostates," and "ethnographers" and "opponents" are neither totally distinct in terms of knowledge, motivation, and relationships, nor are these categories homogeneous with respect to what is known, what is told, why it is told, and how it may be reformulated in the telling. Further, access to knowledge and the influence of both inside and outside influences on the narrator will usually vary with the openness or isolation of the group and the extent to which the group is hierarchically organized. Figure 1 summarizes some of the contextual influences likely to impinge on the different types of narrators.

Believers

The term "believer" is itself a bit troublesome, in that it too involves a claim, one that we as researchers must generally take at face value based on self-reports. The history of the inquisition and other milder tests of "belief" attests to the problematic and troublesome nature of the identity "believer," even for

Figure 1
Contextual Influences on Knowledge, Motivation, and Negotiations for Members, Apostates, Ethnographers, and Opponents

	Extremely Hierarchical Groups	Moderately Differentiated Groups	Equalitarian/Undifferentiated Groups
Believers	Knowledge firsthand Variable domains of knowledge Knowledge domains related to status Positive motivation strong Pressure from group strong External contact/negotiation prohibited	Knowledge firsthand Limited special access to knowledge Limited import of status for knowledge Positive motivation strong Pressure from group moderate External contact/negotiation regulated	Knowledge firsthand Knowledge universal Status not related to knowledge Positive motivation strong Pressure from group minimal External contact/negotiation limited
Apostates	Knowledge firsthand Variable domains of knowledge Knowledge domains related to status Negative/neutral motivation strong Pressure from group variable External contact/negotiation solicited	Knowledge firsthand Limited special access to knowledge Limited import of status for knowledge Neutral negative motivation Pressure from group variable External contact/negotiation available	Knowledge firsthand Knowledge universal Status not related to knowledge Neutral motivation Pressure from group variable External contact/negotiation available
Ethnographers	Knowledge limited and variable Limited domains of knowledge Knowledge related to status/skill Neutral/positive motivation Group pressure stro ng External/internal frames of reference	Knowledge fairly general Variable access to domains of knowledge Knowledge related to skill Neutral/positive motivation Group pressure moderate External/internal frames of reference	Knowledge variable General access to knowledge Knowledge related to skill Neutral/positive motivation Group pressure minimal External/internal frames of reference
Opponents	Knowledge derivative Specialized access to knowledge Knowledge domain related to activity Negative motivation strong Pressure from group strong External contact/negotiation organized	Knowledge derivative Specialized access to knowledge Knowledge domain related to activity Negative motivation moderate Pressure from group moderate External contact/negotiation organized	Knowledge derivative Specialized access to knowledge Knowledge domain related to activity Negative motivation weak Pressure from group weak External contact/negotiation organized

(or perhaps especially for) official representatives of a faith. At an operational level, the category believer is generally used to refer to the collection of "members" or participants who view themselves and are viewed by others as adherents of a faith or group.

What is special about "believer" accounts then is a matter of knowledge, motivations, and context in which narratives are constructed. Believers are insiders, who are positively disposed toward a group, usually avidly so, whose accounts usually are given in the presence of (or with likely access by) other believers. Such narratives are often intended to justify membership which may involve some degree of sacrifice and often the accounts are intended to attract others. Such insiders share some special knowledge of the group, its beliefs, official practice, and actual internal practice, which will not be so readily available to outsiders. However, "apostates" (those who have abandoned the claim to belief) will have as much knowledge of the internal workings of a group as any current practitioner (member in good standing) to the degree that the apostate previously attained a comparable level of membership. To the degree that the ethnographer penetrates, participates in, and is accepted by a group, he or she may have knowledge of the internal workings of a group equivalent to, or exceeding, that of many members.

To be sure, almost by definition, the more esoteric (and closed) a group, the greater will be the difference in what is known by insiders and outsiders, and the more resistant to external scrutiny will be the group. The point here is that rather than focusing *categorically* on the identity of the respondent, researchers concerned about credibility of an account should focus on what knowledge the informant can be expected to have, how the respondent's motives are likely to influence what is communicated, and how that communication may have been shaped by any negotiation of status with groups of others.

Especially in hierarchical groups, members may differ radically among themselves in terms of their knowledge of the practices of a group, because of both personal differences and structural ones. At the personal level will be differences in curiosity, intelligence, dedication to learning about prescribed knowledge, differences in accessing outside and perhaps proscribed knowledge, and the amount of interest in processing such knowledge. The stratification of groups means that in all but the smallest and most isolated communal group, knowledge will vary, often considerably, across types of members. Although movements vary in terms of the degree of stratification, the Rajneesh movement, which forms the basis for our illustrative case study, was not at all unusual as a "new religious movement" in that the adherents were composed of a number of clearly defined strata:

- The spiritual leader (Bhagwan, in that case)
- A principal lieutenant (There and often, the CEO of the faith)
- A core group (There the "Ma-Archy" and a few personal intimates)

- Officials overseeing routine functions (There the managers and the "Peace Force")
- Ordinary members in residence or in regular association
- Peripheral members, aspiring to closer contact or perhaps drifting away
- New recruits or inductees
- Potential recruits who have indicated some interest

While members of any of these categories, certainly the first seven, would likely be classified as "believers," they will differ radically in terms of their knowledge of the inner workings of the group. On the point of knowledge, with some caution in terms of motivation, we could expect to learn a great deal more about some facets of a group from an apostate who was once highly placed than from a current believer who is less so. In some cases, the outsider opponent may have more knowledge of financial or controversial matters; Rajneeshpuram was not unusual in terms of residential hierarchical groups in having had rigid limitations on outside news and contacts. On the other hand, matters of motivational profile, personal practice and belief, and psychological profiles of members will be much better served by emphasizing characteristics of current practitioners.

Especially in reclusive hierarchical groups, believers will be strongly motivated to avoid the appearance of criticizing the group. As Rajneeshpuram was shutting down, lower- and middle-level residents reported having been most concerned that any expression of "negativity" would result in their expulsion. Finally, where groups are sufficiently isolated and regimented to control access by outsiders, believers have little opportunity or motivation to explore their beliefs with outsiders. Consequently, consistent and collective narratives are regularly reinforced. The later discussion of ethnographic practice suggests that this collectively reinforced frame of reference not only influences members, but can exert a powerful influence on the perceptions of the ethnographer-in-field.

Apostates

Bromley (Chapter 2 this volume) uses the term "apostate" to designate ex-members who develop an association with other groups, often those of the anti-cult movement (ACM), and that assumed role involves negotiation of their accounts, usually shaping those accounts in special ideological directions which may be summarized as the "captivity narrative." I use the term "apostate" in the less specifically role-related sense of one who has (or appears to have) abandoned a belief, faith, or cause. Bromley's observations concerning the positive interdependence of the anti-cult movement and "*career* apostates" should caution us especially about how accounts of such "leavetakers" may be shaped by the desire to be accepted by opponents of the group in which they were a member (just as narratives of current practitioners are shaped by their desire to maintain a good impression of themselves within the group of which they are members). Further, the relationship between informants and journalists, law enforcement agencies, and yes, even academic researchers, can shape the narratives jointly produced in their interviews (or interrogations).

Role theorists tend to focus on what I termed earlier "career apostates," persons who assume an active role in the anti-cult movement (Chapter 2 this volume; Bromley and Shupe 1986). While acknowledging that "career apostates" constitute a particularly important variant of more general "leavetaking" because of the role they play as resources for the anti-cult movement, focusing exclusively on those who have made a career of their apostasy would give a distorted view of both those members who subsequently disaffiliate and the processes by which they come to leave new religious movements.

Bromley's analysis (Chapter 2 this volume) of apostate narratives reveals recurrent themes of victimization and coercion, likely shaped at least in part by some of the circumstances of their exits. Such factors may include explanations for their previous affiliation (Chapter 3 this volume), often in conflict with preferences of earlier family and friends, justification for actions which they may now see as undesirable, the effects of "deprogramming" (or re-programming) experiences, and conditions for retaining the attention of the anti-cult movement, media representatives, or publishers. A notable example of the latter is the book *Bhagwan: The God that Failed*, in which Hugh Milne (1986), once a trainer of bodyguards for the Rajneesh community, develops a sensational *exposé* of the movement. Because of Milne's position of considerable trust in the organization, one could argue that he was especially well placed in terms of knowledge. He is most inclusive in his descriptions of negative aspects of the movement, including a number of observations not revealed elsewhere or by others. His story often takes on the "captivity narrative" form identified by Bromley (Chapter 2 this volume). The credibility of his account is, however, rendered questionable by inconsistencies, many claims for which there is no other corroboration, and some items which are simply counterfactual.

A special and extreme case of pressures toward distortion of apostate accounts is likely to be found where members, like the ex-mayor of Rajneeshpuram, become the focus for investigations by law enforcement authorities. In these cases, the motivation to produce something like a "captivity narrative" is perhaps obvious. In the case of central figures in movements this pressure is lessened by the fact that it is less credible, and by the lowered likelihood of a plea bargain. Lower- and middle-status members like the Mayor Krisna Deva, however, may find the temptation to displace blame upward irresistible.

The problem with defining apostates solely as those ex-members (or ex-believers) who have taken on a career role, is that it would lead researchers to minimize the especially valuable potential of those apostates who do not do so. As ex-members, apostates are especially well positioned in terms of knowledge, as well as possibly some elements of motivation. Zablocki's finding that reporting errors were fewer for respondents with "moderate" rather than "extreme" attitudes toward their groups, regardless of whether they were believers, or ex-believers, should be comforting to researchers who are willing to seek out moderate ex-members (and members), for the former may have "insider" knowledge, coupled with an "outsider" detachment. There is also a caution here, since the realities of field research are such that "extremists" (believers and apostates) may be both more visible and more available to researchers than are "moderates."

Ethnographers

Ethnographers, and field researchers more generally, constitute an especially problematic case. Most classical ethnographies are written to some extent from an outsider's perspective, although the ethnographic challenge is to translate in ways that communicate across disparate frames of reference. Further, many ethnographies "have the virtue of a comparative perspective involving an awareness of the theoretical importance of the collectivity . . . to related social phenomena" (Zablocki 1996). However, the practice of ethnography involves meeting people on their own turf, in their daily activities, using their language, and coming to a greater or lesser degree to share, if only temporarily or periodically, their definitions of reality. It is remarkably difficult to spend protracted periods of time alone, or with few outside anchors, among a set of people who have shared definitions of reality without being profoundly affected by those definitions.

To some extent ethnographers must learn to speak the symbolic language of the community in order to be understood and to understand responses; and in that process, they will find their thoughts and observations shifted toward the frames of reference of the community members. Although I neither intended nor did I do anything approaching a classical ethnography of the Rajneesh movement, spending as much of my time with opponents of the movement as with members, I found that those associations shaped my language and thought in ways which required some re-socialization upon my periodic re-entry into the academic world. For example, the question, "How did you become a Rajneeshee?" would produce mild annoyance from sannyasin (members), but "How did you find Bhagwan?" produced extensive accounts. The second question implicitly takes an insider perspective. Confusion inherent in this "shuttle" field observation sometimes caused inadvertent mild suspicion from both sides, since members preferred the term "sannyasin" and opponents used the term "Rajneeshee." Similarly, members referred to "Bhagwan" while opponents used "The Bhagwan." There was a constantly shifting frame of reference, from that of adherents to opponents to an "outside" ethnographic perspective which was different from both.

While it would be comforting to imagine the ethnographer to be free of influence from either members or groups in conflict with the focal group, such detachment has not really been possible since the days of "colonial ethnography." Clifford and Marcus's (1986) book *Writing Culture* contains a provocative set of chapters describing the power relations between early British social anthropologists and their "subjects." The avowed goal was to "translate" the cultures of aboriginal peoples into something understandable to Europeans. However, today aborigine peoples, as well as many religious movements have attorneys, writers, web pages, and other avenues of redress where they feel misinterpreted or compromised. The well-known cases of Synanon and Jonestown, as well as the possibility of litigation and scholarly debate, should alert the academic to the fact that the academy is not as isolated as it once was. Ethnographers are not only open to pressure from the subjects of their inquiries, but from the academy itself which is not totally free from the constraints of "received wisdom" and "political correctness."

Opponents

Narratives of opponents of religious movements are often dismissed from academic discourse, except perhaps as objects of analysis. However, the contemporary anti-cult movement, as well as somewhat less organized opponents of specific groups often have considerable investigative resources at their disposal. Many opponent groups develop substantial archives of legal documents, incorporation papers, public records, and financial documents. To be sure, these archives are selectively (often admittedly) constructed to emphasize negative aspects of the groups studied. The sophistication of new religious movements, and of their opponents, has developed to the point where both attempt to influence journalists and academic researchers. Further, both groups read what is written about them and their interests, and both groups will utilize academic writings about their positions as ammunition in their cause. There are now two forms of feedback between academic discourse and the political discourse surrounding religious groups. First, some groups will modify their strategies after reading of the problems encountered by other groups. Second, religious movements and their opponents will provide information to researchers, and if this information is published in a form which is desired by the group, will cite the analysis as "objective" corroboration in hearings and other formal proceedings.

The norms of academia make us reluctant to believe or to disseminate negative facets of controversial groups; yet some groups do move beyond the pale of legal or academic tolerance and researchers should examine opponent claims with some seriousness, while recognizing the motivations and pressures which shape opponent data collection and archives.

RAJNEESH HUMANITIES TRUST PROGRAM

Let us now move to an illustration of how information from believers, apostates, academics, opponents, and official records can be used to address the credibility of conflicting claims. The following narrative is a reconstruction of a contested incident in the history of Rajneeshpuram, the controversial charismatic commune established by Bhagwan Shree Rajneesh in eastern Oregon. Although the story may at times sound rather like a Gothic novel, the composite of insider observations, outsider observations, and an analysis of records permitted development of a narrative which makes sense of several bizarre and otherwise seemingly unrelated incidents—busing of street people to Rajneeshpuram, announcement of write-in candidates for an election, and salmonella poisoning of a large number of Wasco County, Oregon residents. The discussion following the narrative raises questions about the underlying problems in classifying stories as believer, apostate, and ethnographic accounts. The argument is developed that the more basic underlying problem is one of observers and claims based on differences in knowledge, motivation, and some effects of negotiation in the construction of narratives. Knowledge, motivation, and negotiation are presented as variables which cross-cut the categories believer, apostate, ethnographer, and opponent.

One of the most controversial incidents during the years of Rajneeshpuram involved what appears to have been a concerted attempt by leaders of the commune to sweep the 1984 county elections in Wasco County, the county in which the community had been repeatedly blocked by county commissioners in its ambitious expansion program.

Based on testimony from Krishna Deva, the ex-mayor of Rajneeshpuram, it appears that members of the commune leadership intended to elect residents of the commune to two of the three county commissioner positions in the fall election. To this end, they tried to recruit three sets of potential voters:

• all sannyasin (devotees) who were American citizens but not then resident at the ranch

• non-sannyasin who might be sympathetic to Rajneesh candidates

• and when those recruiting efforts appeared to yield fewer voters than required, large numbers of indigents recruited from the streets of American cities.

It also appears that on two occasions salad bars in The Dalles, Oregon, were contaminated with salmonella, apparently as "tests" to see if considerable numbers of county residents could be disabled. The effort was abandoned only after the State of Oregon closed voter registration and the U.S. District Court declined to intervene.

At the time, allegations about an attempt to sweep the elections was dismissed by commune leadership and sympathetic writers as existing "only in rumors circulated by anti-Rajneeshees." Bhagwan's secretary called a news conference in which she claimed that the election bid of the two write-in candidates was merely a "joke." A call by an Oregon congressman for investigation of the poisonings was dismissed as a "rambling incoherent speech."

Krishna Deva's narrative was in the form of testimony given when he was being investigated for suspected participation in the poisonings and other alleged crimes. As one of the core staff members at Rajneeshpuram, his testimony obviously raised credibility questions, and some of the narrative was frankly astonishing even to outsiders familiar with Rajneeshpuram, though it was savored by the anti-cult movement in Oregon. He was a core practicing member of the community whose testimony was used in subsequent prosecutions of other staff members.

Being unwilling to rely solely on a defector's narrative involving such a remarkable election plot, I constructed the following chronology (presented here in abbreviated form) based on information from extremely varied sources.

1. In August 1984, staff at Rajneeshpuram began calling all American sannyasin (devotees) to come to stay at the ranch for the fall, with offers of ''fellowships'' or ''subsidized rates.''

2. In August 1984, the staff also sent letters to all ''non-sannyasin'' who had ever stayed at the ranch to come to the ranch and participate in ''a special three-month program'' for the fall. Staff response to inquiry about the possibility of a two-week visit was that ''this would not likely be possible.''

3. In September 1994, a massive recruiting effort began with chartered buses sent to major urban areas of the country to recruit ''street people'' to come to Rajneeshpuram as part of a philanthropic ''share-a-home'' program. Over the next month and a half at least 1,455 indigents were transported to the ranch, with the first four busloads arriving September 4–6.

4. On September 9 there was an unexplained outbreak of salmonella poisoning in The Dalles, Oregon which was eventually traced to salad bars in several restaurants.

5. A concerted indoctrination program began at the ranch at this time which urged street people to register to vote in the upcoming election, telling them that the state was trying to deprive them of their right to vote and that groups of people were physical threats to them and the commune.

6. On September 22 (after at least 641 street people had been brought to Rajneeshpuram), a second outbreak of salmonella occurred in The Dalles, this one eventually traced to eight separate salad bars with no common supplier. Samples from the salad bars indicated a single strain of salmonella to be responsible for the poisonings.

7. On October 5 (after at least 1,093 street people had been recruited), Bhagwan's secretary announced the intention to run two write-in candidates for county commissioner positions.

8. On October 7 a ranch spokesperson claimed 7,000 voters at the commune, including 4,000 ''Share-a-Home'' residents (street people).

9. On October 10 voting registration was suspended by Wasco County. (The county received over 2,000 complaint letters from people resident at the ranch who were denied registration.)

10. On October 15 the U.S. District Court refused to order registration to resume.

11. On October 17 (the official deadline for voter registration), five plane loads of sannyasin and one plane of indigents were flown to Rajneeshpuram.

12. On October 18 a spokesperson for the ranch announced the end of the Share-a-Home program.

13. When a federal task force entered the ranch the following year, they found among other things a lab facility in Bhagwan's secretary's residence in which were petri dishes with the same strain of salmonella identified earlier in The Dalles.

Assembling and corroborating elements that went into this tale involved:

• Reports from sannyasin residents at Rajneeshpuram at the time of these events, although none claimed knowledge of the salmonella incidents.

• Mail and telephone contact from recruiters from Rajneeshpuram seeking academics to join them for this three-month period.

• Information concerning timing and numbers of indigents entering Rajneeshpuram from an "outsider," a woman in Madras, Oregon, who managed the coffee shop at the bus station where indigents were transferred from chartered buses on which they came from major cities into school buses for transport to Rajneeshpuram.

• Published accounts of interviews with street people, and an account by an undercover journalist who had posed as a street person.

• Records of law enforcement and other public agencies.

• Personal analysis of 2,000 protest letters sent to the Wasco County voting registration office, consistently displaying the themes of fear and persecution, in many cases in the exact phrasing claimed by expelled street people to have been drummed into them over loudspeakers and in mass meetings. Internal analysis of these documents revealed evidence of systematic "coaching." For example, while many of the street people were quite articulate, something over 100 of the protest letters were below a fourth-grade level of literacy in terms of spelling and grammar, yet appended to each was "cc: Rajneesh Legal Services." It was not credible that individuals who wrote as poorly as these letters indicated would have known enough to send a "courtesy copy" to their attorneys.

CONCLUSIONS

The ethnographer is vulnerable to considerable confusion from moving in the field among people with competing and conflicting definitions of reality. The immersion of participating in ceremony and exchange in a world which is very different from the academic one produces more profound disorientation. As you learn to talk about and experience the world (physically and symbolically) in a believer community, you find yourself seeing and interpreting the world in those terms. The first return to the university after contact with Rajneesh followers and their opponents was a profoundly unsettling experience, because I came to see my own (previous) world through very different eyes. Field researchers do not just study people in the same sense as survey researchers or library researchers. We develop long-term mutual relationships, expectations, and obligations, some of which may make little sense in other frames of reference. To the extent that an ethnographer is successful, he or she will learn to participate in joy, humor, feast, exchange, suffering, and reflection. Yet, we return to the academy and write our own narratives.

To the extent that the ethnographer's frame of reference approximates that of his/her relations in the field and his/her relations in the academy, he or she may be in a sense a "serial apostate." That is, in each setting there are ways of perceiving, describing, and experiencing the world (belief, if you will) which are simply incompatible with each other. The reformulation of field experience into ethnographic narrative in "the objective language of scientific observation and inquiry" (Zablocki 1996) may itself constitute a "negotiated narrative" in a sense related to what Bromley describes with "apostate narratives." Were I to write an academic narrative of my experiences on a vision quest or in other ceremonies, in the language of those experiences, I would likely raise eyebrows in both ceremonial and academic cultures.

The pressure is somewhat different in its direction from the narratives of career apostates which Bromley characterizes, in that, unlike the anti-cult movement, the academic world does not push one toward extreme negative characterizations. Another difference is that while the "serial apostate" may periodically lose touch with (or abandon) some of the beliefs and orientations of the field context or the academic context, he or she has no intention of abandoning either world; there are long-term commitments and obligations in both. The values of both systems forbid some kinds of narrative revelation, and in this post-modern world the narrative of the academic is available for critique by academic colleagues and members of the other culture alike.

Nevertheless, the ethnographic narrative is subject to a number of constraints in terms of its genuineness (authenticity, perhaps). In many cases, other researchers will have experience in the same or similar cultures and this community of scholars impels both conscientiousness and discretion. Further, post-modern religious and other communities have their own web pages and have access to the pages of others on the World Wide Web, as well as access to libraries and professional journals. A prudent contemporary ethnographer, who honors the long-term relationships, will check with the subjects of his or her narratives as to the accuracy and propriety of a narrative. Finally, members of both cultures are likely to scrutinize conclusions, especially novel or unsettling ones, in terms of corroborating evidence. Both groups will ask questions like those suggested earlier for researchers, questions like, "Does the writer have the knowledge implied in the account?" "What is the motive for the account?" "How may the knowledge base, motive, and relationships with others shape and/or distort the account?"

Since most religious movements have some esoteric components, information differentially available to insiders, researchers must access that insider information to understand and account for the beliefs and practices of those movements. The problem is that in many traditions "believers" (or current practitioners) may tend to edit what they report into terms which show the movement in a positive light. Narratives will tend to justify membership and to avoid any revelations which might jeopardize continued affiliation. Ex-members (apostates, if you will) may have both the insider information and be freed from some of the reporting constraints of insiders. However, many apostates have a countervailing set of motivations for bias in the direction of negative reports about a movement, either to justify their disaffiliation, to please relatives who were disturbed by their affiliation, or to ensure their place in groups opposed to their previous affiliation with the religious movement that they describe. While the conventional academic wisdom characterizes the ethnographer as limited in knowledge by virtue of status in the academic setting, academics reporting on cultures other than their primary one will in fact vary radically in terms of the degree of participation in those cultures.

Triangulation across the evidence provided by narratives of believers, apostates, ethnographers (and other sources) is obviously essential, easy to advise, and difficult to meticulously execute. With each type of informant it is crucial that we ask a series of questions. From what frame of reference were the observations made? Does the narrator have, or was he positioned to have, the knowledge claimed? How might his physical and social location have influenced what was available to be seen or known? What is the motivation for the telling? How does his interest, motivation, and intended audience affect what is told and how it is packaged?

Finally, the most useful triangulation does not involve a mere summing (subtracting or averaging) of narratives taken from different frames of reference or informants with different motivations, but rather constructing a coherent overview of a movement or tradition which makes sense of the disparate narratives by relating and evaluating their content in some common frame of reference. We should not automatically assume that a narrative is trustworthy or not because of the type of informant. This will sometimes require some evaluation, through corroborating strategies which are difficult to specify in any general sense. In some cases, something approaching certitude about actual events or behaviors may be arrived at, and we will be able to describe different narratives in terms of the fit between those and that construction of reality. In other cases, researchers will likely be able to do no more than to report and contrast the differences in knowledge, motivations, and perceptions revealed in narratives from different sources. To the degree possible, we seek consistent stories given the expectable, or discoverable, distortions of descriptions from different positions of knowledge, belief, motivation, and social influence.

Finally, it should be noted that while the ethnographic narrative is itself shaped by constraints of both field and academy, we have a dual goal in those narratives: On one side there should be enough insider knowledge to reflect the interrelated web of meanings, beliefs, and perceptions in the culture being portrayed (emic knowledge), and on the other the social analyst seeks to treat that cultural web in a broader cumulative and comparative perspective (etic knowledge).

There is a long tradition of disagreement between researchers who assert that cultural analysis should be based on "emic" principles (insider categories) and those who prefer "etic" principles (outsider categories). There is sometimes the further, almost unstated implication that the etic analysis is (or should be) based in an objective, external reality—the "positivistic truth." See, for example, the contrasting Pike and Harris essays in the book *Emics and Etics: The Insider/ Outsider Debate* (Headland, Pike, and Harris 1990). Identification of *emics* with insider knowledge or meaning categories and *etics* with outsider knowledge or meaning categories is a gross oversimplification of the concepts which these terms are used to reference.

Further, anthropologists are quite variable in the specifics of what they mean by this distinction. Two illustrations of how the *emic/etic* duality is employed by contemporary ethnographers will highlight the contested nature of the distinction. Headland (Headland, Pike, and Harris 1990, p. 22) notes the following common distinction as capturing some facets of the emic concept, but not all of the implications:

One person will shake hands with you by lifting your hand up to about shoulder height and then drop it, another will move your hand less high and then down again, a third will "pump" it up and down two or three times; in Western culture these may be called etic [external "objective," comment mine] differences and can be viewed as various realizations of the one emic element: "shaking hands" [the internal cultural significance of the disparate physical acts, comment mine]. (quoted from Siertsema 1969, p. 586)

Harris (1968, pp. 48–61) develops the case that *emic* does not really correspond to "insider knowledge" in that many (or most) "insiders" do not formulate the distinctions made by an anthropologist in *emic* analysis; they may rather behave as if such internal rules existed, but they are generally unaware of the rules. (I was startled at Rajneeshpuram to find many respondents were unaware of most of Rajneesh's published work; they had been attracted by a single book or discourse.) Harris's distinction may be illustrated by the difference in a Hindu's explanation of why cows (or other meat animals) are not to be killed or eaten as contrasted with an anthropologist or ecologist who might observe that the long-term productivity of land in parts of India is not likely sufficient to maintain so large a population with a meat-based diet (because it takes approximately eight grams of vegetable protein to produce one gram of beef protein). For Harris, *emic* analysis utilizes the meaning categories and linkages of one culture, whereas *etic* analysis emphasizes "explanation of human actions in the environmental, the constraints of the 'real world' surrounding human action" (Pelto 1970, p. 83). In spite of the historical value of the *emic/ etic* distinction in making us more aware that these are different cultural frames, there seems to be an emerging consensus that both types of analysis are important for the understanding, explanation, and prediction of human behavior (cf. Hymes 1990; Headland, Pike, and Harris 1990).

This is not an argument for meshing the two orientations, but rather for understanding and explaining behavior in two different modalities. I could not understand many things at Rajneeshpuram until I learned to accept that Bhagwan's teachings as understood by most of his followers involved a form of radical Advaita Hinduism, radical in the sense that all dualities are dismissed as "illusion" and consequently statements need not be *consistent* from one moment to the next, certainly not from one year to the next. Indeed, many sannyasin would claim that the very notion of *consistency* is illusion. This *emic* knowledge makes it easier to understand the lack of concern for consistency in that community. However, lack of concern for consistency was one of the bases on which enemies of Rajneeshpuram were able to discredit the Bhagwan's varying stories about his reason for moving to the United States—health reasons at one point, and as a religious refugee at another. The surrounding environment, here the European derivative legal and political environment, places great stock in "consistency," especially consistency in stories told to immigration and tax officials. In summary, some of the behavior of sannyasin seemed unfathomable without knowledge of internal orientation and some of the consequences of that behavior mediated by an external legal code are predictable when we view the behavior in "external code." Sannyasin might of course point out that from their frame of reference the notion of consistency is a quaint *emic* distinction in political/legal bodies of the United States. Had they been interested in doing so, the community might have fared better had they learned more of the *emics* of that political culture.

There is a lesson in the classic story of the three blind men describing an elephant as like a thick snake (from the man touching the trunk), a tree trunk (from the man touching the leg), as like a great leaf (from the man touching the ear). The lesson for us is the role of the rhetorically invisible *teller* of the story, who assumes that both he or she and the audience share a mental model of an elephant, and can thus bring some consistency to the contradictory descriptions.

REFERENCES

Brinkerhoff, Merlin, and Marlene Mackie. 1993. "Casting Off the Bonds of Organized Religion: A Religious-Careers Approach to the Study of Apostasy." *Review of Religious Research* 34:235–57.

Bromley David G., and Anson Shupe. 1986. "Affiliation and Disaffiliation: A Role Theory Interpretation of Joining and Leaving New Religious Movements." *Thought* 61:197–211.

Burawoy, Michael et al. 1991. *Ethnography Unbound: Power and Resistance in the Modern Metropolis*. Berkeley: University of California Press.

Carter, Lewis F. 1990. *Charisma and Control at Rajneeshpuram: The Role of Shared Values in the Creation of a Community*. New York: Cambridge University Press.

Clifford, James, and George E. Marcus, eds. 1986. *Writing Culture: The Poetics and Politics of Ethnography*. Berkeley: University of California Press.

Harris, Marvin. 1968. *The Rise of Anthropological Theory: A History of Theories of Culture.* New York: Thomas Y. Crowell.

Headland, Thomas, Kenneth Pike, and Marvin Harris, eds. 1990. *Emics and Etics: The Insider/Outsider Debate.* Newbury Park, CA: Sage.

Hymes, Dell. 1990. "Emics, Etics, and Openness: An Ecumenical Approach." Pp. 84–99 in *Emics and Etics: The Insider/Outsider Debate*, edited by Thomas Headland, Kenneth Pike, and Marvin Harris. Newbury Park, CA: Sage.

Milne, Hugh. 1986. *Bhagwan: The God that Failed.* London: Caliban Books.

Pelto, Pertti J. 1970. *Anthropological Research: The Structure of Inquiry.* New York: Harper & Row.

Pike, Kenneth. 1990. "On the Emics and Etics of Pike and Harris." Pp. 28–47 in *Emics and Etics: The Insider/Outsider Debate*, edited by Thomas Headland, Kenneth Pike, and Marvin Harris. Newbury Park, CA: Sage.

———. 1954. *Language in Relation to a Unified Theory of the Structure of Human Behavior.* 2d ed. The Hague: Mouton [Glendale, CA: Summer Institute of Linguistics].

Richardson, James, Robert Balch, and J. Gordon Melton. 1993. "Problems of Research and Data in the Study of New Religions." Pp. 213–29 in *Religion and the Social Order* (Vol. 3, Part B), *The Handbook on Cults and Sects in America*, edited by David Bromley and Jeffrey Hadden. Greenwich, CT: Association for the Sociology of Religion and JAI Press.

Siertsema, Berthe. 1969. " 'Etic' and 'Emic.' " *English Studies* 50:586–88.

Shupe, Anson. 1996. "Authenticity Lost: When Victims of Clergy Abuse Confront Betrayed Trust." Pp. 261–79 in *Religion and the Social Order* (Vol. 6), *Studies on the Issue of "Authenticity" in Varied Religious Traditions*, edited by Lewis F. Carter. Greenwich, CT: Association for the Sociology of Religion and JAI Press.

Zablocki, Benjamin. 1996. "Reliability and Validity of Apostate Accounts in the Study of Religious Communities." Paper presented at the annual meetings of the Association for the Sociology of Religion, New York.

Index

About the Contributors

EILEEN BARKER is Professor of Sociology with Special Reference to the Study of Religion at the London School of Economics, where she is currently Head of Department. She specializes in the study of new religious movements, with particular interest in changes in new religions, the New Age movement, religion in Eastern Europe and the former Soviet Republic, the Armenian diaspora, and the Republic of Armenia. She is also currently engaged in a large-scale comparative study of religious and moral pluralism. Her publications, which have been translated into over a dozen languages, include *The Making of a Moonie:Brainwashing or Choice?* (1984), which was awarded the Distinguished Book Award by the Society for the Scientific Study of Religion; *Of Gods and Men: New Religious Movements in the West* (1984); *LSE on Freedom* (1997); *New Religious Movements: A Practical Introduction*, 5th ed. (1995); and over 150 articles and chapters. She is past president of the Society for the Scientific Study of Religion.

DAVID G. BROMLEY is Professor of Sociology and an Affiliate Professor in the Department of Religious Studies at Virginia Commonwealth University. His research interests include sociology of religion, social movements, deviance, and political sociology. Among his recent books are *Handbook on Cults and Sects in America* (1993) (edited with Jeffrey K. Hadden) and *The Satanism Scare* (1991) (edited with James Richardson and Joel Best). He is currently working on *Religion and Resistance: Prophetic Religion in a Secular Age*. He is former president of the Association for the Sociology of Religion; founding editor of the Association for the annual series, *Religion and the Social Order*, sponsored by the Association for the Sociology of Religion; and former editor of the *Jour-*

nal for the Scientific Study of Religion, published by the Society for the Scientific Study of Religion.

LEWIS F. CARTER is a Professor of Sociology and Associate Dean of the College of Liberal Arts at Washington State University. He teaches social impact assessment, measurement, both qualitative and quantitative research methods, and courses on environmental, policy, and resource issues. He has published articles on resources and environment, international policy issues, and cultural conflicts, especially those involving religious movements. He authored *Charisma and Control at Rajneeshpuram* (1990), co-authored *Applied Multivariate Analysis and Experimental Designs* (1975), and was the volume editor for *Religion and the Social Order* (Vol. 6): *Studies on the Issue of "Authenticity" in Varied Religious Traditions* (1996).

JOHN R. HALL is Professor of Sociology at the University of California–Davis. His empirical research has focused on collective meanings in countercultural groups, beginning with a study of contemporary utopian communal groups, *The Ways Out* (1978), followed by a cultural history of Jim Jones and Peoples Temple, *Gone from the Promised Land* (1987), and a chapter on the Branch Davidians that critiques binary theories of meaning construction—published in Stuart Wright's edited collection, *Armageddon in Waco* (1995). Using a broadly Weberian phenomenological approach, Hall also has offered a critique of Bourdieu in Lamont and Fournier's *Cultivating Differences* (1992). He has recently completed *Culture: Sociological Perspectives*, an overview of the sociology of culture's importance for cultural studies, with Mary Jo Neitz. He is presently completing a book manuscript that explores sociohistorical inquiries as cultural practices.

DANIEL CARSON JOHNSON is the Sorokin Post-Doctoral Fellow at the Post-Modernity Project at the University of Virginia. His primary areas of interest are in the sociology of culture and religion, sociological theory, and social power. His recently completed book manuscript, entitled *Secularization: The Inherited Models Revisited*, is under review, and he is currently finishing up a second manuscript entitled *The State of Disunion*. This work, co-authored with James Davison Hunter and Carl Bowman, is a comprehensive survey and analysis of contemporary American political culture. Other ongoing projects consist of inquiries into the cultural dynamics that help to build some of our most serviceable public myths. In *Mapping Malaise: The Politics of National Decline*, the focus is on the culturally mediated image of pervasive national decline, while in "Media Constructions of an Angry Electorate," it is on the angry voter, in many ways the bogey-man of American political discourse.

ARMAND L. MAUSS is Professor of Sociology and Religious Studies at Washington State University. Mauss is former editor of the *Journal for the Scientific*

Study of Religion. He is author of numerous books and articles in the sociology of religion, particularly on the Mormons. His most recent book is *The Angel and the Beehive: The Mormon Struggle with Assimilation* (1994).

SUSAN J. PALMER teaches in the Religion Department of Dawson College and is an Adjunct Professor at Concordia University. She is the author of *Moon Sisters, Krishna Mothers, Rajneesh Lovers* (1994) and *AIDS as an Apocalyptic Metaphor in North America* (1997). She is co-editor, with Thomas Robbins, of *Millenium, Messiah, and Mayhem* (1997).

JAMES T. RICHARDSON is Professor of Sociology and Judicial Studies at the University of Nevada, Reno, where he is a faculty member of the Sociology Department, as well as of the Interdisciplinary Social Psychology Doctoral Program. He teaches sociology of religion, sociology of law, social movements, and collective behavior, as well as social and behavioral evidence class for judges in the MJS program. He has been conducting research in minority religions for most of his career, and has authored, co-authored, or edited six books and about 100 articles and book chapters. Richardson is a former president of the Association for the Sociology of Religion, and has served as officer of a number of other professional organizations. He consults on legal actions involving minority religions, and has served as an expert witness in several cases involving such groups.

PHILIP SCHUYLER, an ethnomusicologist specializing in North Africa and the Middle East, has lived and worked for extended periods of time in Morocco and Yemen. His special interests include the ethnography of performance and the interrelationship of the arts. Among his publications are an ethnographic film, field recordings for UNESCO and various American publishers, and numerous articles in both professional journals and the general-interest press, including the *New York Times* and the *New Yorker*. He is currently Associate Professor of Music at the University of Maryland/Baltimore County.

ANSON SHUPE is Professor of Sociology at the joint campus of Indiana University–Purdue University Fort Wayne, Fort Wayne, Indiana. His interests include religion, politics, and deviance. He is author, co-author, or co-editor of two dozen books on religious movements as well as on family violence. In addition, he has written extensively for professional journals, magazines, and newspapers. Among his most notable books on new religions and countermovements are *Moonies In America: Cult, Church and Crusade* (1979) (with David Bromley); *The New Vigilantes: Anti-Cultists, Deprogrammers and the New Religions* (1980) (with David Bromley); and *Strange Gods: The Great American Cult Scare*, (1981) (with David Bromley). His most recent books include a study of domestic violence, *The Violent Couple* (1994) (with William A. Stacey and Lonnie R. Hazlewood) and a study of violation of trust by clergy, *In the Name of All That's Holy: A Theory of Clergy Malfeasance* (1995).

STUART A. WRIGHT is Professor of Sociology at Lamar University. In 1984–1985 he was appointed Post-Doctoral Fellow and Lecturer at Yale University, where he was the recipient of an NIMH grant to study the social and psychological effects of youth participation in new religions. He published *Leaving Cults: The Dynamics of Defection* (1987) on this subject, as well as numerous scientific articles in professional journals and book chapters in edited volumes. Recent contributions include "Leaving New Religions" (with Helen Ebaugh) in the *Handbook of Cults and Sects in America*, and "Reconceptualizing Cult Coercion and Withdrawal," *Social Forces* (1991). Most recently, he is editor of a scholarly volume on the Waco Branch Davidian tragedy, *Armageddon in Waco: Critical Perspective on the Branch Davidian Conflict* (1995).

ISBN 0-275-95508-7

90000>

EAN

9 780275 955083

HARDCOVER BAR CODE

DATE DUE